# EARNING IT

*Joann S. Lublin*

# EARNING IT

## Hard-Won Lessons
## from Trailblazing Women
## at the Top of the Business World

### JOANN S. LUBLIN

**HARPER**
BUSINESS

*An Imprint of* HarperCollins*Publishers*

HarperCollins books may be purchased for educational, business, or sales promotional use. For information, please email the Special Markets Department at SPsales@harpercollins.com.

FIRST EDITION

*Designed by Bonni Leon-Berman*

Library of Congress Cataloging-in-Publication Data has been applied for.

ISBN 978-0-06-240747-4

17  18  19  20    RRD    10  9  8  7  6  5  4

To the most important working woman in my life:

Annie Supman Lublin, my paternal grandmother.

She immigrated alone to the United States at age sixteen

and earned

enough toiling in a sweatshop to bring her parents

from Eastern Europe.

# CONTENTS

Introduction                                                    1

1   Working Women Have Come a Long Way              13
2   Doors Open with a Strong Push                        24
3   Getting Picked: Bloom Where You Are Planted     43
4   Sexual Harassment Never Vanished                   60
5   The Pain of the Pay Pinch                                79
6   Getting Ahead Sooner                                     99
7   Getting Ahead Later                                       116
8   Manager Moms Are Not Acrobats                     133
9   Career Couple Conundrums                            158
10  Male Mentors Mean Business                         173
11  Managing Men Well                                       191
12  Spotlight on Executive Presence                     208
13  Beating Board Bias                                        225
14  Will the Glass Ceiling Ever Shatter?              243
15  Male Champions of Women                          258

Acknowledgments                                           271
Interviewed Executive Women                          273
Notes                                                            277
Selected Bibliography                                      283
Index                                                            285

# INTRODUCTION

Ambitious women today feel little connection with female business executives who overcame obstacles to succeed. Those leaders seem to have catapulted directly into their lofty posts once they got past some setbacks along the way.

But there are powerful parallels between their world and yours, as you'll realize from reading my book.

I know this landscape firsthand. In 1969, I became the first female summer intern for the Washington, D.C., bureau of the *Wall Street Journal*. It was a highly prestigious office of the premier business newspaper in America.

I was thrilled to make my professional debut at such a well-known publication. During my nearly three months at the paper, my byline appeared on five front-page features, including one about citizens' unconventional petitions to Congress. And I learned a lot about big-time journalism from my lanky, middle-aged editor. A veteran of twelve years in the news business, he smoked a pipe and demonstrated a deft touch with words.

But my *Journal* summer stint had an unexpected and unwelcome conclusion. On the day my internship ended, my boss walked me out the door of the office. He then leaned down and kissed me on the lips.

I felt violated. I hardly knew the man. Yet I yearned to be a big-time journalist someday. Mumbling goodbye, I fled the office. I remember thinking, "I can't tell anyone what just happened."

I repressed memories of this horrific incident until 1991, when I helped the *Journal* cover alleged sexual harassment by Clarence Thomas during Senate confirmation hearings for his U.S. Supreme Court appointment. I suddenly recollected my supervisor's misbehavior. I shuddered visibly.

Nor was the unwanted goodbye kiss an aberration when it came to sexist behavior in the workplace. I had landed my summer job as a Newspaper Fund intern after Dow Jones & Co., the *Journal*'s parent, opened that internship program to female journalism majors like me.

As I entered the Washington bureau's conference room for my first staff meeting, every man rose to his feet. I figured a famous politician had arrived. On the contrary. My male colleagues were standing for me in a chivalrous but distinctly unwelcome gesture that I had never experienced in college.

There were other distasteful moments. I refused one coworker's request to make him coffee. I truthfully explained that I didn't know how to make coffee because I drank tea. He silently stalked off. But I doubt he would have asked a male intern to perform such a menial task.[1]

After completing a journalism graduate degree at Stanford University, I got hired in 1971 as the first female reporter for the *Journal*'s San Francisco bureau. I again ran into both subtle and blatant sex bias. Such behavior was socially acceptable during that era.

"Where have they been keeping a dish like you?" male sources often asked me in a teasing fashion. When I covered events at private business clubs that barred women, I was forced to use a special door, usually one near the kitchen in the rear.

In 1987, I was promoted to second in command of the London bureau. I quickly discovered that sexism still ruled in Britain, despite strides being made in the United States. Bosses there needed special permission to let women work past 10 p.m. in factories. Such laws were originally designed to protect the so-called weaker sex, but hindered progress toward gender equality. And though I made more money than my journalist husband, I wasn't allowed under British law to sign our joint tax return.[2]

These setbacks, while sometimes daunting, didn't discourage me. They emboldened my passion to prove that working women are just as capable as men. I shared the *Journal*'s 2003 Pulitzer Prize for stories about widespread corporate scandals that toppled a number of top executives. As the paper's longtime management news editor, I have written extensively and overseen other people's reporting about such topics as women in the workplace, chief executive succession, executive pay, and company boards of directors.

I also inaugurated the *Journal*'s coverage of career issues with the 1993 launch of my monthly column, "Managing Your Career." I currently write "Your Executive Career," a regular advice column that I began in 2010.

Plenty of American working women have pursued similar paths. For a handful at the vanguard, the journey brought them to the corner office of big businesses.

According to Catalyst, a well-regarded organization that conducts research on issues related to women, women ran 4.2 percent of companies in the Standard & Poor's 500 Index as of December 2015. Among the twenty-one in this category: Mary Barra, chief executive of General Motors Co., who took the helm in 2014 after moving up through the ranks of the largest U.S. automaker.

Virginia "Ginni" Rometty also broke the mold, as the first woman to head International Business Machines Corp. Her 2012 promotion came a mere sixty-nine years after the technology giant elected its first female vice president.

Nearly two-thirds of Americans believe that women continue to face a barrier to career advancement, concluded a May 2013 survey by financial services firm Edward Jones. More than 75 percent of millennial women, who reached young adulthood around 2000, identify gender bias as a workplace problem, according to a 2011 poll by the Business and Professional Women's Foundation.

The most common forms cited by the young women? Stereotyping. Unequal pay. Not being treated as an equal. Inequality of opportunities. Being held to different standards. Sexist jokes. And of course, sexual harassment.

Many women reaching the upper rungs of U.S. businesses encountered a variety of setbacks early in their careers. Yet paradoxically, the useful leadership lessons they learned from those challenges propelled their ascent and proved critical to their ultimate success.

A growing number of books promise to reveal "success secrets" for women, usually based on anonymous examples from many walks of life. But this book is very different.

That is because this book is filled with candid and compelling stories about workplace experiences and advancement advice from fifty-two corporate female leaders. Almost two-thirds of the business titans I interviewed are present or past CEOs of public companies, including seven in command of an S&P 500 concern as of December 2015. Insights from women like them, who reached the pinnacle of management, can help you climb your career ladder.

The executive women whose stories I tell in this book represent a unique elite that has radically reshaped the business landscape in the late twentieth and early twenty-first centuries. They dismantled the old boys' club, destroyed myths about capabilities of female leaders, and continue to serve as role models for female associates and relatives.

These trailblazers shared incredible tales of courage, sometimes opening both their hearts and their homes. With great candor, they provided vivid and deeply moving examples of their good and bad work experiences. I met nearly all of the business leaders face-to-face. I describe how they appeared and acted during our sessions so that you can better picture these encounters and understand who these women are. Thanks to them, you'll know what to do when you confront the challenges of the workplace— and equally important, what not to do.

The executives I spoke to exuded grit, resiliency, and a determined unwillingness to admit defeat when they confronted career obstacles. Some got fired for their efforts.

Many overcame daunting personal adversity. Two women suffered strokes at relatively young ages while heading sizable businesses. Others dealt with gravely ill spouses.

One woman who dealt with formidable personal problems while pursuing a high-flying corporate career is Dawn Lepore. In 2010, she struggled over whether she should give up the helm of retailer Drugstore.com. Its $456 million in sales that year made the company one of the largest online retailers in the United States.

Her husband, seriously ill with multiple myeloma, was undergoing a painful bone marrow transplant. She had a daughter in kindergarten and a son in third grade. Along with running Drugstore.com, Lepore sat on the boards of eBay Inc. and the New York Times Co.

"That was the hardest time of my career," Lepore recalled one wintry morning not long after her mother had died. "I didn't know if he was going to die."

During her husband's monthlong hospital stay, she visited him every night after a full day at her Seattle office. She stayed with him until nearly two in the morning.

"He was in such pain [that] he didn't want me to touch him. All he wanted me to do was lay on the bed next to him," she continued. In the wee hours, "I would go home and fall into bed." She then ate breakfast with her children, left for work, and repeated the same grueling routine.

Meanwhile, her housekeeper, on whom Lepore relied during those stressful weeks, stole money from her. She only discovered the theft later. "I wasn't watching any of the money, obviously," she admitted ruefully.

The chief executive burst into tears after informing a male Drugstore.com board member about her husband's life-threatening situation. Sympathetically, the board member leaned over and handed her a tissue. Crying on the job "is embarrassing," Lepore said. But "I was able to run the company."

Lepore cried again when female acquaintances harshly criticized her for continuing to work during this period. "How can you do that?" they demanded. "What kind of message are you sending your children if you are off traveling and your husband is dying?"

The attacks by women her own age flabbergasted Lepore, then fifty-three and at the time her family's sole breadwinner. "I was so angry about that," she said, her blue-gray eyes flashing with fury. "To this day, I am still angry about it."

Battered by such criticism, Lepore wanted to quit every position she held. Her husband urged her not to do so. "If you quit, the cancer would have won," he insisted. "I won't let the cancer win."

She stayed. And he survived.

Carol Bartz successfully confronted a serious personal crisis just as she assumed the No. 1 position for a major corporation. She was informed that she had breast cancer on her first day as CEO of Autodesk Inc., a maker of design software. She disclosed her imminent surgery for the disease at an Autodesk news conference.

"Listen, I was literally one month as a new CEO. I was leaving to go to the hospital the next day. I had cancer. So I was just getting through that at the news conference," Bartz said, her words tumbling out as she sat in the glass-roofed sunroom of her suburban San Francisco home. "Because you are a public CEO, you have to announce," she noted.

"Which breast?" a male reporter demanded, to her dismay.

Despite her achievements in the workplace, Bartz believes that things haven't improved much for high-profile executive women since 1992. "Because of the higher scrutiny today, it is just harder to be a female business leader," she said. You must prove you're the right person to be a boss "*because* you are a woman."

Bartz beat her cancer and led Autodesk for fourteen years,

until 2006. She later joined an even more exclusive sisterhood, by leading a second public company. Yahoo Inc., a struggling Internet business, recruited her for its CEO spot in 2009.

A number of the fifty-two executives whom I interviewed for this book handle the fairy tale of work-life balance with equal aplomb. GM's Mary Barra was married twelve years before she became a mother. When her daughter and son were in middle school, she once found herself challenged about her commitment to career and family by a group of at-home moms at an informal social gathering. All of the women previously had professional careers.

"They said, 'How do you do everything?'"

"I said, 'I don't,'" Barra remembered. She told the women that she had a wonderful nanny and a great house cleaner. Nevertheless, their comments rattled her. "I said to myself, 'Why am I putting myself into this situation?'"

Her husband, a mechanical engineer, restored her equilibrium. "You are allowing yourself to accept guilt you shouldn't accept," he chided her.

The lesson for working mothers? "Figure out what's important," Barra said. "It's about prioritizing." The GM chief continued. "I am there for my kids," she pointed out. "They know generally I am going to be home for dinner." And she attends their sports events, ranging from volleyball to soccer, lacrosse, football, hockey, and cross-country.

Nor does Barra mind when her son or daughter calls her at odd hours while she's overseas for a business trip. "I always have the phone next to me," she explained. "I pick it up and I talk to them. I don't care if it is one a.m. or five a.m."

This book will also equip you to cope with workplace sexism, based on experiences of women such as Patricia "Pat" Russo, a prior CEO of Lucent Technologies Inc. and Alcatel-Lucent SA. She typifies the glass-ceiling crackers I have come to know over the years.

Shortly after Russo joined AT&T Corp. as a twenty-nine-year-old middle manager in 1981, an older male executive unexpectedly walked into her office. "He shut the door, came over, and slapped this wet kiss on me," she recalled thirty-four years later. The un-invited sexual advance shook her up. "That had never happened to me before," she said, waving her hands in the air and looking distressed. "He was a very high-level and influential person," she added. "I was afraid."

The senior executive, who was her boss's boss's boss, invited Russo to go out for a cocktail so they could discuss a special proj-ect that he had assigned her. She flatly refused, and never regret-ted her decision.

"He certainly was in a position to endanger my career," Russo conceded. She made sure other staffers were present any time she conferred with the senior executive. "I would never be alone with him."

The encounter led Russo to conclude that women must learn to defuse situations that could potentially retard their progress in the workplace. In her case, she aimed to exceed superiors' expec-tations for her job performance. She hoped that her work would stand on its own. It did.

Over the past few decades, women like Russo have arrived in executive suites across the United States and Europe. Big-business pacesetters abound. In 2011, Denise Morrison of Campbell Soup

Co. and Maggie Wilderotter of Frontier Communications Corp., a telecom company, became the first set of sisters to lead major U.S. public companies.

Carly Fiorina was the first woman to run a Fortune 20 company, taking charge of technology giant Hewlett-Packard Co. in 1999. She ran for U.S. president in 2016. During her campaign for the Republican nomination, the media panned Hewlett-Packard's financial performance under her watch. One journalist argued that Fiorina's marketing talent overshadowed her capacity to deliver results. I believe that such critiques don't lessen the value of her management insights. You'll also hear from KeyCorp CEO Beth Mooney, the first woman to lead a top-20 U.S. commercial bank.

Some women I interviewed now steer start-ups following successful stints at sizable companies. In 2009 at age twenty-seven, Google alumna Clara Shih cofounded Hearsay Social Inc., a social media management software firm. By 2013, the chief executive had raised $21 million, employed one hundred staffers, and won a board seat at Starbucks Corp.

Getting picked as a public company director represents a critical way to advance a career. You'll gain insights about how to win a directorship and expand the slim ranks of women in boardrooms. The proportion of women on major U.S. corporate boards has changed little during recent years. In fall 2015, more than four of every five directors at the five hundred biggest companies were men.

Many of the executives I spoke to grew up in families of modest means rather than privileged environments. As children, few imagined they might ever be high-powered businesswomen. Fiorina, for example, began her professional career as a receptionist at a commercial real estate brokerage firm one block from Hewlett-Packard headquarters. In her first job after college, Mooney was a bank secretary in Houston.

Despite their typically low-level debuts, these women scored gender breakthroughs and soared in the corporate hierarchy. That's why such high achievers can offer invaluable guidance about handling complicated work situations. Not every story ended happily, of course.

Well-known names will tell little-known tales about how they got going, how they recovered from setbacks, and how they got ahead.

Their experiences offer a road map that will enable other women to find their way when it comes to launching their careers, pursuing crucial promotions, tackling "mission impossible" assignments, inspiring fierce loyalty among skeptical male lieutenants, polishing their executive presences, and much more.

In coming chapters, the stories of several women will illustrate aspects of a common career obstacle, such as a bad boss, resentful peers, or unwanted sexual advances. Chapters also contain concrete leadership lessons that these women gleaned from overcoming that obstacle.

Their lessons are neither sugarcoated bromides nor shrill calls to demand your rights at all costs. These powerful women often reached the apex of companies because they figured out that effective leaders need a complicated but nuanced set of professional experiences and relationships.

Their pointers will guide you about when to push and when to pivot. You'll learn about the importance of being respected rather than being liked by your subordinates. You'll find out how to handle trade-offs between motherhood and a management career. And you'll gain insights on dealing with hearing no a lot before you get to yes about a crucial career move.

The bottom line? It may sound corny, but it's true: Don't give up when things get tough.

These women never did. Using their street smarts, sense of humor, strong belief in themselves, and empathetic ability to walk in employees' shoes, they crafted innovative approaches that helped them win at work. They'll help you win as well—wherever you work.

# 1

# Working Women Have
# Come a Long Way

I own a tattered blue sweatshirt that is one of my favorite items of clothing. In bright gold letters, the shirt says, "You've come a long way Lublin." It reminds me that I was among the women who helped crack the glass ceiling at the *Wall Street Journal*.

Colleagues gave me the sweatshirt as a farewell gift in 1987 when I entered the ranks of management. I left the *Journal*'s Washington, D.C., office, where I had worked as a reporter covering health care, labor unions, housing, and urban affairs. I became second in command to Kathryn Christensen, chief of the *Journal*'s important London bureau. Ours was the first *Journal* bureau led solely by women. Kathryn already had broken the gender barrier as the paper's first female bureau chief in 1982, running the Boston office.

But my small step pales beside the trailblazing strides taken by the fifty-two high-level corporate executives I interviewed for this book. More than half of the thirty-four who currently or previously led a public company were its first female chief executive. Several repeated the feat at their next employer.

Statistically, the status of women in corporate America at all levels has improved dramatically over the years. The ranks of women heading America's biggest businesses hit a record in October 2014, when twenty-six steered such companies. Eight of those experienced CEOs talked to me about their strategies for career success.

That high point for women at the top of management came forty-two years after Katharine Graham, leader of Washington Post Co., punctured the roster of men commanding Fortune 500 firms in 1972. Between 1972 and 2001, no more than four women a year had been members of this exclusive club.[1]

In 2014, women represented nearly 39 percent of U.S. managers, according to the U.S. Bureau of Labor Statistics. Thirty-five years earlier, they held only 25 percent of manager and administrator jobs.

When women reach the executive suite, businesses and their investors reap tangible and measurable rewards. Call it the diversity dividend.

The eighty women who steered Fortune 1000 concerns between 2002 and 2014 delivered shareholder returns, a measure of stock price changes and reinvested dividends, that were three times better than the Standard & Poor's 500 Index, concluded a 2015 simulation by Quantopian, a Boston research firm that provides an investment trading platform.[2]

Businesses with the most gender-diverse leadership were also 15 percent more likely to generate earnings before interest and tax that outpaced their industry, according to a 2014 study of 366 public companies in six countries by McKinsey & Co. The management consultancy tracked women and people of color in both senior management and boardrooms. Women make up about 16 percent of executive teams at the U.S. companies analyzed. Those businesses scored a financial payoff from gender diversity only when "women constitute at least 22 percent of a senior executive team," McKinsey researchers concluded.[3]

A study released in 2016 covering 21,980 public companies in 91 countries found the same strong connection between the presence of female corporate leaders and firms' increased profitability. And a similar McKinsey report in 2007 uncovered what it described as a positive link "between corporate performance and elevated presence of women in the workplace in several Western European countries."[4]

In the United States, the overall economy has benefited from fewer obstacles to women in the workplace. A significant chunk of the growth in worker productivity between 1960 and 2008 resulted from the removal of barriers that kept many white women from realizing their economic potential, economists at Stanford University and the University of Chicago estimate.[5]

Because female pioneers paved the way, businesswomen now standing on their shoulders are having a meaningful impact on management practices. Companies increasingly prefer leaders who can be empathetic and work collaboratively because the businesses compete in an increasingly complex, stressful, and diverse global economy. Such qualities are more common in women, management experts and executive recruiters say.

Female managers are also considered stronger than male ones

in terms of "flexibility and adaptability to change or hardship, and teamwork and cooperation," said a 2014 global study by Mercer, another consulting firm that tracks employment issues.

At workplaces that highly value women's unique strengths, "there tends also to be higher female representation at the higher levels," added the Mercer study, which examined workforce data covering 1.7 million employees in twenty-eight countries.[6]

## A DIFFERENT WORK WORLD GREETED ME

The contemporary workplace barely resembles the one I entered during the 1970s.

In the years following World War II, less than a third of U.S. women held jobs or sought work outside the home. That was partly because many women who had held such jobs during the war faced social pressure to relinquish them to returning soldiers. The picture for women brightened during the 1960s; their participation in the labor force exceeded 40 percent in 1966, a postwar high.

The 1960s saw the publication of *The Feminine Mystique*, a groundbreaking book by Betty Friedan that launched the modern women's movement. Perhaps even more important, the book appeared soon after the 1960 introduction of the birth control pill. Both spurred a surge in female college graduates and the expanded presence of women in professional and business roles.

Landmark federal legislation, such as the Equal Pay Act of 1963 and Title VII of the Civil Rights Act of 1964, also had an extensive impact on women's fortunes in the workplace. Title VII outlawed sex discrimination in hiring, promotion, and compensation.

But working women continued to confront sexism and other obstacles. They usually lacked corporate mentoring programs, paid maternity leaves, high-level female bosses, or even a perquisite as simple as office lactation rooms, where new mothers can pump breast milk privately.

A significant portion of the 152 U.S. newspaperwomen I surveyed for my 1971 master's degree thesis on sex discrimination against female journalists perceived bias in their hiring, job status, and prospects for promotion. Nearly half, for instance, said that they lacked the same chance to be promoted as a similarly qualified newspaperman.

I also uncovered numerous newsroom jobs still linked to traditional sex roles. Jobs generally off-limits to women included reporters who worked nights, sports reporters, crime reporters, photographers, editorial columnists, and senior management.[7] Newspaperwomen in those days typically got assigned to so-called women's pages, covering food, fashion, home furnishings, families, and parties.

I joined a workforce with few female sports announcers, truck drivers, or construction workers. Newspapers' help-wanted ads were segregated by gender. If you wanted the highest-paying jobs, you looked under "Help Wanted: Men." It took several years before court rulings and additional legislation started to turn the tide.

When I arrived at the *Wall Street Journal*, the paper employed 11 women on its 150-person reporting and editing staff. The highest ranked woman held the unglamorous position of copy editor in New York.

As the sole female reporter in the *Journal*'s San Francisco bureau, I sat in an open newsroom surrounded by several men with "girlie" calendars mounted above their desks. To retaliate, I put up a calendar with splashy photos of handsome male nudes. My calendar quickly disappeared. I suspected that one of the guys in my new office took it.[8]

On out-of-town reporting trips, I often had trouble checking into a hotel if I lined up behind a male guest at the reception area. Check-in clerks routinely assumed I was the man's wife!

Other women traveling for work fared far worse. For example, an investment banker for a major New York bank during the 1970s visited distant clients at least one week every month. She flew first class, dressed in a gray suit, a blouse with a bow, and high heels. Prior to one takeoff in New York, she was stowing her bag in the overhead compartment when a male passenger tried to hand her his coat.

"I want you to hang it up," the man insisted. "Please?"

She didn't respond. The man finally understood why. "You're not a stewardess, are you?" he asked.

The woman explained that she was a fellow passenger, not a member of the flight staff.

"Well, you looked like a person in authority," the man replied.

During the 1980s, certain sectors of the economy, notably retailers, makers of consumer goods, and the media, accelerated their progress toward greater gender balance in the workforce, and their efforts opened the executive suite to more women in the years ahead.

Gannett Co., a chain of newspapers and TV stations, offered veteran banker Gracia Martore the job of assistant treasurer in 1985. But she closely scrutinized its management team before accepting. "Cathie Black was running *USA Today*," Martore recalled.

"There were other women who were clearly in key operational roles. So I said, 'Wow, it looks like they are not just putting women in a jar.'" In her mind, she continued, "those people had the opportunity to rise in the organization."

Gannett turned out to be a smart move for Martore. She ascended to CEO of the media powerhouse in 2011 and by spring of 2015, women comprised about 29 percent of the company's senior leadership. When Gannett split into two businesses that June, Martore took charge of TEGNA Inc., the separate broadcasting and digital company. TEGNA has the same share of top women.

The media business is hardly the only industry where women have made tremendous strides. Thanks to a radical shift in sex roles on the job and at home, women have achieved breakthroughs throughout the American workplace. They made up about 47 percent of the U.S. workforce in 2012, and as of November 2015, about 58 percent of adult American women were working or seeking work.

## GLACIAL PROGRESS

But despite women's spectacular gains on the job, their pace of progress remains painfully slow.

We earned only 78 cents for every dollar that men earned in 2013, up from 72 cents in 1990 and 60 cents in 1980, government figures show. Meanwhile, our ability to enter the ranks of corporate leadership has stalled below the corner office.

Women held a mere 14.6 percent of executive officer positions at Fortune 500 companies in December 2013, Catalyst reported.

More than a fourth of these companies lacked a single woman in their highest spots. And the proportion has barely budged since 2010.

There are many reasons for the scant recent progress. Stereotypes persist about women's leadership capabilities. Few male chief executives personally commit themselves and hold their lieutenants accountable for elevating women. So-called second-generation gender bias hurts, too. Unintentional but subtle practices create barriers, such as the backlash that women experience from negotiating hard for themselves.

It's wrong for women "to assume the playing field is level today," said Linda Hudson, a former CEO of BAE Systems Inc., a big defense contractor that's owned by BAE Systems PLC. She was the first woman to head a major Pentagon supplier. "These gains are relatively recent," she warned. "They could be just as fleeting."

That prognosis is particularly true in the high-tech industry, one of the most robust sectors of the American economy. Women's share of jobs in the computer industry has dropped since the 1990s, U.S. Census Bureau data show. In 2011 women were 27 percent of computer professionals, down from 34 percent in 1990. That mirrors the decline in their share of bachelor's degrees in computing science awarded since the 1980s.

Carol Bartz, the former chief of Autodesk and Yahoo, is hardly alone in blaming what she described as persistent "frat boy" behavior in her industry. "They still gather together as males" and refuse to treat women as their equals, she said. Women at small, young firms feel like they "are living in a start-up fraternity house," excluded from the inner circle.

Young women keen to get ahead in high tech must be extremely wary "and stay out of the way of real assholes," Bartz recommended.

Engineers form the backbone of high tech in the United States. Among skilled professions such as law, medicine, and accounting, engineering has the highest female turnover rate, according to a study by a University of Wisconsin researcher of 5,300 engineering alums spanning six decades.

Just 11 percent of practicing engineers are female, even though women accounted for more than 20 percent of engineering school graduates over the past twenty years, the study showed.

Women who left engineering more than five years ago attributed their decision mainly to caregiving duties and the lack of opportunities for advancement, reported Nadya Fouad, chair of the educational psychology department at the University of Wisconsin–Milwaukee.

Female engineers also become flight risks when managers and coworkers belittle or insult them—and they experience a culture that stresses face time and a heavy workload on evenings and weekends, Fouad suggested. During an August 2014 presentation about her research, she alluded to *Lean In: Women, Work, and the Will to Lead*, the phenomenally popular book by Sheryl Sandberg, chief operating officer of Facebook Inc. "Women's departure from engineering is not just about leaning in," Fouad said.[9]

Female tech executives I interviewed identified other challenges facing women in their industry. In technology, "you are going to be the only woman in the room half the time," noted Penny Herscher, executive chairman and former CEO of FirstRain Inc., a small business analytics company, and previously one of the first women to run a U.S. semiconductor business. Though it sounds like a cliché, she thinks women keen to succeed in high tech "need to work harder, be smarter, and be more professional than the men."

Overall, more than 4 in 10 women report that they have personally encountered gender discrimination, most often in the workplace—and 84 percent of women say men get paid more for similar work, according to an April 2013 *Wall Street Journal*/NBC News survey. Perhaps even more disturbing: both findings are little changed from a 1997 survey.[10]

"I don't think things have changed fast enough at the top," complained Denise Morrison, the first female CEO of Campbell Soup, adding that the number of women shrinks once they become middle managers. "We have more work to do in that area because that's the feeder pool" for upper management.

## UNSPOKEN CALCULATION

Yet women often build their own glass ceiling. Among other things, we hesitate to raise our hands for higher-level positions, fearful of disrupting our already hectic and complicated lives.

"Getting rid of these internal barriers is critical to gaining power," argued Sandberg in her 2013 book.[11] She ardently urged women not to scale back their ambitions simply because, for example, they might have children someday.

Mea culpa. By my late twenties, I and three male colleagues in Chicago were rising stars at the *Wall Street Journal*. Our boss sounded out each of us about advancing to bureau chief in a smaller U.S. city.

I spurned his feeler, explaining that I didn't feel ready for that role. But that wasn't the whole truth. Privately, I feared that my marriage to a *BusinessWeek* reporter might not survive our relocation to a small urban area where his employer lacked an office. Nor could I imagine being a high-powered bureau chief and at the same time raising a child, something I longed to do.

For the other three rising stars, it was a different story. Each man quickly took charge of a *Journal* bureau and subsequently rose higher than I ever did. Years later, when I finally applied for a bureau chief's spot, a woman edged me out.

Numerous women avoid line management jobs that bring greater pressure because they involve roles that count toward a company's bottom line. They frequently end up in staff jobs, sometimes labeled the "pink ghetto." Staff positions encompass areas such as human resources, legal, and public relations. About 50 to 65 percent of women at the vice president level and higher occupied staff positions in 2012, according to a McKinsey analysis of the talent pipeline for more than fifty companies. That compared with only 41 percent to 48 percent of men.[12]

But don't despair! In chapters about getting ahead, being a manager mom, male mentors, and managing men, this book will prepare you to navigate the rocky terrain and help you solve key work challenges so that you can reach your desired career goal.

# 2

# Doors Open with a Strong Push

To reach the top, you must often push hard at the bottom. That's what Beth Mooney did by refusing to take no for an answer when she was first trying to gain a toehold in the banking business.

"Tenacity and going for broke is part of my personality," said Mooney, the outspoken head of KeyCorp, a major regional bank. She's the sole female chief executive among the twenty biggest U.S. banks.

After graduating summa cum laude in 1977 from the University of Texas with a degree in history, Mooney interviewed at several Houston banks about joining a management training program. She repeatedly hit brick walls. "Can you type?" bank officials asked her again and again. Though she didn't type very well, Mooney took a job as a secretary for a real estate executive at First City National Bank of Houston.

"I am young. I am ambitious. I need a job," Mooney told herself. Looking back, she realized that "there was a different standard because I was a woman."

Despite her frustrations, the newly hired secretary refused to perform menial tasks, such as fetching coffee for her First City colleagues. In so many words, she remembered saying, "You have two arms and two legs. Go get it yourself."

The next year, Mooney relocated to Dallas for her husband's new job. Eager to escape the secretarial sisterhood, she again applied to be a bank management trainee. "I was determined and desperate," she pointed out.

Three Dallas banks rejected Mooney's application, citing her secretarial background and lack of an MBA degree. With such weak credentials, "you're not going to last," a human resources manager at Republic Bank reproached the eager young woman. Mooney had shown up for the interview attired in the ultimate of that era's business casual: a crisp white blouse and her best Ship'n Shore navy suit.

During her interview, Mooney saw several of the man's colleagues hovering by the door, waiting to go out for lunch. Before heading out to eat with those associates, the HR manager suggested that she make her pitch that afternoon to Keith Schmidt, the bank's head of training.

Schmidt occupied an office outside a training room where analyst trainees worked, lined up in neat rows. Few were women. Stepping out from behind his desk, Schmidt politely but firmly told Mooney that she wasn't qualified to enter the training program, citing her insufficient education. In response, she spent almost three hours trying to knock down his objections. She pretended to understand a credit file that he handed her. She promised to obtain a business degree.

"I wasn't leaving until he said yes," Mooney told me years later. She remembered thinking, "This is the first time I have gotten this far. I have to make this work."

Schmidt didn't throw her out of his office. He finally looked hard at Mooney, who was seated on a chair facing him. "I have never seen anybody want something so much. I won't sleep nights if I tell you no," the training chief said. "I don't think you are going to succeed. But go prove me wrong."

She promptly agreed to a $14,000-a-year salary, roughly $5,000 less than what most Republic Bank trainees earned at the time. But it was $4,000 more than her secretarial wage, and the bank paid for her graduate school tuition as well. Mooney, along with another female trainee, ended up outperforming everyone. They won full-time bank positions faster than any male trainee.

In May 2011 Schmidt sent Mooney a handwritten note, not long after she moved into the corner office at KeyCorp. He recollected feeling perplexed at how her name had suddenly shown up as a notation in his office calendar the day they met. But once they met, he wrote, "I realized I was in the presence of somebody who was special and I got intrigued."

Mooney called Schmidt to express her lifelong gratitude that he had played such a critical part in opening professional doors for her.

Mooney isn't unique. A number of high-powered corporate leaders I interviewed started out in traditional female occupations, such as waitress, bank teller, teacher, house cleaner, or production assistant. They often found ingenious ways to emphasize the skills that they had developed during their entry-level jobs.

Rather than shrink from early career impediments, you should persuade somebody to give you a break, several women advised. Carly Fiorina, the real estate brokerage receptionist turned CEO of technology giant Hewlett-Packard years later, expressed that sentiment well. "You absolutely have to have people who will take a chance on you," she said. "Be open to people helping you."

## GET GOING IN LOTS OF WAYS

Despite the great strides women have recently made in corporate management, those eager to move up today still need a strong door opener at the start of their professional lives.

Kathleen Ligocki, CEO of Agility Fuel Systems Inc., a developer and maker of natural gas fuel systems for vehicles, learned this lesson early. Being a woman opened doors faster than she expected at the outset. In 1979, the recent graduate of Indiana University with a degree in Chinese history and Renaissance art applied for the entry-level job of factory foreman at a GM electronics assembly plant in Kokomo, Indiana. She wrangled an interview despite her lack of an engineering degree.

"They are interviewing almost all engineers and businesspeople," Ligocki recollected between bites of lunch at a French bistro in Manhattan. "I get to the end of the day and sit down with this kind of old-style HR guy." The human resources manager worked in a small cubicle on the factory floor and Ligocki, a fast talker with fiery red hair and a cheek-to-cheek grin, held her hands in the air to illustrate the man's narrow workspace.

"I really want to hire engineers on this job," the manager told Ligocki. "But I have an attrition problem because all these engineers want to design integrated circuits. They don't want to work in this factory environment."

He kept talking. "I have a diversity metric, whatever the hell that is," he said. "So I want to hire an otherwise unemployable diversity candidate. And that would be you."

Ligocki took the $14,400-a-year job. She later became the first woman to steer Tower Automotive Inc., a major supplier of vehicle parts, and obtained the top job at Agility Fuel in late 2015 after leading Harvest Power Inc., an organic waste management concern, since 2014.

In my case, I hurt my head from banging it so often on newspapers' closed doors. I spent four years repeatedly seeking summer internships. At one point, I applied to more than a dozen newspapers a year in advance. None showed the slightest interest, even though I was an ace reporter on my campus newspaper.

The Newspaper Fund, a nonprofit foundation created by Dow Jones, publisher of the *Wall Street Journal*, opened its internship program to aspiring female journalists like me the year that I applied. Dow Jones had created the fund to attract male liberal arts majors to journalism. My 1969 selection as a Newspaper Fund intern generated summer offers from several big newspapers besides the *Journal*.

As my college graduation approached, I pushed hard for full-time employment in journalism. An editor at *Newsday*, a Long Island suburban newspaper, wanted to interview me for a permanent position. We had met during my prior pursuit of a summer internship there. "Make sure you wear that cute miniskirt you wore the last time," he said.

During the interview, the *Newsday* editor described openings in its revamped women's section and bragged about how the paper was closing the gender pay gap now that men had also begun working for that section. I refused to be pigeonholed into writing about food and fashion.

Accepting the *Journal* offer was easy. I had no other prospects.

## THE SERENDIPITOUS STRANGER

When it comes to breaking into the business world, you never know who might become a crucial early ally. For Liz Smith, then an aspiring young writer from the Philadelphia suburb of Yardley, it was a stranger in a Manhattan elevator. He turned out to be a star player in corporate America who was willing to offer her an unexpected toehold in his world.

Smith has come far from that life-changing day. She is chief executive of Bloomin' Brands Inc., owner of such immensely popular restaurant chains as Outback Steakhouse and Bonefish Grill. Smith and her family live the good life in St. Petersburg, Florida. Their nearly 7,100-square-foot Mediterranean Italianate home overlooks the scenic Intracoastal Waterway. Bought for almost $3.5 million in 2010, it has five bedrooms, 7.5 bathrooms, and a three-car garage, according to Zillow.com.

"I come out here to chill," Smith said on a warm, cloudy morning in January 2015 as she strolled to the edge of her dock. The family's small motorboat and their kayaks bobbed alongside it. Dolphins frolicked nearby.

Back in her high-ceilinged living room, Smith perched on the edge of a pale beige couch, ignoring the clatter from the kitchen, where her husband was whipping up pancakes for the couple's two teenage sons. She talked passionately about her college dream of writing the great American novel.

"I was a very idealistic English major from the University of Virginia," said Smith, an ebullient woman who raises her dark eyebrows for emphasis. If someone had told the newly minted graduate in 1985 that someday she would run a major public company, "I would have laughed and thought that was absurd," she said.

Being a novelist required "a long road that didn't pay much," observed her father, then the CEO of Commodore International Ltd., an early maker of personal computers. He proposed that she earn some money before earning a doctorate in English.

"My natural inclination was publishing," Smith said. "If I wasn't going to write a book, then I was going to circumvent the rules of having a real job by actually working in books." She moved to Manhattan, sharing an Upper West Side apartment with her sister and making the rounds of publishing houses. "My dream job was to work at Farrar, Straus and Giroux Publishers," she said, "because it was the imprint of Flannery O'Connor, my favorite writer."

Reality hit her like a harsh slap. The Phi Beta Kappa graduate was only qualified to be an executive assistant. Typing manuscripts paid little. "Not enough to be able to rent a closet from a friend of mine," Smith said bitterly.

Deciding not to settle for such options, Smith accepted a back-office administrative role at Morgan Stanley while she sought a meaningful position in publishing. One spring day in 1986, she paid a visit to her brother, a Paine Webber broker, so she could print out her résumé at his midtown office on Sixth Avenue. In the elevator, Smith struck up a conversation with an affable stranger dressed in an expensive suit with a starched white handkerchief. He seemed amused to see a young woman wearing jeans and flip-flops in a fancy office building. "Where are you going?" he asked.

Smith explained that she had just graduated from college, was uncertain about what she really wanted to do, and felt frustrated by her inability to find a decent job in publishing. "I was refreshingly unrehearsed and honest," she remembered. Luckily, they were riding a local elevator, giving her time to tell her tale.

The stranger turned out to be a Paine Webber senior vice president and a key player in its brokerage division. In retrospect, Smith suspected that "he had gotten a lot of very uptight young go-getters dressed to the nines telling him they wanted to be the next whoever."

The man also knew her brother. "The next thing I knew," Smith said, "he encouraged my brother to have me apply to one of the training programs there." The stranger from the elevator helped her land an interview and be chosen for the firm's two-year financial analyst program.

Nearly all of Smith's two dozen fellow trainees had degrees from Ivy League colleges in business or economics, along with relevant internships. But the competition didn't deter her. "I really dug in out of fear and insecurity, and became a strong analyst," she said.

Much to her surprise, Smith loved investment banking. "Working with really bright people on deals that were in the paper," she recalled. "The acquisition of Greyhound Bus Lines, a financing deal for an NBA team. Not exactly what I thought I could be doing as an English major."

Smith forgot about the great American novel. Instead of a doctorate in English, she earned an MBA. "It was a very fortuitous elevator ride," said Smith, with a look of mischievous glee in her wide-spaced hazel eyes. The encounter made her recognize the importance of speaking up with authenticity, even in the most unlikely setting.

## BREAKING GROUND IN UNFAMILIAR TERRITORY

An important door opened for Abbe Raven during a visit to Macy's department store in Manhattan in the winter of 1982. Largely thanks to that visit, she reached the peak of A+E Networks, whose ten cable television channels include History, Lifetime, and A&E.

Raven majored in theater at the University of Buffalo and by age twenty-two had become the youngest woman stage manager in professional theater in New York City. She subsequently spent five years teaching high school English and drama until late 1981, when she decided that she wanted to switch to television. But "I wasn't a TV person," recalled Raven, leaning forward on the gray couch in a glass-walled conference room at the ultramodern A+E headquarters on Manhattan's East Side. Clad in a short purple dress and black tights, she recounted her early struggles to shift professional gears.

Nobody is going to hire you without any television background, industry people warned her over and over. Raven brushed aside their warnings. "I can do this," she reassured herself. She had demonstrated the same sort of stubborn determination at age sixteen, when she declared her desire to go into show business. "I come from a working-class family," she recollected. "We had gone to Broadway twice."

Raven targeted Daytime, a start-up women's cable network that eventually evolved into A+E Networks, but at the time was a fledgling operation. She wrote to Daytime producers. "Nothing happened," she said. "I had no connections." She saw a full-page ad in the *New York Times* promoting the network's March 1982 launch by inviting the public to meet Daytime stars and programming executives in Macy's third-floor lingerie department.

Raven outfitted herself in a smart black polyester pantsuit with a vest. (She didn't yet own a skirt.) The publicity event attracted hundreds of women, and after it ended, dozens of well-dressed job seekers, each clutching a résumé, rushed the stage to buttonhole a Daytime programming executive. Raven was stuck at the back of the crowd. "I said, 'Okay, forget it,'" and she headed down the escalator to the second floor.

There, Raven changed her mind. "I said to myself, 'Stop. This is your shot. You can't go.' I turned around and I went back upstairs. By then, the crowd had thinned out a little."

The head of programming was already putting on her coat when Raven introduced herself, mentioning her theater major in college and her desire to break into television by joining Daytime.

Clearly impatient, the executive quickly inquired about Raven's professional theater experience. The fact that the young woman had managed stage productions made an impression. "You can work in television," the executive concluded. "Absolutely. Go for it." She gave Raven her business card and the name of a lieutenant in charge of Daytime's television studio whose title was production vice president. "I have no idea if he needs anybody," the programming boss said. "But give him a call."

Raven left Macy's in a trance. "This is it," she inwardly exulted. "My break."

She telephoned the vice president five times a day for the next ten days. He never called back. "On the tenth day, I did the old trick of calling at six thirty or seven at night, and he answered the phone. He said, 'I have seen your name on my call sheet many times.'" His tone turned brusque. "What do you want?"

Nearly frantic by this time, Raven talked faster, describing how she had met the top programming executive. "I am a production manager," she told him. "I've worked in theater. I really want to break into television."

He seemed indifferent to her pleas. "I have a million people calling," he replied.

Raven decided to take a more aggressive tack. "Just meet me," she pleaded. "I will come by tomorrow."

"Okay, I will see you tomorrow at two," he said reluctantly.

The vice president occupied a small, cluttered office that overlooked the studio near the Hudson River on Manhattan's West Side. It was Raven's first visit to a TV studio.

But she couldn't get any further than a foot in the door. "I have nothing here for you," the man said. He reiterated what he had said on the phone. "I have a million people from broadcast television who want to get a job in cable television," he continued. "You have no experience, I can't hire you."

Raven ignored his rejection. "I am really, really good," the twenty-nine-year-old applicant declared. "I will do anything, whatever you need done." She insisted that she would start at the bottom, despite her years as a stage manager and high school teacher.

The studio boss again refused to hire her. The interview was over. They both stood. As Raven reached his door, she turned and made her promise again. "Really, I would do anything."

Her ardent willingness to perform menial tasks ultimately dented his resolve. "Do you see those scripts over here?" he asked, pointing to three piles of scripts on the floor. Each pile stood three feet high and every script needed to be photocopied. "My secretary is going in the hospital tomorrow," he explained. "Would you do that?"

Raven said that she would copy the scripts. She started the next day in a job for which she was initially paid about $3.50 an hour. Her official title was production assistant. But "the secretary never came back," she noted. "I ended up basically being his secretary."

Raven rose through the ranks and became a senior vice president by 1994. She attracted attention for launching the History Channel the following year and growing it into a leading cable network. In 2005, A+E elevated her to chief executive, making her the first woman in its top job. And while a power transfer between women rarely happens in the corner offices of corporate America, it did at A+E Networks. After Raven mentored her lieutenant Nancy Dubuc for years, the company decided that she should hand Dubuc the reins in 2014.

## FATHERS MATTER

My interview for a college summer internship with the *Washington Daily News*, then one of the city's four major newspapers,

abruptly ended when an editor wanted to know which section employed my father.

"He doesn't work here," I confessed.

"Sorry," the editor replied. "We only hire employees' children
for summer jobs."

In this situation, I was the loser. But with most industries and
professions dominated by men, several female executives I interviewed gained an early advantage by having a well-connected
father.

Among them was Sally Smith, now CEO of Buffalo Wild Wings
Inc., a fast-growing restaurant chain based in Minneapolis.
Growing up in Grand Forks, North Dakota, she often discussed
business with her father, president of a small bank. She worked at
the bank as a file clerk beginning when she was sixteen.

Smith soon developed strong opinions about the status of
women. She remembered a summer evening during her college
years when her father was in the kitchen cutting up a half side
of beef for his annual office barbecue. He employed a few female
officers, but only invited male executives to the event.

"My dad was not sexist," said Smith, dressed in a gray wool
sheath dress and calf-high leather boots during our conversation
at her Buffalo Wild Wings office, framed by an oversize map of the
world. "He had three daughters. He very much encouraged us."

But her father's attitudes did not always seem to extend to his
workplace, a state of affairs that mystified his ambitious daughter. "Why wouldn't you have the women there?" she demanded
when she heard about his plans for the barbecue. "How are they
going to get to know the people they work with?"

"The jokes might be inappropriate," her father replied. For her, this was an unacceptable answer. "I said, 'Dad, they can hold their own,'" she recalled telling him. "'It is up to the men to watch their language. Not to be concerned about the women. I am sure they have heard these words before.'"

The next year, the women attended the barbecue.

Graduating from the University of North Dakota in 1980 with a degree in accounting, Smith debated whether to join the Minneapolis office of Peat Marwick, a Big Eight accounting firm that had zero female partners at that location. Its managing partner telephoned her father because they had belonged to the same college fraternity. "We had a chance to interview your daughter," the executive said. "We would really like her to come work for us. As she is making her decisions, we hope you will put in a good word."

Eager to please her father, Smith accepted Peat Marwick's offer. "I went in not knowing the managing partner," she said, "but knowing that he was watching out for me."

## HELPFUL HUSBANDS

Spouses can open doors, too, as Sara Mathew, a former chief executive of Dun & Bradstreet Corp., discovered.

Mathew's husband, Jacob, played a vital early role in her progression from an accounting clerk in 1982 to chief executive of the credit report giant in 2010. In hindsight, "I would not be where I am if I didn't have Jacob in my corner," Mathew said. "A person who gets me, knows who I am. Who encouraged me all the way through."

Mathew had never worked before emigrating to the United States from India in fall 1980 at age twenty-five. She arrived after an arranged marriage in the couple's native land.

One afternoon as we nursed cold drinks at a sleek Manhattan hotel bar, she described her childhood as the daughter of two physicians. On this occasion, she wore pressed jeans and a simple sleeveless blouse, as she was headed for the airport. "My parents raised me to be married," said Mathew, a gregarious talker with flowing dark hair. "That's what it means to be a 'kept woman.' You marry somebody rich."

Mathew attended college in India and spent summers taking vacations with her family there. She enjoyed playing tennis in the cooler hills.

Mathew first met Jacob ten days before they wed. Their nuptials took place two days after her final exam for a master's degree in finance and accounting. Her fiancé, a product development manager for Procter & Gamble Co., worked in research and development at the headquarters of the big consumer products company in Cincinnati, where he already owned a modest trilevel home. The $62,000 he had borrowed to pay for the $65,000 house frightened his bride. In India, families typically bought their residences with cash.

"We don't own the house," Mathew said, recounting her anxious thoughts as she embarked on married life in a new country. "I have to pay off that debt. I have to work. His debt is now our debt."

Originally, she thought that working would be fun. But finding a job turned out to be no fun. She knew little about job hunting in America, and searching for employment then was a low-tech task. Because her résumé contained no work experience, she filled the single-page document with detailed descriptions of her two degrees.

In 1981, Mathew found a temporary, low-level position at a local manufacturer of office safes, and worked there off and on for more than a year while she kept trying to find a real job. "Every Sunday, I got the newspaper," Mathew recollected. "Sunday evening, I circled every job I thought I qualified for. Monday, I sent out all the résumés. Friday, usually the reject letters arrived."

Mathew had been turned down for dozens of the forty permanent spots she had sought before finally landing an interview at a local Avon Products Inc. facility. The hiring manager, attired in a no-nonsense business suit, looked the young applicant up and down when Mathew arrived, dressed in brown pants, a casual red shirt from India, and a long-strapped bag slung over her shoulder.

"I must have looked like a hippie," she said. "I knew I wasn't dressed right." Hardly to her surprise, Avon rejected her.

So Mathew bought a copy of *Working Woman* magazine, a self-help publication launched in 1976, and figured out what she should wear for such occasions. She splurged on a navy skirt suit, a white oxford shirt, a red silk tie, navy pumps, and a shiny briefcase.

Armed with more appropriate attire, Mathew decided to explore opportunities at P&G, where her husband helped open a door. He gave her résumé to his boss, who put it into the company's recruitment system, and P&G invited her for an interview.

"I didn't know what I was going for," Mathew admitted. But,

she added, "I came out at the end of the day with an offer." The job paid $350 a week. She mistakenly thought P&G wanted to hire her as a cost accountant, a professional position that involves tracking costs. "I don't think I heard them because I was so excited."

She returned home, walking on air thanks to the offer. Her husband asked her why she would be paid weekly rather than monthly. "What's wrong with that?" she wondered as they chatted in their small kitchen.

Jacob explained that he and his fellow managers were paid monthly while clerical workers received weekly paychecks. "Don't take it," he urged his wife. "If you start as a clerk, you are never going to get anywhere."

Mathew stood her ground. "I am going to take it," she replied firmly. "If I don't like it, I will try something else."

Though her husband finally supported her decision, his hunch proved right. "When my first paycheck came," Mathew remembered, "it said, 'cost accounting clerk.'" But she was nonetheless elated. "I didn't even want to cash it. It was the first time I had ever owned anything. I was so proud."

Within fifteen months of her arrival in November 1982, Mathew was chosen for a managerial post, earning $25,000 a year. In 2013, her final year as Dun & Bradstreet CEO, she earned a package worth $5.2 million (including stock grants). Her total compensation hit a peak of about $6.7 million in 2011.

Mathew had come a long way from making $350 a week decades earlier. Yet she never regretted commencing her career as a low-level P&G clerk. "Starting there," she said, "taught me a lot about how we sometimes treat people."

## LEADERSHIP LESSONS
## FROM "DOORS OPEN WITH A STRONG PUSH"

- Be tenacious about looking outside your comfort zone for an open door and finding someone to champion your candidacy. That's especially important when obstacles loom, as they invariably will. You can't shrink from those barriers, advises Beth Mooney, chief executive of KeyCorp.

- Find influential internal allies. Linda Hudson, former CEO of BAE Systems, sought such early ties among the men she worked with in the male-dominated defense industry and cemented her connections by exceeding their expectations. "If I focused on what I did, they would forget I was female."

- Try to avoid letting preconceived notions influence your judgments of employees. Mindy Grossman, chief executive of HSN Inc., a retailer known for its home-shopping network, embraced this idea after she ran into gender stereotypes while trying to open doors early in her career. She vowed to someday become a boss who looks at who a person really is.

- Confront self-doubts about your capabilities. Clara Shih, CEO of Hearsay Social, the social media advisory firm, battled the self-esteem demon when she was an academic star at Stanford University. "If you hear that voice, you need to overpower it with another voice that says, 'I do belong,'" she recommends. "Catch yourself."

- Be willing to start at the bottom. Abbe Raven, former leader of A+E Networks, still swears by this tactic. "I hear people say, 'Don't be a secretary,'" she remembers. "Excuse me, that's how I learned finance," she continues. "If you are good, you will shine."

- For your professional debut, seek a workplace where you have a fighting chance to succeed. Janet Dolan, the first woman in senior management and later the CEO of Tennant Co., a maker of industrial cleaning products, suggests trying to make sure that your first workplace is known for being a pretty good environment for women.

- Aim for early jobs that measure success quantitatively, such as by the number of items sold. "Then, it is not about who you are," says Maggie Wilderotter, former executive chairman and CEO of Frontier Communications. "It is about what you deliver."

# 3

# Getting Picked: Bloom Where You Are Planted

As their careers progressed, the women I interviewed didn't always get their preferred pick of managerial positions. For some, that turned out to be a lucky setback.

Case in point: Andrea Jung, who would one day take command of cosmetics giant Avon Products. The day that Jung found herself summoned by the chief executive of Bloomingdale's, she was twenty-five years old and making $23,000 a year as a swimwear buyer there.

On that day in late 1984, Jung already harbored lofty ambitions. Her ultimate goal was to run a trendy ready-to-wear division at the glitzy Manhattan department store. Jung had turned Bloomingdale's conservative swimwear department into a fashion destination by stocking a wide assortment of hip and sexy bathing suits.

"I felt ready, and my results were great," she remembered as we conversed in her small office in Times Square crammed with Avon mementos such as a hand-stitched pillow that read, "Behind every great woman is herself." Jung was wearing her trademark pearl necklace, which matched the elegant white orchid on a corner table.

Marvin Traub, Bloomingdale's larger-than-life leader, had transformed the store from a low-rent dry goods emporium into arguably the city's hottest retail destination during the 1970s and 1980s. He knew Jung casually. She was the daughter of Chinese immigrants, and they had met when she filled in for an absent translator so Traub could entertain a China delegation assembled in the corporate boardroom. At the time, Jung's wardrobe was so modest that she had to borrow a suit from Bloomingdale's sportswear department for the event.

"From that point on, he took an interest in my career," Jung said. "I always felt like we had a connection. He would look out to see how I was doing."

Five years after Jung translated for Traub, his secretary called her "and asked me to come upstairs that day and meet Mr. Traub." The secretary didn't explain why.

The young buyer felt nervous about seeing the CEO again, partly because she had just been passed over for the ready-to-wear promotion that she yearned for and offered what she regarded as a less attractive advancement: a job as merchandise manager for the intimate apparel division. Jung believed that selling underwear, widely considered an old-fashioned segment of the women's apparel market, was a low priority for her employer's big brass.

The same man had run that department for thirty years. He

and his buyers toiled in a windowless office in the store's subbasement. The adjacent subway rumbled loudly.

She rode the elevator to Traub's corner office, which was located behind the towel department on the seventh floor of the company's flagship store. Large windows overlooked the corner of Lexington Avenue and Fifty-Ninth Street, one of the city's best-known intersections. "He had photographs of himself with every imaginable designer," she recalled. "He was the iconic retailer of his day."

Traub sat in an armchair facing Jung, who was perched on a couch. "In his inimitable style, Marvin described the potential to transform lingerie into an exciting department," Jung said. He challenged her to take the role and create a new vision for that department of Bloomingdale's.

Jung asked for a day or two to decide, but she finally accepted the offer. In the ready-to-wear division, "I wouldn't have learned what it was to dive into something where at first you feel like you are in over your head." Taking such a dive, she acknowledged, "does test your ability to really become a leader."

Arriving in the subbasement headquarters of the lingerie department, Jung suddenly recollected a poster of a potted plant that hung on a wall of the store's human resources office. "Bloom Where You Are Planted," the poster urged. Jung began to suspect that she might benefit from stepping into what she perceived as an undesirable management position.

For the new merchandise manager, grasping the complexities of a different product line while leading a dozen older associates was a challenge. Jung listened intently before making bold changes to the assortment of intimate apparel that the store carried. Among her changes: adding bright-colored bras and panties to the conventional mix of beige and white underwear. The new items sold out, and the department flourished during her two-year tenure.

"It was a career-defining moment," Jung said. She never forgot that Bloomingdale's assignment.

Joining Avon in January 1994 as its president of U.S. product marketing, she discovered a direct-sales company with a stodgy and outmoded brand that was strongly identified with the staid Avon Lady. "The passion to reinvent the brand probably came from those early-day assignments," Jung said. In 1999, Avon directors elevated her to chief executive, making her the first woman to reach its apex.

Taking a different managerial spot than the one you really want "can end up being the very best thing that happens to you," Jung observed. And, she added, this sort of threatened career setback can be "a very integral part of becoming a better leader."

## THE MAINE CAPER

Andrea Jung won a chance for a significant promotion within a few years of launching her career. Anne Mulcahy trod a much slower path to management, but eventually ran Xerox Corp., the giant copier and printer company.

She became a Xerox sales representative in 1976. "Sales had the purity of quantitative results," Mulcahy remembered, speaking with a fierce earnestness amid the noisy lunchtime clatter of a Manhattan restaurant. She reminded me of a schoolteacher, with wide-set eyes that peer through her black-rimmed glasses.

At the outset, however, Mulcahy got little pleasure from selling Xerox products. "A lot of cold calling, a lot of rejection," she recalled. "I don't think I was a naturally gifted sales rep," she said. "If you are not doing well, it leads to a tough outcome."

One of two Xerox saleswomen in the Boston area, Mulcahy harbored a deep fear of failure. She forced herself to work harder and longer than anyone else. She performed well. After selling for almost six years, the rep raised her hand to be a Xerox sales manager. Repeatedly.

She interviewed for about a half-dozen sales management jobs, but always without success. Being a woman, especially an unmarried one like her, represented a disadvantage in those days, especially in a large and traditional business, she concluded. "I wondered whether there was a priority around men with families," she said in recounting her frustrations.

Male bosses who interviewed Mulcahy about openings in the company often seemed to merely go through the motions of considering her candidacy. They grilled her about such tangential issues as how she would handle traveling alone on business trips.

"I don't even understand what the problem is," she replied, keenly aware that her male counterparts were never asked about this matter. "To me, it was not fair," she said. "Rather than get defeated, I got mad."

At one point, Mulcahy applied for the open position of sales manager in Maine, a state she had never even visited. "It was a loser assignment," she observed. With its far-flung and largely rural population, Maine consistently ranked among Xerox's worst regions.

As she relived those tense times from 1981, Mulcahy unconsciously switched to the present tense. "It is a team of old codgers

•

that had been up there, lived up there," she told me. "Hadn't been successful ever. All guys."

Because Xerox did so little business in Maine, accepting the job meant she would have to travel extensively on small planes so she could make the rounds of remote paper mills. "I don't know what made me do it," she said. "I don't think there was even anyone else interviewing for the assignment." She now realizes that she was driven by hopes for a chance to demonstrate her capacity to lead.

Mulcahy interviewed for the Maine job in the big Boston office of one of the company's branch managers. "Do you even know where Maine is?" he barked at the young woman sitting opposite his desk. He strode over to a large map and pointed. "Here is where you are, and here is Maine. Why do you want this job?"

"I want a challenge," Mulcahy replied.

Although no one else had raised a hand for the job, the branch manager initially resisted committing himself. Mulcahy's seventh try finally brought her into the management ranks at Xerox.

Taking the position in Maine turned into a smart career move for the novice sales manager. By Mulcahy's second year on the job, Maine ranked among Xerox's three top-performing regions in the Northeast. "We did spectacularly well, something that had never happened before," she recollected.

But the branch manager, who was now her supervisor, refused to recognize her part in the state's impressive sales figures. "He would attribute it more to good fortune than talent," Mulcahy said. "He was not a fan." And when the man left Xerox to launch a rival business, she continued, "he took all of the sales managers in Boston with him with the exception of me." She landed her next promotion only after he resigned.

Mulcahy gleaned a crucial career lesson about jerk bosses, an all-too-common species back then and still today: "Learning to work for assholes is a really important thing to do. And surviving them."

## BAD BOSSES BEGAT BETTER BOSSES

Some women assigned to a bad boss took advantage of the arrangement to figure out how to be better bosses. Among them was Carol Bartz, the former CEO of Autodesk and Yahoo. The sharp-tongued woman once worked for a man who insisted that she stay silent during the meetings he conducted.

"He didn't want to hear what I had to say because I was probably right," Bartz recalled. In response, she vowed, "'I am not going to do this, I am going to remember how this felt.' That's when you really advance in your own personal style."

Geraldine "Geri" Laybourne, one of a handful of early staffers at Nickelodeon, the cable TV network for children that she later ran, thrived despite an equally daunting experience with a bad boss. Laybourne was recruited as the network's program manager in 1980, based on her experience as a teacher. At Nickelodeon, she initially reported to a veteran of the advertising industry.

"He was very much a command-and-control patriarchal manager," Laybourne said. "He was the very best teacher I ever had because I kept a notebook of 'what I will never do when I am a boss.'"

She especially resented his insistence on hoarding critical information. "His idea of managing was, 'If I hold all the information, people will have to come to me and I will be important,'"

Laybourne continued. "I was trained as an open classroom teacher. The role of an open classroom teacher is to find out how you can nurture each one of your students." The experience taught her that a good boss should not terrorize employees or make them feel inadequate.

Laybourne scribbled numerous pointers in her notebook, which she accumulated during four years of observing the shortcomings of her Nickelodeon supervisor. They included:

- Bullying is not attractive.
- Getting angry with people doesn't work.
- Sharing mistakes is better than covering them up.


## SWEET REVENGE

Melissa Dyrdahl turned the tables on a bad boss and came out ahead. Dyrdahl, who subsequently became chief executive of Ella Health Inc., a start-up firm that provides women's health care services, found herself in this awkward situation during the early 1990s. At the time, she was a thirty-something senior manager for Claris Corp., the software unit of then-named Apple Computer Inc.

Male colleagues encouraged Dyrdahl to apply for her departing boss's job. Moving up to the director level would be a major promotion. But she knew nothing about two of the six areas that he oversaw.

"I decided all on my own that I wasn't qualified," Dyrdahl admitted, sitting barefoot in the living room of her California hilltop home. She gazed out its soaring windows, which offered a picturesque vista of the distant Silicon Valley and San Francisco Bay beyond. "I somehow wasn't going to be able to do a good job."

Crossing her arms and clenching her teeth, Dyrdahl looked pained as she described her tale of self-sabotage. "Almost all the leadership in this company was men," she said. "Which I think subconsciously is another reason why I was a little hesitant. So I just didn't throw my hat in the ring."

Yet the successful candidate, a recruit from Apple, grasped just two of the six areas that the job required. He was a boyishly handsome man with a turned-up freckled nose who offered big-company experience plus plenty of personal charisma. As it turned out, those assets didn't suffice.

Within two months, Dyrdahl realized that he was as dumb as a rock. "He doesn't work very hard. He shows up at nine, leaves at five," she said, ticking off the man's shortcomings on her fingers. "This guy has skated by on his charm and good looks."

Watching her new superior perform poorly, Dyrdahl came to see her own management potential in a fresh light. "You can take what you know and still be a successful leader even if you don't know everything," she told herself. Her comments sound like a management truism, but they still represent a useful insight.

Claris pushed out her bad boss after less than a year. When that happened, Dyrdahl expressed interest in succeeding him during a meeting with a vice president.

"The guy is leaving and I want this job," she said confidently. "I know I can do it better than he can. I can manage these other functions, too. The ones I didn't know." She and the vice president had a thirty-minute conversation as they sat around a coffee table in his office at Claris headquarters in Santa Clara.

"You can do this job," he agreed. And Dyrdahl did.

Her 1992 promotion proved a crucial career milestone. Dyrdahl subsequently became a senior vice president of software manufacturer Adobe Systems Inc., where her boss was Chief Executive Bruce Chizen. He recruited her from Claris, where they had worked together for years. By 2003, she managed 250 staffers and a $100 million–plus budget for Adobe.

## THE WILD WEST OF TECH

From the outset, tech industry veteran Diane M. Bryant worked vigorously to fit in with the industry's notoriously rough-and-tumble male culture. Her efforts bore fruit in a critical way: she earned respect from a male peer, who later helped her deal with a misogynist male boss.

She joined Intel Corp. in 1985, after completing a degree in electrical engineering at the University of California, Davis. "It was the Wild West days of Silicon Valley," recalled Bryant, who is now an executive vice president of the big semiconductor company and oversaw 29 percent of its $55.4 billion in revenue during 2015. Like much of the tech industry, Intel remains a man's world, with men comprising about three-fourths of its U.S. workforce.

"I took the stance that I am going to be one of the guys," Bryant explained. "To be successful, you have to embrace the majority." She said she quickly figured out how to swear like a sailor, down single-malt scotch, and drive a stick-shift BMW.

By 2003, the year she turned forty-one, Bryant had moved up to a senior management role. She led engineering teams that developed Intel server products. Her boss was the general manager of the entire server business. (A server is a computer that provides data to other computers in a network.)

But her supervisor repeatedly refused to let her attend quarterly business reviews with an important customer. He gave no explanation for his actions. In retrospect, however, Bryant thinks she knows what motivated him. "He hated women," Bryant said. "He hated me more."

She renewed her request as her boss wrapped up a staff meeting in his conference room at an Intel office outside Portland, Oregon. She made a strong pitch. The customer with the coming review needed to discuss topics that were clearly her responsibility, Bryant insisted.

"He looked at me and said, 'Diane, the customer does not want to talk to a woman.'" The comment infuriated her. "His own stupid gender bias was stopping me from talking to the customer," Bryant said. She subsequently learned that the customer had no problem dealing with women in the workplace.

As it turned out, the unit's assistant general manager overheard their boss's brusque remark. "He was mortified," Bryant remembered. Conferring privately with her afterward, the man volunteered to rectify the situation. He made sure that she got to attend Intel's next meeting with that customer.

Bryant arrived late the night before the session in Texas, where the customer was located. She entered a noisy bar filled with twenty-five guys from Intel and the customer having drinks. Their consumption of booze was well under way, and she heard men curse and loudly challenge one another about who was the most macho. Not a single female patron was in sight.

Bryant vividly recollected the well-meaning bartender. "She jumped out from behind the bar, ran over and stopped me at the door, and said, 'Honey, I wouldn't come in here if I were you.'" Bryant barged past her. "I know these guys," she explained.

Bryant said she gained valuable insights about the customers' needs during their eight-hour visit the next day, and in the process forged long-term business relationships. But she decided that staying in her boss's unit would not boost her Intel career. Luckily for her, he quit midway through her quest for an alternate supervisor at the company.

## MAKING PEACE WITH MALE PEERS

Several female leaders devised different clever tactics to get accepted by male peers during the early days of their careers, laying a foundation for their later success.

That's what Mary Barra did in 1983, three decades before General Motors tapped her as its first female CEO. The daughter of a veteran GM die maker, she grew up in a household where neither parent had earned a four-year college degree.

Barra remains as unassuming today as she did when she entered the auto industry. Dressed in casual black slacks and matching jacket, the powerful executive initially didn't want to be photographed on the spring afternoon that we met in her thirty-ninth-floor office atop GM headquarters, a black-sheathed glass skyscraper with a sweeping view of the Detroit River. She had been up since five thirty that morning, so "my makeup is gone," she murmured.

With dark circles under her eyes and her shoulder-length hair slightly disheveled, Barra settled herself at a conference table. Her nearby desk was outfitted with a simple black chair with a webbed back, old-fashioned "in" boxes at either end, three piles of paper, and no personal touches. An oversize poster of a red Cadillac ATS, a compact luxury sedan, hung on the wall behind her wooden desk.

In her first full-time job after she finished her college degree in electrical engineering from the company-owned General Motors Institute, Barra worked as a controls engineer for a GM plant in Pontiac, Michigan. The facility made a sporty car called the Fiero. It used innovative production methods, such as breaking down barriers between salaried managers and hourly line workers.

Barra's job involved making sure that the factory was running as it should and that equipment was properly maintained and repaired. To accomplish these tasks, she needed cooperation from its virtually all-male workforce. "I was working on systems all through the plant," Barra recalled.

But every time the young engineer walked past one corner of the factory floor, an assembly worker directed a shrill wolf whistle in her direction. She finally stopped and stared at him. "What are you doing?" she asked.

Trying to attract your attention, he replied.

She suggested that he do so by simply saying, "Hi." "And I will say 'Hi,' instead of me walking quickly and ignoring you," she promised. The man stopped his wolf whistles. The two began to greet each other with a wave or a hello.

Mutual respect emerged from their more personalized interactions, Barra said, adding, "We transitioned from a nameless type of walking by to 'Hey, I know you. You know me. Hi!'" Noisy cat-calls from other male workers dwindled, too.

The former wolf whistler helped shape Barra's future leadership style, a key aspect of which consists of trying to look at the world through other people's eyes. "I have this fundamental belief that everybody is pretty rational," she told me. "If you can understand what is motivating them or change what is motivating them, you can accomplish things. So I have always wanted to understand. Maybe that is the engineering part of me."

## THE TIE WAR

Kathleen Ligocki, the Agility Fuel CEO who arrived at GM as a twenty-two-year-old diversity hire, won respect from fellow fore-men following her unusual war over their required ties.

They worked together at a hot, old, and noisy electronics facility in Kokomo, Indiana, that assembled speakers, among other items. Ligocki managed about two hundred workers on the speaker line. "Fast, fast, fast work," she recollected. "All handwork at the time. Almost all women, except for the leaders, who were all guys."

Ligocki and nine male foremen reported to the assembly plant's general foreman. Twenty years her senior, the general foreman had never before had a woman on his leadership team.

As a uniform, she wore a GM blouse with her first name custom-stitched on the front. "The guys wore traditional long- or short-sleeve button-down shirts with ties," she said. "They could ditch the ties for the summer."

Ligocki started in June 1979. Because of the overhead ovens, summer temperatures in the plant often skyrocketed. And the assembly lines lacked air-conditioning. That year, the hot weather lasted past Labor Day, when the tie rule officially resumed.

One sultry September day, Ligocki's fellow foremen grew cranky about having to don their ties again. The temperature near the speaker assembly line exceeded 155 degrees, Ligocki estimated. The foremen marched into their boss's office to complain that while they had to wear ties, she didn't.

The general foreman then called Ligocki to his office, a glass cube in the middle of the speaker assembly line. The cramped but air-conditioned cocoon contained a desk, a credenza, and a few chairs. Hundreds of factory workers, mostly women, watched an unusual drama unfold inside his workspace.

"I didn't sit down because I didn't know what he wanted," Ligocki said. "He starts talking in a roundabout way. 'We are a team here. We all want to be equal. I want to treat you like I treat all the guys.'"

Her boss finally made his point. "You know the guys all have to wear ties. We think it would be fair if you would wear a tie, too."

The request surprised Ligocki. "I am looking at him thinking, 'I am getting fashion advice from you?'" She asked whether she had to still wear a bra.

"Oh, oh yes," the general foreman answered.

"Well, maybe the men can wear bras," Ligocki shot back.

Caught off guard, her stunned boss blushed a deep red as she walked out the door. He immediately brought the foremen back for another chat. The men strode into his office, smugly confident that Ligocki would soon share their sartorial misery.

"In the glass box, you could see him relaying what I had told him," she recalled. "And you see the same look on their faces. They are shocked, speechless."

Female workers on the speaker assembly line watched the whole dramatic scene play out. "The guys all come out and they are like, 'Well, I am not wearing a bra! That's really stupid,'" Ligocki said. The story spread like wildfire down the lines. "The women just gave the men hell for the rest of the day," she added. "I never got fashion advice again."

But the foremen still had to wear ties. I wondered how standing up for herself humorously with the general foreman changed Ligocki's working relationship with her male colleagues.

"Earned cred," Ligocki said. "That's how guys deal with each other. They go toe-to-toe. It is like male belly bumping."

The tie requirement "was a ridiculous rule," Ligocki said, noting that a foreman could easily injure himself by leaning over dangerous equipment with a dangling tie. "Nobody should have been wearing ties."

The Indiana plant changed the rule several years after she left. Foremen no longer had to don ties once interior temperatures hit a certain level.

"Her refusal to model herself after men didn't slow her one bit," Anne Doyle wrote about Ligocki in her 2011 book, *Powering Up! How America's Women Achievers Become Leaders*. "She rose to hold multiple CEO positions in the fiercely competitive global auto industry."[1]

## LEADERSHIP LESSONS FROM "GETTING PICKED"

- Your experiences with a bad boss can teach you how to become a better manager.

- Take stock of your managerial strengths rather than focus on your weaknesses. That especially can make a difference when you're competing for a promotion. Notes Melissa Dyrdahl, a former Adobe Systems senior vice president: "Don't assume that this other candidate deserves all the credit."
- Make sure your supervisor knows what you really want career-wise and take the same approach with your key lieutenants. Teresa Taylor, a former chief operating officer of Qwest Communications International Inc., recommends regularly informing higher-ups about your willingness to relocate for a better job, for example.
- View your management career as a zigzag. Stepping backward into a less glamorous role can enable you to step forward into a better one. Andrea Jung, a prior Avon CEO, believes women face more zigzags than men "but actually should be able to cope with them better."
- Use humor rather than anger to deflect gender stereotypes, gaining respect from male peers by connecting with them as one human being to another.
- Stand out on a trivial project by going the extra mile. Meg Whitman, CEO of Hewlett Packard Enterprise Co. and Hewlett-Packard CEO until the company's 2015 breakup, recalls writing "the definitive memo" about the size of the hole in a shampoo bottle cap during her early days at Procter & Gamble. What initially struck her as a stupid assignment became a defining moment. She decided to always do "the very best job that has ever been done," no matter how seemingly trivial the task.

# 4

# Sexual Harassment Never Vanished

The scourge of sexual harassment in the American workplace persists despite decades of outcry, litigation, legislation, and awareness training for workers.

Long after becoming the first woman to run a Fortune 20 company, Carly Fiorina remembered her early encounters with sexual harassment. And even as recently as 2015, the year Fiorina launched her bid for the White House, young women regularly approached her to share their tales of being harassed or demeaned by men.

While a young saleswoman for AT&T, Fiorina once rebuffed an amorous middle manager at the company's Mountain Bell unit in Denver. The two had spent much of the day visiting customers, and that evening, when they met for drinks in the hotel bar, she realized that the man viewed her as his next sexual conquest.

Although she escaped to her hotel room, "he called throughout the night and was angrier every time," Fiorina said in *Tough Choices: A Memoir*, her 2006 book. The next day, when she arrived at the

Mountain Bell office in Denver, she was greeted with unwelcome stares from her coworkers. "Eventually, I was told that the man I'd rejected the previous evening had come into work that morning bragging about the great sex we'd had the night before," she wrote.[1]

Fiorina described the incident in greater detail along with how she dealt with it during our subsequent interviews. Rather than fume, she told a trusted male associate about what had really happened. "A guy who was well respected in the office and knew me and believed me," she said of the man she confided in. As for the middle manager whose behavior had so upset her, she decided to exclude him from a major business pitch she made to a U.S. government agency.

"I don't think revenge is the right term," Fiorina said. But, she noted, "there are consequences to choices. The consequence for him was that he had destroyed a working relationship." And, she added, "he was a higher level than I was. I had no power. I just cut him out of what I was doing."

Thanks to Fiorina's instrumental role in winning the contract with the federal agency and the successful installation of AT&T equipment, the company promoted her to sales manager. The Denver harassment incident made a deep impression on Fiorina, helping her figure out how women should deal with offensive treatment on the job. She noted in her book, "We can only be diminished if we choose to allow it."[2]

## THE PERSISTENT SCOURGE

Sexual harassment has long represented an occupational hazard for women. As I wrote in a front-page article in the *Wall Street*

*Journal* in 1981, unwelcome physical or verbal advances usually directed by men at women pervade the workplace and increase employee absenteeism and turnover.[3]

Little has changed since then. One in four women has experienced sexual harassment in the workplace, Langer Research Associates found in a 2011 poll of 1,018 American adults. And 64 percent of both genders still viewed sexual harassment as a problem, a figure that soared to 88 percent for women who had been harassed.

One woman who recently fought back against inappropriate behavior toward women on the job is Christina Young. While a managing director at Steven Hall & Partners, an executive pay consultancy, she sued the firm over sexual harassment. Her 2014 lawsuit claimed that male colleagues routinely talked about erections and masturbation in the office, and that one of them read erotica aloud. Young also alleged that a male managing director encouraged female managing directors to perform oral sex on potential clients to help the company obtain new business. The company declined to comment about its subsequent settlement of the suit.

Young's case was far from unique. Sexual harassment has grabbed recent headlines amid a flurry of fights involving high-level women in such industries as retail, venture capital, technology, and executive recruitment. American Apparel Inc. was ordered to spend more than $3 million to resolve arbitration claims of sexual harassment and defamation in 2014 and 2015, court documents showed. The company disputed liability in the arbitration claims.[4]

Allegations of sexual harassment also emerged during a closely watched trial in 2015 involving gender bias. The case pitted Ellen Pao, a former partner at Kleiner Perkins Caufield & Byers, against that prominent venture capital firm. Much of the testimony focused on an affair that Pao had had with a married colleague. She claimed that the man had relentlessly pursued the relationship but retaliated against her when she broke it off.

During a business trip, the same man appeared at the door of a hotel room of another female partner wearing only a bathrobe, that woman testified. Pao further testified that yet another male partner gave her a book of erotic poems on Valentine's Day.[5]

In March 2015, the jury ruled that Kleiner Perkins had not sexually discriminated or retaliated against Pao when she complained. She filed to appeal the trial loss, but later dropped her appeal. The trial came in the wake of repeated allegations of unfair treatment of women in Silicon Valley, including several sexual harassment suits by former executives of tech start-ups. A subsequent survey of more than two hundred tech industry women with at least ten years of experience lent credibility to allegations raised in the industry suits. Nearly all of the women worked in the San Francisco Bay area. A surprising 60 percent of those polled said they had experienced unwanted sexual advances.

Nor is such behavior entirely random. Women in male-dominated organizations who display assertive, dominant, and independent personalities find themselves the primary victims of sexual harassment, a 2007 academic study concluded. "Sexual and sexist comments, unwanted sexual attention, and sexual coercion [are] primarily targeted at women who step out of place by having masculine characteristics, or 'uppity women,'" wrote

Jennifer L. Berdahl, then a management researcher at the University of Toronto. "This suggests that sexual harassment is driven not out of desire for women who meet feminine ideals but out of a desire to punish those who violate them."[6]

Penny Herscher of FirstRain, the business analytics firm in San Mateo, California, she led between 2005 and 2015, believes sexual harassment remains prevalent because of how society treats women. "It is very deep and very fundamental," she said.

Herscher knows that reality all too well. In 2013, an attractive FirstRain employee complained about unwanted advances from a man who worked for a large corporate customer. "She showed me a text," Herscher said. "It was really inappropriate, sort of badgering her to go out with him."

The young woman refused to date the customer. "She said, 'I don't want anything to do with this man, but I also don't want to hurt FirstRain,'" Herscher recalled.

Seeking to resolve the issue as calmly as possible, the FirstRain chief executive encouraged the staffer to offer a reasonable excuse for rebuffing the man's advances. "She told him she was in another relationship," Herscher said. "He backed off." And FirstRain kept the account.

Herscher herself is no stranger to sexual harassment. She remembered an especially disturbing instance that occurred in 1989, when she was a twenty-nine-year-old business development manager at Synopsys Inc., a maker of design software. She and a male customer whom she knew casually were strolling down a corridor en route to a meeting at his employer, a major semiconductor company in Silicon Valley. "He put his hand on my butt and was fondling my butt as we were walking along,"

Herscher said. "It was not an accident. It was really creepy," she added. "There was nobody else around."

Worried about alienating an important client, Herscher didn't formally complain about the fondling incident. Later that day, she told her boss what had happened and asked him how she should handle the matter.

"Oh, just let it go, ignore it," he replied. But during their sexual harassment awareness training at Synopsys later that year, both Herscher and her boss were informed that California employers are required to protect their employees from such behavior. "He looked at me and he realized that he had given me the wrong advice," she said.

## ESCAPE FROM A STALKER BOSS

By six thirty one morning in 1982, an investment banking trainee named Dina Dublon was hard at work on a New York trading floor at Chemical Bank. The young woman was expecting her first child that December, but she didn't feel ready to divulge her condition to her coworkers.

Her boss, a married vice president, guessed that she was pregnant. When he walked over to her desk and asked if she was having a baby, she recalled, "I blushed and said yes."

Sitting down beside his trainee, he whispered in her ear, "This could have been mine."

"That is not something you can say," Dublon retorted, infuriated.

Yet she was torn. The man had been an exemplary mentor. He

had patiently taught her how to trade, listening in during every business call. "He was willing to put in time and effort and explain," Dublon said. "He was an amazing teacher." Like many women, she agonized over how to cope with a distressing but widespread dilemma: a sexual harasser with some positive attributes.

Dublon, who was born in Brazil and raised in Israel, had followed her husband to America for his postdoctoral studies. She completed her MBA degree before becoming a trainee at Chemical in 1981 at age twenty-eight. "My gender was a factor in my getting hired," remembered Dublon, as she perched on a high-back leather chair near tall, glass-front bookcases in the library of the Yale Club in Manhattan.

For her group of twenty-one trainees with graduate degrees, Chemical had recruited eighteen women and assigned them to a large trading floor dominated by hundreds of men.

"We had the double burden of joining a very homogeneous, young, white male group that had undergraduate degrees," Dublon explained. "We were both the women and the ones with graduate degrees. So there was tissue rejection in many different dimensions."

Male traders occasionally pestered female trainees by telling dirty jokes. Some made lewd, loud comments about one woman's large breasts. "The overall environment was hostile," Dublon said. She and one other trainee were the only women from the initial eighteen who remained by their second year. The rest quit Chemical, upset by the macho behavior.

Why did Dublon stay? "I had to figure out how to deal with that particular element of a professional relationship," she said. "As opposed to, 'This is something to get angry about.'"

At the outset, her supervisor sometimes put his arm around her shoulder and tried to lure her into an affair. He also stalked her once. "He followed me on the subway," Dublon said. "He followed me when I went shopping after work. He stood in front of my apartment door as I was walking into my apartment."

Reliving those difficult days clearly troubled Dublon. She gazed fixedly at the overly bright chandelier hanging from the library ceiling as she described the harassment. Although her objections stopped her boss's stalking, his offensive comment about her pregnancy proved the last straw.

"I was going to figure out a way to move away from him," Dublon said. In 1983, she took a temporary special assignment elsewhere within Chemical. She assisted a senior vice president in creating a system to remove interest rate risks from various divisions. The executive had chosen her partly based on her knowledge of interest rate management, which she acquired under her old boss's tutelage.

The sexual harassment taught Dublon "the importance of being comfortable in delineating boundaries and the line you don't cross," she explained. The strength she gained from having to deal with such experiences helped propel her eventual ascent to chief financial officer of JPMorgan Chase & Co., a large U.S. bank and the country's largest by 2015. After retiring early from JPMorgan, she pursued a second career as a professional corporate director at Microsoft Corp., PepsiCo Inc., and other major companies.

In my case, I finally tried to take a stand against sexual harassment at the *Wall Street Journal* after unpleasant incidents affecting me and some other female coworkers. I especially remember the time in the mid-1990s when my bureau chief and I were interviewing a prospective reporter. The three of us squeezed into a tiny, windowless office at our Manhattan headquarters. The applicant, seated next to me, was an outgoing and friendly guy from the West. Too friendly, as it turned out.

When the interview drew to a close, the man suddenly reached over and squeezed my knee hard. "I know we're going to have great fun working together," he said with a broad grin.

Horrified, I strongly argued against hiring him. My boss disagreed, blaming the applicant's offensive behavior on his laid-back lifestyle. But the new hire never fit in well at the *Journal* and lasted less than three years.

## HARASSED WOMEN LEARN TO LEAD IN MANY WAYS

Linda Hudson rose from being an engineer to being the first female head of a major Pentagon supplier. She commanded BAE Systems, whose products include combat vehicles, until January 2014.

At the beginning of her four-decade career, Hudson frequently faced sexual harassment during business trips, industry conferences, and facility visits. "There were all kinds of evil and ugly things that happened in the workplace," she told the *New York Times* in 2009. "I know what it's like to have to find the skills to cope with that and still do well."[7]

During our interview, Hudson said that she used to see pictures of nude women on desks and be greeted by catcalls as she made her way through factories. She was especially annoyed when male factory workers "accidentally" rubbed their arms across her chest.

But Hudson feared that an overly emotional reaction or complaint might cut short her advancement. "I wasn't going to let this defeat me," she said about the harassment. "You had to learn to deal with it." For example, she would make comments to the men about their inability to recognize her value to their organization. "That was their problem, not mine," she pointed out.

Coping with such incidents also shaped Hudson's leadership style. As chief executive of BAE, she tried to eliminate inequitable treatment of employees throughout the U.S. defense contractor. She required that middle managers and executives take a two-hour class about "unconscious bias" so they could recognize how hidden preferences for members of certain groups often influence crucial workplace decisions.

She also put in place a system where a woman or a person of color participated in panels that interviewed potential middle managers and executives. As a result of Hudson's efforts, the number of women and people of color in senior management climbed nearly 10 percent between May 2011 and May 2013.[8]

## HUMILIATED BY A HOIST

Brenda Barnes significantly reshaped Sara Lee Corp. after her promotion in 2005 to chief executive. The major producer of such popular consumer items as baked goods, sausage, and coffee was the biggest Fortune 500 company run by a woman at that time.

Tragically, a serious stroke cut short her stewardship five years later at age fifty-six.

Barnes had spent twenty-two years moving up in management at Pepsi and ultimately headed Pepsi-Cola North America, its highly profitable beverage business. It was there that she turned a demeaning encounter with sexual harassment into a powerful lesson for her male top managers.

While second in command of Pepsi-Cola North America during the 1990s, Barnes attended a company-sponsored dinner for major customers at a hotel in the Caribbean. As the evening drew to a close, a drunken senior executive of a large grocery chain approached her. "This guy picked me up under my arms, and he was holding me up in the air," she said. "My legs cleared the air."

Barnes felt totally humiliated. "What the hell?" she demanded of the executive. "Put me down, please!"

He laughed, but kept her airborne.

Suddenly, half a dozen men who worked for Barnes rushed to her defense and formed a circle around their uplifted boss. "The guy who was holding me put me down," she said. Barnes's deputies escorted her out of the dinner.

During subsequent team meetings, she cited the humiliating episode to reinforce her message that her male lieutenants should treat their female employees with dignity and should intensify their efforts to mentor and promote women. "Play an active role in making it right. You can't take a backseat on this," she instructed them. "This is not just a women's issue." A good leader, Barnes concluded in hindsight, creates a corporate culture that teaches people right and wrong behavior.

## "FUN TO SEE YOU TWO IN YOUR PANTIES"

Sexually harassed women should figure out a strategy to win justice without placing themselves in harm's way, recommended Dorrit J. Bern, the former chief executive of Charming Shoppes Inc., a women's plus-size retailer. "Be absolutely frank but [with] a very business and not personal point of view." Attired in blue jeans and an embroidered work shirt, she peered over half-moon glasses while we spoke at New Jersey's Newark International Airport shortly before she flew home to Florida after visiting relatives in New York.

Bern heeded her own advice in different ways. She accompanied her mother, a merchandise buyer, on business trips to New York starting at age twelve. She was still in her twenties when she became one of the youngest divisional merchandise managers for the Bon Marché arm of Allied Department Stores in Seattle. As a thirty-year-old rising star in 1980, she was responsible for the junior division, its biggest apparel unit, when an older divisional merchandise manager propositioned her. Bern was married and the mother of a young son at that time.

The merchandise manager, who was also married, reminded Bern about their imminent buying trip to New York during a meeting in his Seattle office. "He came from around the desk and he closed the door," she remembered. "He said, 'I want to see you in New York.'"

Clueless about his intentions, Bern invited him to join a business dinner in New York. The five-foot-ten woman and her slightly taller colleague stood facing each other.

"He said, 'You don't get it,'" she recalled. "And he put his arms around me and kissed me." Bern stepped back, glared at him, and replied frostily, "I guess I do get it. Don't you ever, ever do that again. And we will never have dinner together, even if it is in a group of people."

Frightened by her antagonism, the man asked Bern whether she intended to tell their boss about his sexual advance. "I said, 'No, I am not. The last thing I want is a scandal and drama.'" But inwardly, she seethed. "I really wanted to kill the guy." She avoided talking to him throughout their New York trip and as much as possible once they were back in the office.

"I am disappointed in myself that I couldn't figure out a way to get back at him," Bern admitted. "He had a different business than I had. It wasn't like I could influence his budget. I couldn't drag all his merchandise off the floor. I couldn't eliminate all his sales associates."

But eleven years later, in 1991, Bern won justice for harassed female subordinates at Sears, Roebuck & Co. Four years earlier, the retail giant had hired her as its first female national merchandise manager, overseeing women's apparel. Two twenty-something assistant buyers came to her office on the thirty-sixth floor of the Sears Tower in Chicago, upset because of tasteless comments by a veteran male executive in one of the divisions that Bern supervised.

Sitting in front of her desk, both women started to cry. "I stand up and come around from my desk and say, 'What's going on?'" Bern said in recounting the incident. "I put my arms around them."

According to the pair, the executive made his crude remarks while he and the young women conferred about the underwear business. "Are these the panties that you wear?" he asked them. "It would be really fun to see you two in your panties."

Bern summoned the man to her office. The harassment accusation shocked him. "Please believe me," he said, his voice breaking, as he leaned forward on her desk with his arms stretched wide. "I didn't mean to offend. I just thought I was being funny."

But Bern was reluctant to overlook what had happened. "It would compromise me," she pointed out. "I made it very clear as a leader where the boundaries were." Sears had already banned offensive sexual conduct in the workplace. Bern set a stricter standard, telling her employees that she also disapproved of sexist comments.

She fired the executive the same day. At 5 p.m. she brought the female assistant buyers back to her office and told them about his dismissal. "They were thrilled," Bern remembered. "They couldn't believe that I would follow through with his termination because they knew he was a very capable executive. And that the company was a big company with a lot of senior management that were men," she said. "They thought he would be protected. Which happens a lot."

## BATTLING THE BEER BARON

Charlotte Beers, a brash trailblazer in the advertising business known as the "queen of Madison Avenue," realizes that her gender helped her to succeed. And I realized that the moment I stepped inside her elegant Fifth Avenue apartment across from leafy Central Park in Manhattan.

The living room was outfitted with peach-colored couches, bold red walls, and a roughly eighteen-foot ceiling covered with gold-leaf paper. "It looks like a bordello, don't you think?" said Beers, who was wearing black slacks and a matching sweater set off by an oversize gray scarf.

In 1992, Beers became the first female leader of Ogilvy & Mather Worldwide, a multinational advertising agency, and billings grew substantially during her five years there. Twenty years later, she dispensed advice about the importance of women not being intimidated by men in the workplace during an event to promote her new book, *I'd Rather Be in Charge: A Legendary Business Leader's Roadmap for Achieving Pride, Power, and Joy at Work.*[9]

She learned to handle men's intimidating behavior toward women early in her advertising career. Hired by J. Walter Thompson while in her late twenties, Beers was one of the few female account executives at the ad agency when management gave her its $30 million Sears account because they considered her gender an advantage. "They didn't say, 'Now Charlotte, we think you are the best,'" she recollected. "They said, 'Go and stand out because you are a girl,'" she added. "One of the guys used to say to me, 'Do you have a shorter skirt than that?'"

Beers figured out how to turn such attitudes to her advantage. Key product lines at Sears included tools, "not exactly a girl's territory," Beers observed. The company had twice rejected her agency's proposal to advertise its Craftsman drill. So in front of thirty skeptical male Sears executives, she took apart and reassembled a power drill as she praised its double-brass balls. "They all started laughing," she remembered. As a result of her efforts, Sears soon began its first U.S. ad campaign for drills in years.

Nevertheless, Beers was ill-prepared for being sexually harassed by a senior executive at a major client of Tatham-Laird &
Kudner, a small and struggling ad agency that named her its first
female chief executive in 1982, when she was in her forties. As
part of its turnaround push, the Chicago agency landed a $20 mil-
lion account with a beer brewer. "It is the biggest new client we
have ever had," Beers said. Tatham had spent six months pursuing the account, edging out nine other agencies.

So she immediately accepted a New York dinner invitation
from a top officer at the brewer, even though he didn't oversee its
advertising and she didn't know him. "Why would he invite me
to dinner?" Beers asked herself in retrospect. "I didn't look into
that." She now thinks the beer baron just wanted to check out the
only female executive at her agency.

She met the man at the elegant 21 Club, where he had been
drinking with liquor industry buddies. During their drive to a
restaurant for dinner, the executive announced that he had to
stop at his employer's residence in the Helmsley Hotel and collect
some documents to review with Beers.

"You know what?" the man said. "You should come up and see
our company apartment. It has been amazingly redone." Beers
agreed, thinking to herself, "The guys back in the office will be
gaga if I was at this famous beer company's private apartment in
the Helmsley."

She and the executive boarded a private elevator. "I noticed he
was swaying," she recalled. "I thought, 'I made a mistake. This
man is drunk.'" Terrified once she realized that her companion
reeked of alcohol, "I started getting a high panic."

The pair stepped into a pitch-black apartment. They couldn't find any lights. The man nudged her into a corner. Beers stumbled onto a bed, and the hefty executive jumped on top of her.

She put her hands on his massive shoulders and said, "'You don't want to do this,'" she remembered. "And I shoved. I didn't have any hope of making much progress, but in fact he rolled off of me like a little ball. I think he was just brought to his senses. He rolled over to the side of the bed and began sobbing."

Shaking all over, the frightened CEO fled the apartment. But then, a fresh dilemma loomed: Should Tatham drop the account? Beers woke up male colleagues with a late-night call to tell them about her frightening encounter. They were furious. The agency's single biggest account wasn't worth keeping, some of her associates argued.

"That's ridiculous," Beers replied. "We worked too hard for this." She felt responsible for her bad judgment as well as for everyone else in the agency.

After a sleepless night, Beers called the executive at six the next morning. She was ready to test her leadership philosophy of "quid pro quo," which involves offering someone respect and generosity during a difficult situation. You must make yourself uncomfortable to their advantage, she noted.

Beers hoped to preserve her agency's relationship with the executive. "I needed to not have him frightened into creating a defense," she explained. On the phone, she spoke in a tone that gave no hint of her anger about the incident. "You were not yourself last night," she told him. "Obviously, I can't work with you anymore. It would be uncomfortable for both of us."

Recalling their exchange more than three decades later, Beers continued, "I say, 'I have a solution.' And I name a guy who is going to take over the account."

"That's a good solution," the executive replied with relief. Then, Beers pledged to never discuss their evening again. "If I can overlook what is a very serious indiscretion on his part," she said, "he can guarantee the successful evolution of the business." That's exactly what's happened.

The moral of the story for contemporary women facing sexual harassment in the workplace? "You can outthink any man who is on the move," Beers said. "They are afraid of getting caught." But with the beer baron, she conceded, she lacked a ready defense against his sexual advances because "I was a mighty CEO. I thought I was impervious. And the message to women is you are never impervious to that."

## LEADERSHIP LESSONS FROM "SEXUAL HARASSMENT NEVER VANISHED"

- Seek justice on the job rather than individual revenge for mistreatment at work. Melissa Dyrdahl, head of a start-up and a former Adobe Systems executive, believes that you must take your ego and personal feelings out of the situation.
- Get high-level help if harassment endangers your career or your physical safety. Dorrit Bern, an ex-CEO of retailer Charming Shoppes, suggests finding a female executive within your organization whom you can trust. That's especially important if you're a newcomer. "When you start a new job, the unwritten rules are unclear, such as whether the culture will tolerate sexual harassment by men against women," she says.
- Act as a role model for your subordinates by enforcing standards of acceptable decorum in the workplace.

- Pick your battles and don't overreact. Carol Bartz, a former chief of Yahoo and Autodesk, urged her middle daughter not to complain to her employer because a sales manager kept asking her out for a date. "You haven't earned the right to make a big deal of this," Bartz told her. "Just stay out of his way."
- Look for indirect influence so you can stand up for yourself. "We all have more power than we realize," notes Carly Fiorina, a former chief of Hewlett-Packard. Dina Dublon, an ex–finance chief at JPMorgan, also never felt unable to oppose harassment. "You just push back as equals," she says.
- Avoid office parties with heavy drinking, late business dinners, or other potentially risky venues. Melanie Healey, the first woman to run the North American unit for Procter & Gamble, recommends thinking twice before you have a glass of wine alone with a male associate after work. "Make sure you are not sending any signals that could be misinterpreted."

# 5

# The Pain of the Pay Pinch

Money talks. Especially for young women who start out with little money.

Diane M. Bryant, now a well-paid Intel executive, grew up hoping that a decent wage might someday enable her to escape a dangerous home life and support herself.

Bryant, raised in Sacramento, California, is the daughter of an abused homemaker and a violent ex-convict. Her father spent five years in San Quentin prison for armed robbery before her birth and bounced from job to job while Bryant and her sister were young. "He was always in and out of jail," she said.

Their father once beat her mother so badly that she lost her hearing in one ear. "And he had us all emotionally terrorized, frequently threatening to kill us," Bryant recalled. Her mother tried to flee their home, but she and her daughters never went far because she had no money of her own.

"I told myself, 'I would never be financially dependent on

another person,'" Bryant said, her words pouring out in a nonstop staccato. She was forced to fulfill her pledge sooner than she expected because her father decided to stop supporting her once she turned eighteen.

On that milestone birthday, she drove home from high school in her tiny Volkswagen. "Everything I owned was on the front lawn," she remembered. Her father stood outside, with her mother sobbing nearby.

"Whatever you can fit in your car, you can take," he announced. "What you can't fit is mine."

One item that Bryant couldn't fit inside the car was the orange ten-speed bike she had bought and treasured. "I had to leave it," she said, her voice quavering with emotion. "I had to leave a lot of stuff." Gypsy-like, she moved from friend to friend until she finished high school four months later and got her own apartment.

"I still had a long row to hoe to financial independence and success," Bryant added. "I was motivated to get a degree that paid a bunch of money." Enrolling at a junior college, she squeezed in classes between her three jobs as a waitress and hostess.

A fellow calculus student told Bryant that she could earn a decent living if she majored in engineering. "He said, 'You can make $30,000 with a bachelor's degree.'" Even though she had no clue what an engineer did, that sounded like smart advice.

Bryant joined Intel, the semiconductor giant, as a $30,000-a-year electrical engineer in 1985. Today she enjoys a multimillion-dollar annual package of cash and stock awards as a senior executive of the company.

In this respect, Bryant is not alone. A number of female corporate leaders I interviewed accomplished financial independence that far exceeded their wildest fantasies. Gracia Martore, for example, is the daughter of a builder who died before she completed high school. She majored in history and political science at Wellesley College. As a bank management trainee, her first job after graduation, she made $8,500 in 1973. As CEO of Gannett, the media giant, she made $12.4 million in 2014. (Gannett split in June 2015, and Martore took charge of TEGNA, its separate broadcasting and digital company.)

Several executive women I met pocketed sizable rewards only after they pushed for more equitable financial treatment. Deft pay negotiations for themselves and female colleagues often made them stronger leaders.

But the gender pay gap continues to affect women on all rungs of the corporate ladder. The persistent difference between how much men and women earn represents a powerful symbol of women's slow progress in the workplace. Based on current trends, U.S. women will not achieve pay equality until 2058, according to a 2015 report from the Institute for Women's Policy Research, a nonprofit think tank. A typical working woman loses more than $530,000 over her lifetime due to the gender wage gap, the report said, and such losses are even greater for those with higher levels of education.

The pay gap still yawns wide for unionized staffers at Dow Jones, my employer. On average, Dow Jones women get paid about 87 cents for every dollar paid to their male colleagues, according to a 2016 analysis by the union that represents such employees. Dow Jones CEO William Lewis promptly launched a deeper review of pay practices. Management found that employee pay didn't vary because of gender or ethnicity, but promised a follow-up salary analysis.

Various factors account for the gender gap, such as job choices, career interruption, levels of work experience, union membership, hours worked, and available child care. In many cases, women bear a certain responsibility for their pinched pay. They don't get the money they don't ask for. In a 2014 survey of two thousand men and women by *Glamour* magazine, only 39 percent of women said they asked for a higher salary when they started a new job. But 54 percent of men did so. Among those already employed, 43 percent of women said they had ever asked for a raise, compared with 54 percent of men.[1]

Paula Rosput Reynolds got a close look at how men and women bargain differently about pay while chief executive of insurer Safeco Corp. and previously at AGL Resources Inc., an energy holding company. "Men are much more inclined to come in and say, 'I am unhappy with my pay' than women are," she said during our chat at the Algonquin, a restored historic hotel in midtown Manhattan. "I have had many more conversations with men about what they were going to be paid than with women."

Women don't make pay demands "because they are more respectful," Reynolds observed. "They don't want to be a squeaky wheel."

Negotiation researchers like Linda Babcock agree. An economics professor at Carnegie Mellon University, she has spent years studying why women frequently hesitate to pursue raises and fail to negotiate over pay as well as men when they do bargain. Her research found that gender differences in starting salaries play a significant role in long-term earning differentials between men and women.

Babcock's conclusion? Women who seek more money are perceived as less nice. "Just asking for it creates this backlash," she explained. The phenomenon is known as the "social cost" of asking.

"They're seen as more aggressive than men, and that's a negative thing," she said. "Greedy is okay for men, but not for women." Equally troublesome, societal norms about how women should behave change at glacial speed, warned Babcock, the mother of a teenage daughter. "I am hoping that by the time my daughter retires, the wage gap will be a thing of the past."

Satya Nadella, chief executive of Microsoft, caused a firestorm over the issue during a technology conference for women in 2014. He told his audience that women shouldn't ask for a raise because the system will give them the right pay increases as they go along. His comments implied that women should simply wait to be rewarded for their hard work. He later apologized in an email to Microsoft employees.

Ellen Pao, the venture capitalist who lost a sex discrimination suit against a prior employer in 2015, sought to correct women's disadvantage as pay negotiators when she was interim chief executive of Reddit Inc., a small Web company in San Francisco. Reddit created a take-it-or-leave-it policy for starting pay, with one offer weighted more toward equity and the other toward cash.

In explaining the rationale for this policy, Pao said pay negotiations put women at a disadvantage because men bargain harder than women, and she didn't believe in penalizing poor negotiators with low pay.[2]

Some successful executives I interviewed failed to seek initial pay raises that they probably deserved. Brenda Barnes, the former CEO of Sara Lee, made $10,000 a year at her first full-time job as a distribution manager for Wilson Sporting Goods in 1976.

She conceded that she earned little because she was too humble at that stage of her career. "I wasn't really pushy on my behalf," she said.

But Barnes improved with experience. During her command of Sara Lee, she once confronted fellow directors about her pay package. They wanted to lower her $1 million salary because she was radically shrinking the size of the big manufacturer. "I said, 'This is not a fair way of looking at how you are paying me.'"

Barnes pointed out that she and her management team were achieving a Herculean task. "The board did get involved and realized I was raising reasonable points." Her salary rose along with the value of her Sara Lee shares because investors liked the fact that she was selling some of the company's assets. During her five-year tenure, Sara Lee shed more than 40 percent of its business. "We all made money," Barnes noted. "I ended up a very wealthy woman."

As did a number of the female chiefs I interviewed. Among the highest paid in 2014: Irene Rosenfeld of Mondelēz International Inc., maker of Oreo cookies, Ritz crackers, and Trident gum, with total compensation valued at $21 million; Hewlett-Packard's Meg Whitman, at $19.6 million; IBM's Virginia Rometty, at $17.9 million; and GM's Mary Barra, at $16.2 million.

## EARLY PAY BATTLES COUNT

Cathie Black resisted being underpaid from the outset of her career. She eventually became president of Hearst Magazines, a major publisher of popular publications such as *Cosmopolitan* and

*Esquire*, and has been called "the First Lady of American Magazines."

Raised in Chicago, the daughter of a food broker and homemaker, Black sought an entry-level publishing job in New York after graduating from Trinity College in 1966 with a degree in English literature.

She needed to find work before finding a place to live. "My dad said I couldn't sign a lease until I had a job that could pay for the rent," Black told me the winter afternoon we met at NeueHouse, a shared workspace on Manhattan's Lower East Side. She wore a gray cape draped over a black sweater and skirt, glasses perched on the edge of her nose as she leaned forward in a low tan armchair. But she knew almost no one in the publishing industry, and her summer work experience consisted of clerical or retail sales jobs.

Condé Nast, the powerhouse magazine publisher, offered the new college graduate an editorial position that paid $65 a week. "I cannot afford to work for that," Black insisted.

"I know that, dear, but there's an awful lot of women who are supported by their parents who come here to work at Condé Nast," a personnel official replied. "It kind of is what it is."

Black rejected the job, then landed a better position paying 46 percent more. *Holiday* magazine hired her for $95 a week to sell classified advertisements over the telephone to hotels and resorts. "One of the things that drew me to *Holiday* was the fact that my title would be sales assistant rather than secretary," she wrote in *Basic Black: The Essential Guide for Getting Ahead in Work (and in Life)*, her 2007 memoir. "The job responsibilities and salary might have been exactly the same, but I figured I'd get an even better job next time by holding out for a more impressive-sounding title to start with."[3]

It was a savvy move. Eighteen months later, her boss quit, and Black decided to pitch *Holiday*'s publisher about succeeding her as manager of classified advertising. She arranged an appointment with the publisher, an industry veteran whom she barely knew. Attired in a suit and heels, she marched into his office down the hall at *Holiday*'s Manhattan office. The twenty-four-year-old assistant took a seat opposite him and described herself as driven and capable of advancing to manager, she recalled during our interview. "I would work harder than anybody else he could find."

The publisher offered Black the promotion plus a $3,000 raise, bringing her total annual salary to about $8,000. She wasn't pleased, because her former supervisor had made about $13,000. Informing the publisher that she had an inkling about how much the prior manager had earned, she announced, "I expected that that was what I would be offered."

The man was shocked. His face turned beet red. "He looked apoplectic," Black said, "like, 'Who is this little whippersnapper?'" He nevertheless sweetened the pot by $1,500, and Black took the promotion.

The gutsy encounter taught her the importance of women bargaining hard over pay. "Women forever have had a real issue with negotiating," Black said. "Women, I think, are instinctively embarrassed. They don't think it is the right thing to do."

Black came to view conversations about compensation as a game in which a woman should anticipate the worst possible outcome. At *Holiday* magazine, she remembered thinking, "What's the worst that could happen? He could take the job offer away," she pointed out. "But I am the devil that he knows. Better than hiring somebody from the outside who frankly would cost more," she continued. "He probably weighed that in his mind."

Black progressed to being an advertising manager for *Ms.* magazine and publisher of *New York* magazine, the first woman in such a role for a weekly consumer publication in the United States. She tapped her pay negotiation skills again during a summer of talks in 1983 with Al Neuharth, the irascible newspaper baron who led Gannett and had launched *USA Today* the year before with hopes of creating a national circulation daily. Neuharth wanted Black to take a job in corporate media sales, but she preferred to run his new newspaper, which at the time was bleeding red ink.

Neuharth ultimately offered her the presidency of *USA Today*. He balked at her insistence on an employment contract, however. For new executives, such a contract typically guarantees a sizable exit package if their job doesn't work out. Black already held a high-profile position at *New York*, and the survival of *USA Today* appeared uncertain.

"I am not going to come without a contract," Black remembered telling Neuharth.

"Well, we don't have contracts," he replied. "Nobody in the company has contracts."

Black sought advice from a lawyer friend. As a compromise, the attorney drafted an offer letter in which Gannett promised her lucrative severance pay if she got forced out. "Neuharth fought it tooth and nail," Black said. But she stood her ground, and he reluctantly accepted her demands. By 1991, *USA Today* had become the nation's largest-circulation daily paper.

Despite her negotiating acumen, Black has had some career

missteps. She lasted just three months as chancellor of New York City's schools, the biggest U.S. school system. Criticized for her lack of experience in education or government, she resigned in April 2011.

Nowadays, Black still urges women to assert themselves when it comes to pay. Whenever compensation is being discussed, she recently told a group of advertising industry women, "negotiating is expected."

How firmly should women stand their ground during pay talks? "It depends on how good you are," Black told me. "If you are thought of very highly in that company, if they talk to you about your future, then you have got leverage."

Black's experiences illustrate why ambitious women must devise smart strategies in bargaining for their compensation. "Women are good pay negotiators when they recognize the value they have and make it visible," said Deborah M. Kolb, founder of the Center for Gender in Organizations at Simmons College. "If you have good information, pay disparities disappear."

Not everyone might agree with Kolb. And good information goes beyond knowing how much money people inside and outside an organization earn. "It includes learning about what others negotiated for as well as what they got," Kolb said in *Negotiating at Work*, a 2015 book she coauthored.[4] But men tend to be more effective at forging professional networks and sharing information, noted Babcock, the Carnegie Mellon economist, who also has coauthored books about women and negotiation.

I paid a price for my ignorance about a perquisite obtained by some *Wall Street Journal* colleagues. In 1973, I requested a transfer to our Chicago bureau from San Francisco in order to follow my husband, who was about to begin work on a graduate degree in journalism at Northwestern University.

The *Journal* transferred me but refused to cover our moving costs because I initiated the relocation for personal reasons. I later discovered that our editors didn't always enforce this policy. Shortly before my transfer, the *Journal* footed relocation bills so a male reporter based in New York could move to the San Francisco area to live closer to his seriously ill mother.

## KNOWLEDGE IS POWER

Challis Lowe knows all too well that knowledge is power when women seek fair pay deals, based on her stints as the highest human resources executive of three major businesses: Beneficial Corp., Ryder System Inc., and Dollar General Corp.

Lowe typically commanded a sizable pay package in those posts. At Ryder, a commercial truck leasing and logistics company, she made more than $740,000 in 2002. Her Ryder pay deal was a far cry from her compensation in 1977, the year I wrote a front-page profile of Lowe for the *Journal*. Then thirty-one, she was earning only slightly more than $25,000 a year as a middle manager and the first black female officer of Continental Bank.[5]

Lowe had dropped out of Southern Illinois University during her final year because she was pregnant with her first child. She ultimately finished her studies through college-level equivalency exams. She entered the business world after two years as an elementary school substitute teacher.

Lowe has always been a shy person who speaks in soft tones.

But once she reached upper management, she spoke up to make sure she got paid what she felt she deserved. "As the senior HR executive, I was in the best position to know how people were paid," Lowe recollected when we reconnected with a hug in the Algonquin's lobby bar. The retiree still dressed like an executive, with a brown-and-white tailored jacket and silver pendant earrings.

Lowe negotiated her pay by digging hard to find out what people she considered to be at the same level of the organization were making, even if they worked in far different areas than her own. Lowe's approach paid off handsomely when Beneficial wooed her to be human resources chief of the consumer finance concern in Peapack, New Jersey. At the time she held that role at Heller Financial, a Chicago commercial finance company. Switching employers would represent a risky move, uprooting the Chicago native and making her the highest human resources executive at a U.S. public company for the first time.

Because hers would be a staff job rather than one that involved generating revenue for the business, Beneficial intended to pay Lowe about 25 percent less than operational executives with profit-and-loss responsibilities. She instead wrangled the same hefty compensation paid to business unit chiefs. Her argument was that she needed the parity to give her clout when she revamped the corporate culture.[6]

Lowe believed that she couldn't shake up the organization without extensive cooperation from the heads of Beneficial's business units. "My argument there was, 'This is my group of people I have to work with in order to get this job done,'" she said. "'They have to see me as a peer and not as a subordinate.'"

Already unsure about relocating to accept the job, "I was definitely willing to walk away," Lowe noted. "When they came back with an offer that was twenty-five percent higher, I said, 'Maybe this is what I am supposed to do.'" She joined Beneficial in 1997.

Unearthing details about a little-known management perk proved lucrative for Lowe at a different employer in 2009. Ascension Health, the country's largest Catholic health care system, recruited her to run its human resources activities and wanted her to move to St. Louis, where the system is headquartered. Unwilling to relocate from her permanent home in Miami, Florida, Lowe asked about possible special deals for current senior executives at Ascension Health.

She discovered that its finance chief had also refused to relocate. Ascension Health paid for the St. Louis apartment that he occupied during the week along with his weekly commute to and from California. "This is a really big perk," Lowe pointed out. "I asked for an apartment in St. Louis that they paid for." Throughout her four years, Ascension Health also covered her flights. She commuted to Florida in the winter and Chicago in the summer.

## SHOWDOWN OVER A BIASED PERK

A brouhaha over gender bias in managerial perquisites created tremendous angst for Anne Mulcahy years before the longtime Xerox staffer reached its corner office. While in her thirties, she became a Xerox branch manager for the first time soon after she gave birth to her first son in 1983. She commuted nearly 130 miles a day between her home in Westport, Connecticut, and her office in Hartford. At the time, she earned about $55,000 a year.

Xerox had hired Mulcahy's second in command just before her promotion. A Fairfield resident, he had a slightly shorter commute than she did. "I happened to see a copy of his offer letter, and they are paying him for his commuting expenses and his parking," she remembered. As a result of this arrangement, the man pocketed several thousand dollars a year for those outlays. "It was a lot of money at the time."

Yet Xerox paid Mulcahy nothing for her commuting costs. "Hey, it must have been a mistake," she complained to her boss.

The boss had a ready answer. His circumstances are different than yours, he explained. Mulcahy realized he was describing the fact that her deputy had a wife who stayed home with their children while Mulcahy's husband worked for Xerox. Their cordial conversation suddenly turned confrontational. "I don't think you want to go there," cautioned Mulcahy, a low-key individual who rarely gets angry.

Her boss grew testy. "Don't you make a big deal out of this," he retorted. His apparent gender bias astonished Mulcahy. "I hadn't come across anything quite that blatant," she said. "We left it at an impasse."

At home that night, Mulcahy asked her husband about the best way to handle the unfair compensation arrangement.

"You have to pick your shots," he proposed. "But it sounds to me like if you don't deal with this one, it just builds over time," he continued. "You won't be treated equally."

Mulcahy decided to inform the regional human resources office about the disparity. Six weeks later, she received a surprise raise of about $1,500. "This was called an equity adjustment or something," she said. "It was a way to get me off the case, but not let me feel I had won."

Why didn't she demand the same extra sum as her second in command? Mulcahy answered that she has a very strong sense of when to push and when to pull back at work. "It is good to take it as far as you can and not put your job at risk," she said.

The incident did cause repercussions within Xerox, however. Mulcahy earned a reputation as a middle manager who took pay negotiations seriously. She valued that reputation. "You have to let people know that you expect to be fairly compensated and will not live with that kind of treatment," she said.

Mulcahy also deepened her involvement in the Women's Network, a Xerox self-help group she had cofounded. Based on compensation problems that she and her female associates faced, the network inaugurated one of the first pay equity studies at Xerox. The 1980s study identified gender pay gaps for which there was no good business reason and produced "a whole bunch of adjustments for women," she reported.

Mulcahy now views the incident involving the commuter benefit as a pivotal moment in her development as a leader. "There are moments of truth within your career that really do influence the rest of your career."

## GOING FOR THE EXECUTIVE SUITE GOLD

Other high-level women helped narrow the gender pay gap by toiling behind the scenes on behalf of other female executives. That's what Lowe did at Ascension Health, Ryder, and Dollar General, a discount retailer.

Such lobbying efforts remain critically important today because men still outearn and outnumber women in senior management.

In 2014, there was a $10,000 difference in average salaries for male and female executives, according to a global survey of 907 executives by the Association of Executive Search Consultants. The report cited the lower representation of women in the highest positions as the driving factor for the disparity.

Ninety-three percent of the gender gap in executives' total compensation stems from the fact that women receive a lower portion of rewards from bonuses and stock grants, concluded a 2015 study of senior management at the 1,500 biggest U.S. businesses by the Federal Reserve Bank of New York. "The fact that female top executives perceive limited access to informal networks, gender stereotyping, an inhospitable corporate culture, jointly with their younger age and lower tenure," the study authors wrote, "suggests that they might be considerably less entrenched and exert lower control on their own compensation than their male counterparts on average."[7]

Such findings don't surprise Lowe, the veteran human resources chief. She said she always made sure "that senior women get paid more and in one case, substantially more, as a result of the fact that there were men in roles that were similar who were getting paid a whole lot more than they were."

She scored her biggest victory at Ascension Health. One day in 2011, she walked into the corner office used by her boss, president of the health care system, and showed him disturbing results from her annual analysis of internal pay patterns. "We are sitting at the conference table and I pull out the study," Lowe recalled of their meeting.

Compensation for its regional heads was supposed to be based on the amount of hospital revenue from their area. While the woman who ran the largest region earned more than $600,000 a year, that was far less than two men overseeing smaller regions. One man made in excess of $800,000.

"There is an issue here," Lowe warned him quietly. "The African American female who runs the largest region in your organization is paid less than two white men who run smaller regions."

Her boss offered an excuse. "Well, she has been at the job less time than they have."

But the woman had held her position for five years and enjoyed stronger job performance ratings than those male counterparts, Lowe retorted. "You don't get paid by how long you have been at the job," she persisted. "You get paid by performance and scope. Her performance is outstanding, and her scope is bigger than theirs. She needs a raise."

The president leaned forward slightly. "What do you suggest we do?"

Lowe upped the ante. "We give her a big raise."

"Can we do it in two installments?" he asked. Lowe rejected his idea, arguing that a gradual pay adjustment was unfair to an experienced female star.

"Okay, I guess we are going to make somebody happy," he said, smiling.

Looking back, Lowe believes the Ascension Health president never intended to aggravate the gender pay gap. "He really wanted to do the right thing. He didn't have anyone before tell him what the right thing was."

Nor had the female regional head ever pushed for pay parity herself. Grateful for the promotion, Lowe recollected, "she never questioned how much she was making relative to the other regional managers."

The president immediately gave the underpaid woman a

$200,000 raise. Since then, the woman has been promoted once more and has become a member of the Office of the President. "She is now responsible for all those regional managers," Lowe said. "So, there is no question about the fact that she is paid more."

## SECRET BOARD BUDDY

Paula Rosput Reynolds, the two-time public company CEO, has played a similar secret role of pay advocate for executive women as an independent director at eight other public companies. She currently holds three such board seats. She wore a gray-and-white suit that matched her salt-and-pepper short hair on the day that we talked.

Like Barnes, Lowe, and other corporate leaders I met, Reynolds polished her pay bargaining skills by negotiating effectively on her own behalf. "I did come in well prepared on what I thought I should make," she recalled. Indeed, a board member at a company where she was a top executive once declared, "It's a hard day's work when you have to negotiate Paula's pay."

Nowadays, Reynolds sees the career progress of many women slow after they reach middle management. "Pay disparity surfaces when finally they get a boss who says, 'I am going to take you up'" into senior management, she said. Their pay remains out of whack because their male counterparts moved up faster.

The issue arose a few years ago while Reynolds and another woman served on the board compensation committee at an energy industry business. Committee members convened in a room across the hall from the boardroom. Taking a seat at the head of the table, the chief executive described his plan to elevate a female senior vice president to an executive vice presidency and boost her pay more than 20 percent.

Reynolds was unimpressed. Despite the $100,000 raise, she pointed out, the executive woman would make less money than comparable executive vice presidents, all of whom were men. The gap equaled about 15 percent.

"I know," the CEO replied. "But it is a big jump for her."

Reynolds pressed further. Even with the extra money, the promoted woman would still earn less than the company's target amount for such high-level positions, based on a comparison with its competitors. "You have got to have a commitment that says over a very short period of time, you get her there," Reynolds remembered saying. "You cannot leave her down here if you are satisfied with her work."

The chief executive recognized the gender pay gap. "He just figured that it would get fixed over a longer time horizon," Reynolds said. She and certain other members of the compensation committee persuaded him to move faster to end the disparity in pay.

The following year, the company significantly increased the executive vice president's pay once again so the woman now earned about the same as her male peers. She continues to flourish there, Reynolds noted, and has become "a great advocate for other women."

## LEADERSHIP LESSONS FROM "THE PAIN OF THE PAY PINCH"

- Defuse tense pay talks with a "velvet glove" in which you ask smart questions and exhibit empathy for the other side.

- Keep your boss well informed about your accomplishments so you can win the raise you deserve. Cite relevant facts to clarify your expectations, and stand your ground.
- In pursuing an executive position, hire an attorney to help you wrangle a generous employment contract, and request comparative pay data from a compensation consultant.
- Find out how much people at the same job level earn inside and outside the company, even if your role isn't identical, so you can decide whether to make a fuss. That's crucial because "women are generally not paid the same as men who are in comparable roles," notes Challis Lowe, a veteran top human resources executive.
- Use your professional network to learn about little-known executive perquisites. "Do your homework. Talk to people in the industry," suggests Dorrit Bern, a former CEO of retailer Charming Shoppes. Before taking its highest spot, she persuaded board members to pay for a Philadelphia apartment and her weekly flights home to Chicago.
- Be willing to jump ship to achieve pay equity. "Women are so damn loyal," complains Paula Rosput Reynolds, a prior chief of Safeco and AGL Resources. "Men threaten to leave and get raises to stay. Women just stay."

# 6

# Getting Ahead Sooner

You won't get ahead in mid-career unless you're ready to put your career on the line.

Many executive women I met made their marks midway through their careers by tackling risky roles, especially ones that involved a "mission impossible." Taking this gutsy approach wasn't always easy, as Liz Smith, chief executive of Bloomin' Brands, the casual dining chain, found out firsthand.

By the 1990s, Smith was in her thirties and already on the fast track at Kraft Foods Inc. The giant food company had promoted Smith to senior product manager of its popular Jell-O products, and she assumed that she would soon advance to business director of a big Kraft brand.

Jell-O was part of the company's desserts division, which was then led by Irene Rosenfeld, the current head of Mondelēz International, manufacturer of Oreo cookies, Ritz crackers, and other products. In the fall of 1996, Rosenfeld summoned Smith to her corner office at divisional headquarters in White Plains, New York. Kraft had acquired Callard & Bowser, a tiny distributor of Altoids mints. The 250-year-old breath mint was imported from Wales and sold in distinctive tins. A colorful, older Englishman ran the distributorship from Elmsford, a short drive from White Plains.

Rosenfeld wanted Smith to help integrate Callard & Bowser into the Kraft organization, overseeing its loose network of confectionery brokers and reporting to the Englishman. Though the Altoids business was small, "I saw enormous potential if we could have a bold, creative leader," Rosenfeld explained to me. "Liz was a very bright, very aggressive young woman," she went on. "We were going to lose her if we didn't continue to challenge her."

But Smith was flabbergasted by Rosenfeld's request. "How have I fallen so far from grace?" she recalled thinking. "What could I possibly have done to get myself so far off field?"

Smith saw the move as a dangerous career detour. "I was at the marquee brand at the mother ship," she said during our interview at her Florida home. "I never heard of this place. It didn't sound like the fast track." In a slightly quavering voice, she asked her division chief what she had done wrong.

Rosenfeld viewed Callard & Bowser differently. "I want you to figure out what this place is all about," she told Smith. "It is going to stretch every muscle you have. You won't have the comfort of having this large organization around you."

When Smith resisted, Rosenfeld underscored her promise that the move would hasten her professional growth. "This is going to be the best thing for you," the executive emphasized. "You are going to be in the engine room. You are going to be building. You are going to be learning."

Smith accepted the Callard & Bowser job, partly because she knew she would be in a strong position to take charge after the Englishman retired. But she had to turn a deaf ear to the reactions of her colleagues in White Plains, who buzzed about the exile of Jell-O's top product manager. "I remember someone said, 'Liz Smith went from the big house to the outhouse.'" And initially, that was exactly how she felt.

Several other women I interviewed took tough operational assignments, and in doing so achieved success that enhanced their reputations as rising stars.

"The chance to work on something that seems very difficult or challenging by definition gets more visibility," noted Andrea Jung, the former Avon CEO. Not long after the big cosmetics concern hired her as a marketing manager in 1994, she pursued an initiative to give her new employer a coherent global profile. At the time, Avon was very decentralized, with regional fiefdoms that developed their own versions of Avon products.

"The unpopular project of trying to create a global brand strategy and going up against the fiefdom leaders in addition to my day job was a huge one," Jung recollected. Despite the challenges, she succeeded, and Avon put together a formal global marketing organization eighteen months later. Jung credits this mission impossible project with propelling her subsequent Avon promotions.

As a current board member of General Electric Co. and Apple Inc., Jung regularly scrutinizes emerging talent at both corporate giants as part of the board's management succession planning, and she's impressed when women bosses demonstrate leadership acumen outside their regular routine. "That is, I think, one of the best ways to get ahead," Jung suggested.

But embracing a difficult work assignment when you're a midlevel manager can be tricky. For starters, you probably have comparatively few internal allies, a short track record, and incomplete leadership skills. "It's going to be uncomfortable at first," cautioned Robin Ely, a professor at Harvard Business School who has studied gender issues for thirty years.

Complicating matters, women keen to get ahead often find themselves trapped in a double bind, Ely's research shows. Female leaders are expected to be collaborative, caring, and helpful rather than exhibit typically masculine traits such as decisiveness and assertiveness.

"There's a contradiction," Ely observed. "If I act like a leader, I am violating the gender stereotype. And if I act like a woman, I am violating the leadership stereotype." As a result, she said, women are often forced to choose between being liked and being seen as competent.

Ely raises this issue during training sessions that she runs for high-potential businesswomen. Participants frequently say, "I traded off likability for competence a long time ago." She proposes an alternative strategy: anchor what you're trying to accomplish by clearly linking your supervisory behavior to your team's specific goals.

Managerial women who step into risky roles face another challenge, known as the "glass cliff." These positions become precarious because their organization is in crisis or they lack needed resources. That, in turn, increases the managers' chances of failure.

The notion of the "glass cliff" was explored in a 2005 study by two British psychology researchers who scrutinized the performance of the hundred biggest public companies in the United Kingdom before and after they appointed a male or female board member.

The study found that during a period of overall stock market decline, companies with consistently bad performance in prior months were more likely to have placed women on their boards. The authors called this a glass cliff, which they described as "an additional, largely invisible, hurdle that women need to overcome in the workplace."[1]

Yet the chance of failure didn't deter most women I interviewed from taking a mission impossible and becoming more resilient as a result of their inevitable setbacks. "Taking risks and being willing to push yourself in a position where you're looking at a cliff," said Beth Mooney, the KeyCorp CEO, "is part of life and part of building a career." That's because "you learn what you're made of," she added.

And in a risky situation, "you already have more upside," said Kathleen Ligocki, the Agility Fuel chief executive who previously drove Tower Automotive out of bankruptcy. "You have a better opportunity to take ownership of something."

This was the lesson that Liz Smith ultimately learned. On her first day at Callard & Bowser in 1996, the then thirty-three-year-old manager walked past the 1950s-era furniture that filled the company's handful of ground-floor suites in a large Elmsford office building. Her peers, most of whom were men, "were shocked at how young I was," she recalled. "Everyone stands up out of their cubicles and comes out of their office and stares at me."

Smith was soon outraged to hear about a chore assigned to the firm's executive assistants: cleaning dirty dishes left by higher-ups in the office kitchenette. Every assistant was a woman, she said, and "everyone had a dish day."

Smith and her new boss clashed early on over this chore. "For the first few weeks, we stared at each other," she remembered. Then "I let him know that I thought 'dish day' was probably not appropriate," she continued. "I said, 'I know they are the executive assistants, but they happen to all be women. So it just feels like it is very sexist.'"

"I hadn't thought about it that way," her boss replied. "I just view it as part of that responsibility."

Jokingly, he assured Smith that he wouldn't assign her a dish day. But his humor didn't placate her. Forcing female executive assistants to wash the dishes, she told him, was humiliating for every woman in the office. "I got him to understand the importance of perception."

The compromise? Everyone except the boss agreed to wash their own dishes in the kitchenette.

Gradually, she came to regard the Callard & Bowser president as a high-integrity leader and mentor. "I really had to just check my stereotypes at the door," she said, "because it would have been very easy to write him off as this sexist Englishman."

For instance, her boss refused to install voice mail for himself or his associates because he preferred the personal touch. "Every single one of our customers and every single one of our vendors deserves to be greeted by a live voice," he told Smith. "It is very disrespectful to dump somebody in a mailbox and have them wonder whether you are ever going to return their call."

His approach impressed Smith, and she began responding

faster to her business calls and email. "To this day, I like to think I am pretty good at getting back to people."

What initially seemed like a dreaded career detour turned into an important stepping-stone. Smith said she earned the trust of candy brokers by listening to them intently, then brought their informal network up to Kraft's professional standards. She also attracted expanded corporate promotional support for Altoids based on her presentation to senior management. "We were able to take it from a sleepy brand in a specialty network to a mass brand that still had the cachet," she said.

In 1997, she succeeded her boss at the helm of Callard & Bowser. Joining and running that business "developed every muscle I had," Smith admitted. Two years later, Kraft made her a vice president, and by 2001, she was leading one of the company's large divisions.

## DOUBLE DUTY

Gracia Martore took a different route to getting ahead in management. She didn't hesitate to accept a risky role midway through her Gannett career, even though the decision saddled her with double duty for years. "I love new challenges," said the former chief executive of the U.S. chain of newspapers and TV stations who now runs TEGNA, a Gannett spin-off.

Martore traced her career trajectory as she sat in a dark brown leather armchair in a corner office of Gannett's midtown Manhattan operation. Wearing a simple black pantsuit and scant makeup, she recalled that she loved newspapers, even as a child in a Boston suburb. She started reading the *Boston Globe* with her father at the age of five. Stock tables, she confessed, "were intriguing to me." The double-duty opportunity arose in July 1995, a decade after she left banking to join Gannett. Martore, then forty-three, was Gannett's vice president of treasury services.

Her boss, Doug McCorkingdale, the company's vice chairman and chief financial officer, called her into his imposing office at Gannett headquarters in Arlington, Virginia, a space several times larger than her digs down the hall. "He was at his very large desk and I was across from him," Martore recalled.

She knew that Gannett's first full-time head of investor relations had just announced her resignation. "Would you be interested in doing this?" McCorkingdale asked his busy lieutenant. "You have some spare time," he jested. "You could just fit this in."

Thrilled by the offer, Martore jumped at a chance to deal with Wall Street for the first time. "Sure, I would love to do it," she said.

Walking back to her office, Martore regretted her sudden decision. She couldn't sleep for several nights. Tossing and turning in bed, she worried that she might screw up, hurt Gannett's shareholders, and ultimately lose her job. "I had seen other IR people say things that had an immediate impact on their [employer's] stock price," she observed. She had never held a job where she received instant feedback about her performance, and "that was kind of scary."

Martore nevertheless decided to fulfill her commitment to McCorkingdale. "It was a new challenge," she said. "Doug was testing me."

The former investor relations manager was able to spare only a few hours to brief Martore about how to handle shareholders.

So, she said, "I talked to every IR person, sell side analyst, and shareholder that I could."

Martore flourished running investor relations even though the double duty increased her average workweek to seventy hours from fifty hours. She juggled her new job along with her other responsibilities for another year after she became Gannett's finance chief in 2003.

The experience transformed Martore into an ardent advocate of calculated career risks. "If you don't stretch and get out of your comfort zone," she pointed out, "then I am not sure it is going to be all that interesting a career."

Right after landing Gannett's highest job in 2011, Martore stressed the importance of smart risk-taking in videocasts and at town hall meetings for her employees. As she urged the entire company to take such risks, "I remembered my 1995 meeting in the CFO's office," she said.

Not every colleague shares Martore's fearless attitude. She repeatedly gets turned down when she offers risky promotions to qualified women. They cite "all the reasons why they can't do the job," she noted. "Men, even though they have the same inability to do the job, will sit there and say, 'I can do that. That's no sweat.'"

## PROJECT IMPOSSIBLE

Other women turbocharged their mid-career progress by tackling a project that appeared doomed.

One such woman was Victoria "Vicki" Holt. A chemistry major at Duke University, she began her eighteen-year career at

Monsanto Co. in a sales job and today leads Proto Labs Inc., a medium-size manufacturer of custom-made product prototypes and parts.

Holt won command of a public company for the first time in 2010, when fellow directors of Spartech Corp. asked Holt, then a senior vice president of PPG Industries Inc., to complete the restructuring of Spartech, a maker of plastic packaging products. "I thought I would like to try my hand at being a CEO," she said. "'It is worth the risk,'" she recollected telling herself.

Spartech announced Holt's appointment the same day that the company reported a swing to a loss in its third fiscal quarter due to a sharp increase in bad debt, higher raw material costs, and delays in plant consolidation. "In the first ninety days, I found the company was a lot sicker than any of us on the board thought," she said.

Holt is a tall, genial woman with a narrow face who often slaps her thigh for emphasis. The day we chatted at a small, round table in her office, she was dressed in a black shirt with PROTO LABS stitched below the collar and khaki slacks. She described this chapter of her career at the company's two-story headquarters in a farming hamlet outside Minneapolis. Her office overlooks a field where deer occasionally wander.

Jumping into a risky role is nothing new for Holt. In 1983, when she was just twenty-six, she was the first woman to get profit-and-loss responsibility at Monsanto's big chemicals unit when she took charge of a $30 million operation that made additives for items such as paint. "It was a lot of fun," she said, because the relatively small size of the additives operation gave her a fairly free hand.

But after Holt moved up to running a larger product line that made chemicals for swimming pools, she found herself with a task that wasn't fun: negotiating with a Japanese chemicals maker over a joint manufacturing agreement worth millions of dollars.

When she got this assignment in the late 1980s, few women worked in the managerial ranks of Japanese companies. Not surprisingly, executives at the Japanese manufacturer considered Holt an oddity. "They had never done business with women before," she remembered. Her height of nearly five feet, nine inches exacerbated the awkward situation.

Holt's boss, a man named Dave, accompanied her to an early bargaining session in Tokyo. The Japanese executives, seated at a table opposite the Monsanto team, repeatedly posed questions to him because they couldn't believe she was in charge of their pending deal.

Even though her boss insisted that she answer their queries, the Japanese men responded merely by catching Holt's eye momentarily. "The next question would come and they would turn to Dave," she recalled. "And Dave would say, 'Vicki, I think you have this answer, right?'"

Her boss had a strong motivation for putting the ball in her court. "He didn't have the answers. It wasn't his business. It was my business," Holt said. The Japanese eventually played according to the Americans' rules, and lobbed their questions at her.

Holt thinks that she finally gained their respect because "they knew I knew my business really well. I was transparent, honest, yet demanding."

In 1988, seven months pregnant with her daughter, she flew to Tokyo to sign the accord. Both sides celebrated over dinner at a traditional Japanese restaurant where patrons sat on the floor. Describing the evening, Holt leaped up from her office conference table and reenacted the setting, assuming a cross-legged position on the floor. "I had to get up," she said, roaring with laughter. "I can never forget that night. My back was so sore!"

By the fall of 1990, Holt was preparing to leave the pool chemicals operation in St. Louis and relocate to California. Her Japanese manufacturing partners, sorry to see her go, organized a goodbye party for her in St. Louis. One Japanese man cried. "I was very touched," she said. "I may have had a tear in my eye as well."

Holt knows that women often run into their first significant obstacles midway through their careers. They can overcome such obstacles, she said, if they assist colleagues in getting their work done and accept assistance from individuals who care about their success. "People want to get the work done."

## TAMPONS ATOP THE TABLE

The year was 2001. Melanie Healey, a rising star at Procter & Gamble, and key executives in its feminine care business stood around a conference room table at the unit's global headquarters in Cincinnati. They stared at dozens of tampons, sanitary napkins, and panty liners piled atop the table, representing their worldwide assortment. "They are all pretty much white," recalled Healey, who recently had been named North American general manager for those products. "Very antiseptic looking."

Inwardly, she raged. "They do nothing for me as a woman," she said to herself. "They are not appealing." She thought that P&G treated the natural function of menstruation "as if it is a problem when it is not."

With these thoughts in mind, Healey addressed her colleagues boldly. "I said, 'This looks like we are looking at a bunch of Band-Aids,'" she remembered. "There is something completely different we could be doing with this category," she continued. "Why don't we design products that delight women, that make them feel better about having periods?"

Her comments broke an unspoken rule at her tradition-bound employer because she couldn't cite any relevant market research. "P&G is a data-driven company," she explained to me. "You do take a personal risk when speaking up with any forceful nature without it."

She said she spoke bluntly during the 2001 meeting because she felt so passionate about the issue. "It is a subject I still feel strongly about."

Healey, who was born and raised in Brazil, had joined P&G, a major consumer products maker, as a brand manager in Brazil in 1990. She often embraced uncomfortable situations, such as by taking an unpopular position while she climbed the management ranks of P&G's health and feminine care businesses.

"I am a person who my entire life has gotten out of my comfort zone. It is part of who I am," explained Healey, attired in an off-white jacket with gold trim on the afternoon we lingered over a late lunch at the Algonquin Hotel. "My parents did it to me early on, and I did it to myself later on."

For example, she said, her parents transferred her from a British school to a Brazilian school at the start of fourth grade. At the time, she spoke Portuguese so poorly that she had to repeat the previous grade.

"They took me out of my comfort zone," Healey said of her parents. "I was pissed, but anger is a motivator." Upset about being left back, she worked diligently to learn Portuguese and ended up skipping fourth grade. She faced a similar challenge when she arrived in the United States for the first time just five days before the beginning of her freshman year at the University of Richmond. She graduated with a degree in business.

She started working in the United States when P&G promoted her to the feminine care products post, an appointment that yet again pushed her beyond her comfort zone, largely because a huge price increase was hurting the unit's sales and profits. "We had to rescind the increase," Healey said. "This was a messy situation."

Her gutsy outburst in the conference room about the feminine care products grew out of her desire to fix the business, and the move had long-term repercussions for both P&G and her career. Until her outburst, the company's developers of those products focused on engineering ones that absorbed well.

Healey, who then had two young children, tried to push her alternate approach for the products by describing what she called the Sesame Street effect. When you put Band-Aids on kids' wounds, she pointed out to colleagues at the meeting, they keep crying. "But if you put a Big Bird Band-Aid on that wound," she said, "they are going to be the happiest kid in the world. So where is the Sesame Street effect?"

Some men at the session looked a bit bewildered. But others grasped Healey's point. P&G soon revamped the design of its feminine care products, and launched a tampon known as Tampax

Pearl. "We redesigned the package to look more like a handbag," Healey said. "You lifted up the flap rather than tearing open a strip."

The previous packaging had been somber and unadorned, but the new tampon came in a shiny box decorated with a picture of a strand of pearls. Thanks to all of these changes, Tampax Pearl got 17 percent of the tampon market in 2004, a year when sales of the product rose 24 percent, according to market researcher Information Resources Inc.[2]

"The consumer loved it," Healey reported of Tampax Pearl. "This was the first time there was a tampon designed with her in mind versus the machine in mind." She then spearheaded a worldwide campaign so young women would treat their period as something positive. "In a lot of parts of the world, there are no facilities to take care of it," she observed. "Their level of confidence drops because now they are self-conscious about the fact that they have their period." P&G also created BeingGirl.com, a website for teenage girls that proved a highly popular marketing vehicle.

The campaign helped earn Healey the global presidency of the feminine care products unit. In 2009, she became the first woman to lead the North American arm of P&G. She stepped into that spot at a time when the recession had persuaded numerous consumers to reduce their spending on everyday items and switch to lower-cost brands from P&G's premium ones. Her business struggled to regain lost sales and market share.

Healey's attempted turnaround proved such a trying task by 2011 that she felt ready to resign. "I am quitting," she told her teenage daughter upon her return home after an especially bad day at work. "I've had enough."

"Mom, you can't quit," her daughter protested. "You are not just my role model, you are my friends' role model."

Healey finally retired at age fifty-four in July 2015 after failing to win the CEO position at P&G. But she'll likely soon find a different corner office, executive recruiters predict.

Healey offered strong advice to midlevel women who are unsure whether they should accept a mission impossible role. If the role involves something you care deeply about, she said, "you just make the impossible happen. You are unstoppable."

## LEADERSHIP LESSONS FROM
## "GETTING AHEAD SOONER"

- Thoroughly explore possible downsides and upsides of a risky role in mid-career.
- Make sure you have a clear sense of how your boss defines success before you take a mission impossible.
- Don't accept such an assignment if you feel set up for failure. "You are doomed" unless you get a sufficient budget and final say over the composition of your team, cautions Abbe Raven, a former chief executive of A+E Networks.
- Close your knowledge gaps rapidly and focus on making a memorable impact. Anne Stevens, a former CEO of Carpenter Technology Corp., a developer and maker of specialty alloys, frequently took midlevel management jobs she knew nothing about. "The key is asking the right questions," she says. She learned quickly by asking her team questions for which she lacked answers.

- Getting out of your comfort zone develops leadership muscles. Mission impossible experiences can also build your image as a valued change agent.
- Don't overly criticize yourself when an assignment doesn't work out. Ellen Kullman, a former chief executive of DuPont Co., sticks to a "no regrets" policy. "If it doesn't work out, I am not going to sit there and lament it."

# 7

# Getting Ahead Later

Getting ahead later in your career can be tricky, even if you've grabbed a foothold in higher management. You could face harsher gender stereotypes about your capacity to lead. You will find fewer role models, given the scarcity of women at the top.

Another potential roadblock arises from the so-called imposter syndrome: you worry about being exposed as a phony because you feel that you don't belong in a high-powered position. Research shows that imposter anxieties often arise among competent, successful people with unusually high fears of failure or of making mistakes.[1] The problem appears more common among women. It's a hot topic nowadays, as a flurry of books, speakers, online communities, and workshops attempt to help women cope. One workshop features "Imposter Syndrome Bingo," a playful way to identify the behavior.

Several executive women I met conquered such fears and thrived. Their courage typified what I observed in a number of the leaders: an ability to rebound from adversity and advance further.

Among those who confronted the imposter syndrome was Dawn Lepore, the former CEO of Drugstore.com. After she graduated with a music degree from Smith College, Cincinnati Bell trained and hired her as a computer programmer. "I wasn't good enough to perform music," she recalled. "I was fascinated about how you use technology to solve business problems."

In 1983, while in her twenties, Lepore joined Charles Schwab Corp. as manager of the information center for the investment brokerage. She spent years climbing its management ladder, yearning to be named chief information officer someday. Yet for years, she also doubted she qualified for the senior role, which involved running all of the information technology operations.

A voice in Lepore's head kept telling her, "'I can't do it, I can't do it, I can't do it. I can never do that, I can never do that, I can never do that,'" she said, repeating her words for emphasis. "'I am a music major. I don't have the background.'"

Lepore finally decided she should at least try to capture the coveted spot. "The way you focus on your job changes when you consciously admit to yourself you want a position," she pointed out. But "you become very vulnerable because if you don't get it, you fail."

Lepore already was a Schwab vice president in the late 1980s when a new chief information officer arrived, and she was curious how an outsider like him would handle the high-level post. "I watched what meetings he had. I watched how he communicated. I watched everything he did," she said. "So I got better and better at my job."

Within a year, the new CIO promoted Lepore to senior vice president and began grooming her and others as his possible successor. "There came a point when I thought to myself, 'Maybe I could be a CIO,'" she remembered.

A few years later, Schwab needed to install a new generation of technology for the entire company. "They were looking for somebody to head this, and nobody raised their hand," she recollected. People said, "'We don't need to change. It won't work,'" she added. She raised her hand, hoping to demonstrate she might be a strong contender for chief information officer.

"You had to be able to show you could take on something you didn't know anything about," she explained. "Call it courage. Call it naïveté. Call it stupidity. But I took on the project."

Though far from finished, the technology initiative was making progress at the time that the chief information officer retired in 1994. Lepore, then thirty-nine years old, succeeded him. Her willingness to take risks was the main reason she got the plum position, Schwab's leaders told her.

Yet despite the biggest promotion in Lepore's career, external forces kept her demons of self-doubt alive. Some older board members questioned the wisdom of putting such a young woman in charge of Schwab's technology. "Are you sure she can do it?" the directors asked a senior executive.

Lepore soon attended her first professional event for top technology officers like her. Walking into a large hotel ballroom, she found herself surrounded by five hundred men. Every man wore a blue suit, and she was the only woman. "I literally couldn't breathe. I was like, 'Oh my God,'" she said. "I felt so conspicuous that everybody turned around and looked at me. At least that was my perspective. I am not sure if they did or not."

Feeling very intimidated, Lepore barely spoke to any of the men. "A lot of these guys were experienced in technology," she continued. "I didn't have a computer science degree." In hindsight, she thinks she should have expected and prepared to be the sole female executive at that industry event.

Her first eighteen months as Schwab's CIO proved tough, too. "I was promoted over my peers. Everybody was watching me," she recalled. "I thought I had to be perfect."

Lepore subsequently advanced to a vice chairman of Schwab, and left in 2004 to run Drugstore.com. Walgreen Co. bought the online retailer in 2011.

She believes the imposter syndrome still haunts women today. "The talk in your head could be your biggest enemy," Lepore often counsels younger women. "Courage is incredibly important."

Some other women I interviewed contend that strong self-confidence should trump any imposter fears about taking a top-level job. After all, "if you don't have confidence in yourself, you shouldn't be aspiring to get ahead," said Pat Russo, a former chief of Lucent Technologies and Alcatel-Lucent. She is presently chairman of Hewlett Packard Enterprise, created when Hewlett-Packard split into two companies in November 2015.

## KNOCKING DOWN DOMINOES OF DOUBTS

Until 1998, Ellen Kullman never doubted her ability to manage increasingly larger management posts at DuPont, the maker of Kevlar body armor and Teflon nonstick pan coating, and which she later led.

Kullman is a native of Wilmington, Delaware, the headquarters city for DuPont. As a young girl, she aspired to be an astronaut. She received a degree in mechanical engineering from Tufts University, then worked for two other major corporations before DuPont hired her as a marketing manager in 1988.

She became its first female vice president at age thirty-nine in 1995. Even though Kullman had scant manufacturing experience, DuPont assigned her to manage a business with six plants, plenty of hazardous materials, and big customers. The unit sold titanium dioxide, a pigment used to whiten paper. "They were taking a chance," Kullman told me. "This was my dream come true. It's what I always wanted to do: run a business."

Three years later, however, a radically different opportunity threatened the self-confidence of the DuPont corporate officer. On a Monday in mid-August, Kullman ran into Chief Executive Charles "Chad" O. Holliday, her boss's boss, at company headquarters. She had just returned from a weeklong summer vacation with her husband and their three young children.

Holliday greeted her as he left the Wilmington building for lunch. "I will see you this afternoon at four thirty," he said. Kullman knew nothing about their appointment. Nor did her colleagues at the suburban office of their titanium dioxide unit. "What did I do wrong? What did the business do wrong?" she wondered. She feared that she might lose her job. Usually, you don't get called downtown to headquarters if things are going well, she noted.

Kullman sat facing Holliday at his desk in his ninth-floor corner office. He described DuPont's interest in launching a division based on its safety heritage. But he mentioned no details about what products or services the venture might provide. "I

have no idea why he is talking to me about this," Kullman recollected thinking.

Holliday explained that he wanted her to spearhead the new
division, offering her a free hand to craft its game plan.

"You want me to leave my job and you want me to start a business?" she replied, incredulous. "There's no definition of what the
business is. There's no people. There's no assets."

"Yup, pretty much," Holliday said.

His vague proposal puzzled her. "Is it because I am doing a bad
job?" Kullman asked herself. She requested several days to weigh
the offer.

She sought guidance from her husband, Mike, a DuPont middle
manager. "I don't think this is good for your career," he told her
during a chat in their kitchen that evening. "What do you get out
of it?"

A fellow vice president also urged her to reject the offer. "He
reminded me that success in this company is all based on assets
you have and the number of people you have working for you,"
Kullman said. The titanium dioxide unit had $2 billion in annual
sales and about two thousand employees at the time.

Worried about the dubious lateral move, Kullman lost sleep for
a few nights. She grilled Holliday again about the proposed venture during their next session in his office. "What is this going to
do for my career? What are your expectations?" she asked. "How
do you define success? Isn't this going to appear like I failed at the
job I am in?"

Holliday, a relatively new chief executive, instead focused
on the bigger picture. "It's about creating the new DuPont," he
declared.

Kullman finally took the job. "I felt I would learn a lot about me and about starting a business and doing something different," she said. "This would either be the best decision I ever made or the worst decision I ever made."

Nevertheless, Kullman hedged her bets by requesting a "get out of jail free" card from Holliday. He promised to find her a different DuPont position six months later if she concluded the nascent safety consulting unit wouldn't succeed. The August 1998 official announcement about its creation said Kullman would become a member of the CEO's operating group as well.

Yet not a single colleague called to congratulate her. Nor were any DuPont administrative assistants willing to work for her at her new organization. She persuaded a retired assistant to rejoin the company.

During her four years at the helm, the safety consulting business expanded at a compound annual rate of 15 percent. Kullman further enhanced her DuPont reputation by subsequently building another new division. In January 2009, she moved into the corner office vacated by Holliday.

I asked Kullman how contemporary female executives should react to the prospect of a challenging higher management role. "Be pretty sure about how you will benefit from this," she suggested. "Will this play to your strengths or to your fears?" Arranging a fallback position is critical, too. In her case, she reminded herself, "I have a good set of skills. I will find something fun to do."

Kullman stepped down from the helm of DuPont in October 2015, as the company slashed its outlook and announced plans to speed up cost cuts. In retiring early at age fifty-nine, she said that she had accomplished her goals for transforming her longtime employer.

## COPING WITH STRESSFUL SETBACKS

Staying ahead as a business leader can turn out to be as daunting as getting ahead, a predicament that Cheryl A. Bachelder encountered in 2003.

Now chief executive of Popeyes Louisiana Kitchen Inc., a fast-food restaurant chain, she was then in charge of KFC restaurants. Tricon Global Restaurants Inc. had recruited her two years earlier to be the first female president of a unit known for its popular fried chicken. She reported to David Novak, CEO of Tricon, which changed its name to Yum Brands Inc. in 2002. She brought thirteen years of food marketing experience at Domino's Pizza Inc. and RJR Nabisco Inc.

"This was supposed to be the pinnacle position of my career," Bachelder wrote in her 2015 book, *Dare to Serve: How to Drive Superior Results by Serving Others*.[2]

Unfortunately, Bachelder inherited a mess. "KFC was a troubled brand," she said during our interview at the New York office of Popeyes' public relations firm. "Declining sales and guest traffic. Declining restaurant profits. Terrible relationships with their franchisees," recalled the executive, a lanky woman with chocolate-brown hair who stands six feet tall. "Those are the things that I think are fun. I look at them and say, 'I understand what's wrong and I know what to do.' I thought the brand could be revitalized."

Bachelder's KFC tenure began well, as she rolled out new advertising and products. But she was diagnosed with breast cancer eight months after she arrived, then worked during her treatment. And soon, she said, "everything I touched turned to mud."

KFC suffered negative press coverage over lawsuits linking obesity to fast food. Its new advertisements and products lost popularity, upsetting franchisees. Bachelder figured she had time to correct the problems. "A brand that has been performing poorly for a long time is not a fast turnaround," she explained. "My strategy was a long-term strategy."

Looking back, she recognizes that she lacked sufficient self-confidence to defend her long-term view. "I should have been braver, firmer, clearer with my management," she admitted. The top brass of Yum Brands preferred short-term results. "They operate very much in the here and now. So I was kind of going against the grain of their culture," she said.

In September 2003, the forty-seven-year-old KFC president attended a funeral for a relative of an employee. She mused about how she had failed to fulfill the chief executive's expectations for her unit because "I could not give him the improvement he needed."

During the funeral, Bachelder decided to offer her resignation upon her return to KFC headquarters, a massive replica of the White House in Louisville, Kentucky. She mentally rehearsed what she would tell her boss: "This is obviously not working for either of us.'"

Bachelder and Novak unexpectedly met halfway down a hall near their respective offices. "He was coming to see me, and I was going to see him." She stepped into his corner office, whose walls contained about two thousand photographs showing every Yum Brands staffer whom he had handed a company award.

The two executives sat down on a couch. "This is not working out, and we are going to make a change," Novak flatly told his lieutenant.

"I agree," Bachelder replied. "This is not working out for either one of us."

Being fired embarrassed, saddened, and hurt her. An unflattering photograph of the ousted KFC president appeared in the Louisville newspaper under the headline, "Cheryl Bachelder Replaced," she recollected. "My kids had to see it in school. A really ugly day."

The KFC experience profoundly changed her leadership style. "It certainly shaped how I run Popeyes," Bachelder observed. Assuming command in 2007 as the chain's first female CEO, she heard the familiar refrain of weak sales and tense relations with franchisees. But she now understood that a publicly held company must perform well every quarter and embrace a clear, long-term strategy. She also altered how she dispenses pink slips, and tried to treat fired staffers with greater dignity. "I spend more time and detail around those decisions than any other decision," she said.

Working with Popeyes franchisees, Bachelder reduced costs, sped up service, and revitalized the brand through remodeled restaurants and new menu items. The turnaround resulted in a 190 percent gain in the Popeyes share price by March 2014.[3]

"This success story would not exist without KFC," Bachelder told me. "You have to be humbled, and you have to find the better rules to lead by," she continued. "The leadership rules that I now know to be phenomenally effective came from what did not work."

Careful listening is one of Bachelder's rules. A few years ago, Popeyes franchise owners strongly rejected a proposed design for remodeling the restaurants. "Lack of passion for the new design would doom the results of the remodel program," she said in her book. Her team started over, taking two years to develop a more acceptable design. Franchise owners liked the new look so much that 80 percent of restaurants remodeled in two years, "a task that would typically have taken five or more years," Bachelder wrote.[4]

Getting dismissed from a senior-level spot was an equally meaningful wake-up call for Meg Whitman, the former chief executive of eBay and Hewlett-Packard. (She presently leads Hewlett Packard Enterprise.) But unlike Bachelder, whose firing consumed a full page of her book, Whitman said nothing about her removal from the highest spot at FTD, a provider of floral products, in her 2010 memoir, *The Power of Many: Values for Success in Business and in Life*. FTD was her first CEO stint.

"Probably the most frustrating and, ultimately, least successful executive experience in my career," Whitman wrote in her book. "I finally quit that job."[5]

She revealed what really happened during our March 2015 interview in a conference room at HP's sprawling campus in suburban Palo Alto, California. "In the end, I got fired," she told me. The ruddy-complexioned chief executive often blushed when she spoke. She wore a quilted Burberry jacket and scuffed jeans that Friday afternoon because she was leaving for a ski weekend in Telluride, Colorado.

Whitman is a Harvard MBA who received her undergraduate degree in economics from Princeton University. When wooed to take charge of FTD in 1995, she was in her late thirties and held a senior management role at Stride Rite Corp. She was a veteran of other big businesses such as Procter & Gamble and Walt Disney Co.

A group of FTD investors led by Richard Perry, the head of Perry Capital, was shifting the member-owned cooperative into a for-profit business before they took the company public. "It seemed like an exciting opportunity and I took it," Whitman said in her book. She arranged a long-distance commute between her home in Brookline, Massachusetts, and FTD headquarters in Detroit.[6]

The investors gave Whitman lofty marching orders: rapidly reverse FTD's multimillion-dollar losses and instead make millions of dollars in profit.

The company struggled with high levels of debt and low employee morale. Meanwhile, many florists stuck with the roughly eight hundred staffers whom Whitman laid off because they had long done business together. "We massively tried to redo the relationships with the florists in the face of a new competitor called 1-800-FLOWERS," she said during our lunch interview. "It was hard."

Perry pulled Whitman aside during an FTD florist convention in Arizona near the end of the CEO's second year. Although the company had stopped bleeding red ink, its profits still lagged behind the investors' ambitious goals. "I love you to death, but you are not doing the job," he told her.

"You know what?" Whitman replied. "This is fixable, but it is not fixable by me." To her surprise, Perry concurred.

Whitman had expected that he would volunteer to help her finish fixing FTD. "I was pretty bummed out," she told me. "I felt I failed. I probably should have figured out how to do this."

She telephoned her husband with the bad news, flew home, and began job hunting. She didn't wallow in self-pity, because "I tend to move on to the next thing," Whitman said. But she vowed to dig deeper before accepting other opportunities. Toy maker Hasbro Inc. hired her as general manager of its Playskool division.

The technology neophyte landed her second CEO post in 1998 at eBay, then a funky start-up that let people sell collectibles and other items to the highest bidder via a virtual flea market. During Whitman's decade at its helm, eBay grew from 30 employees and $4 million in annual revenue to more than 15,000 employees and $8 billion in revenue. Her stake in the Internet auctioneer eventually made her a billionaire, the first woman CEO to join that elite club in the high-tech industry.

On the other hand, Whitman neglected to investigate whether a campaign for California governor represented a viable career option before spending two and a half years and $144 million of her money on an unsuccessful run in 2010. She shelled out more than any other self-funded political candidate in U.S. history.

"I actually am quite game to take on big challenges and I am not easily cowed. Sometimes, I probably don't see all the negatives," Whitman conceded. But "I am a much better CEO because I ran for governor and lost," she said. "I developed a much thicker skin."

You can glean an important insight from the serious setbacks that Cheryl Bachelder and Meg Whitman encountered far along in their career trajectories: to get ahead at that point, you must learn from your occasional backward fall so you can avoid making the same slip twice.

## "TALK ME OFF THE LEDGE"

Luckily, Mindy Grossman never fulfilled her fantasy of a despondent fall from her high-rise apartment. "I don't know anyone who hasn't had a 'Talk me off the ledge' moment,'" the HSN chief executive told me.

She has run the shopping service since 2006, when it was the biggest unit of IAC/InterActiveCorp. At that time, "Home Shopping Network had a reputation of C-list celebrities selling rhinestone jewelry and miracle skin creams to couch potatoes."[7]

Grossman came to HSN after six years at Nike Inc., where she oversaw its $4 billion global apparel business. "People thought I had a midlife crisis," she remembered the December day we conversed in her Manhattan corner office, where the floor-to-ceiling window overlooked bustling Madison Avenue far below. Four television screens displaying HSN shows filled one wall, while a single white orchid sat atop a small side table.

"I was forty-eight, and if I was going to take a risk, now was the time to take a risk," Grossman continued. The fast-talking New Yorker wore oversize rings on each hand and glasses with bright green frames. She said she expected the HSN position would also broaden her skill set.

Grossman was its eighth leader in ten years. "There had been no investment put in the business," she said. "There was mold on the buildings."

The HSN leader acted swiftly to revive the retailer, rolling out a new strategy in fall 2006 and relaunching the brand in August 2007. She and fellow executives then spent months getting ready to spin off from IAC and go public. HSN made its debut as a publicly traded company in August 2008, amid a widespread economic collapse.

Its stock price tumbled from about $10 initially to less than $1.50 by December. People feared HSN might violate debt agreements. "That was probably the watershed leadership moment of my life," Grossman said, gesturing widely with her hands. "The world fell apart."

Between summer and the end of 2008, she had trouble sleeping, gained twenty pounds, and developed stress eczema. "I was a mess," Grossman recalled.

The worried chief executive turned to her husband, Neil, for a pep talk. They lived in a twenty-third-floor Manhattan apartment, and she used to walk outside on its patio. Grossman said she implored him, "'Talk me off the ledge.' Because I knew I had the lives of six thousand people that are family and everything else to think about every day."

Her husband encouraged her to keep those HSN staffers focused on her vision for the company. Grossman intensified employee communication efforts, doubling her usual number of town hall sessions. As a leader, she realized, "you have to have the confidence and you have to motivate and keep people going."

Grossman also realized that things would gradually improve for HSN because "we had a very agile business model." She spread shopping content from static TV shows to interactive offerings on small screens of mobile devices. HSN progressed from losing millions of dollars a year in 2008 to earning more than $130 million in 2012, and its share price rebounded.[8]

Throughout Grossman's life, colossal challenges have rarely impeded her progress. She attributed her resiliency to her mother, a high school dropout. "She was very clear that there were no impediments. You decide what you want to do and you do anything." Her father worked nights in the produce business. Both expected their adopted daughter to become a professional. She graduated from high school at age sixteen.

But Grossman abandoned college during her senior year at George Washington University, where she had majored in English literature and philosophy. In 1977, she obtained an entry-level job in the New York apparel industry as an executive assistant. She never completed her college degree.

In her view, female executives considering a risky career move such as reinventing a business should envision the possible corporate and personal benefits. "The impact that you can have . . . is much greater than doing the safe thing," Grossman said.

## LEADERSHIP LESSONS FROM
## "GETTING AHEAD LATER"

- Be braver than others about taking high-risk roles in higher management. "You look for opportunity amid chaotic times," recommends Cheryl A. Bachelder, leader of Popeyes Louisiana Kitchen.
- Ignore issues that you can't control and focus on issues where you have the greatest chances of success.
- Pick team members who can help you thrive because they care more about the company than themselves. "The ones who are about themselves, they will screw you. They will screw the company," cautions Paula Rosput Reynolds, who has twice led publicly held companies. "They are flameouts."
- Defuse your imposter anxiety by initially pursuing a small-scale

assignment. "If you step forward," says Kathleen Ligocki, the current CEO of Agility Fuel and a former chief of Tower Automotive, "you learn if you are agile enough."

- When you assume a top-level role, ask a powerful internal ally to watch your back. In addition, "you have to be careful that you are not going to be the sacrificial lamb," cautions Dawn Lepore, a former chief executive of Drugstore.com.

- Be receptive to criticism about your performance and fix your mistakes fast. Speaking of negative feedback, "it is almost better if it is out there on the table" because colleagues will have that in mind anyway, advises Ilene Gordon, CEO of Ingredion Inc., a major supplier of sweeteners and starches for the food industry.

- In case you can't fix your flubs, make sure you have a fallback position.

# 8

# Manager Moms Are
# Not Acrobats

Forget the myth of work-life balance. "Telling a woman to balance her home and work life is impossible unless she is an acrobat," said Melanie Healey, the first woman to run the North American unit of Procter & Gamble, the world's largest consumer products company.

Healey knows plenty about the impossible balancing act that working mothers face. In 1992, when she was a thirty-one-year-old marketing manager at P&G, the company offered her a chance to leave her native Brazil and join its soap division in Mexico. She eagerly accepted the expatriate assignment, and her husband, Bruce, lined up a new job there.

Shortly before the couple moved abroad, Healey learned that she was pregnant. She and her husband had been trying to conceive for four years. "I had been through two operations," she said during our interview. "I was told I would probably never have kids of my own."

She strode into the office of the company's general manager for Brazil and sat down opposite his desk. "I said, 'Look, I am pregnant. I don't know if you guys want to be transferring a pregnant expat because I plan to take my maternity leave,'" she recalled, adding, "'I waited a long time to have this kid.'"

Healey intended to take off four and a half months, including the month before her due date, as required under Mexican law. "We are going to transfer you anyway," her boss replied. Six months pregnant, Healey rented a house with her husband a mile from her P&G office in Mexico City.

She figured living close to work would help ease the demands of being a mother who worked outside the home. But P&G failed to assign someone to fill in for her after her son was born in 1993. In response, she invited members of her work team to her home for lunch every day of her leave. "We would debrief," she said. "I would give them the orders of the day, and off they would go."

When Healey returned to her office full-time, she reported to a different boss than the supportive one she had worked for at the beginning of her leave. "This general manager had a reputation for working long hours, slave-driving his team," she said. "He gave me five impossible tasks."

Unfortunately, the myriad challenges that Healey confronted trying to maintain her career after having a child are hardly unique. Manager moms carry a double load, toiling hard both at the office and at home. To succeed, they require the uncommon combination of highly committed employers and highly involved husbands. "We all need to encourage men to lean in to their families," Sheryl Sandberg, chief operating officer of Facebook, wrote in her 2013 book, *Lean In.* "Unfortunately, traditional gender roles are reinforced not just by individuals, but also by employment policies."[1]

A handful of American businesses assist new parents in bold ways. In summer 2015, for example, Netflix Inc. began to give both mothers and fathers up to a year of paid leave after the birth or adoption of a child. Accenture, a large professional services firm, now allows mothers and primary caregivers to skip out-of-town business trips for a year after they return from parental leave.

And Yahoo extended its paid parental leave policy to sixteen weeks for mothers and eight weeks for fathers, although the company presented a somewhat mixed message to staffers when its chief executive, Marissa Mayer, announced that she would take little time off after she gave birth to twin girls in December 2015.

More than 80 percent of the corporate leaders I interviewed have children, and the proportion of mothers was even higher among the experienced chief executives. Fulfilling their dual roles caused guilt pangs, juggling of domestic tasks, career zigzags, and occasionally, stress-related illnesses.

At the same time, parenthood also made many women better bosses; some learned the importance of choosing their priorities while others set up a child care facility for employees' offspring. Their parenting skills, such as patience, consistent problem solving, and setting clear expectations, also transferred well to their supervision of subordinates. At the same time, women with high-powered corporate jobs offer positive role models to their sons and daughters.

But the more extensive presence of mothers in the executive

suite hardly means that women don't have problems when trying
to combine parenthood and careers, I wrote in an article in the
*Wall Street Journal* in 2010. Fathers were more likely to move into
management than mothers in most major industries, according
to a U.S. Congress Joint Economic Committee summary of a Government Accountability Office report that I cited.[2]

Younger mothers sense the greatest career disadvantage, a
2013 survey by the Pew Research Center found. Fifty-eight percent of mothers aged 18 to 32 said parenthood made it harder
for them to get ahead at work, compared with only 19 percent of
working fathers in the same age range. Equally disturbing, these
so-called millennial parents increase their post-parenthood work
hours after becoming parents more than earlier generations did,
according to a 2015 study by Ernst & Young, a professional services firm.

Among parents of all ages who work full-time, 41 percent of
mothers report that parenthood interferes with their career advancement. That compares with 20 percent of such working fathers, a 2015 poll by Pew found.

The prior year, a federal jury in California ordered AutoZone
Inc., an auto parts retailer, to pay a former sales manager named
Rosario Juarez $185 million in punitive damages because the
company had demoted her upon finding out she was pregnant and
later fired her. AutoZone had claimed that Juarez was a poor performer. The jury award set a record for a pregnancy discrimination
case. Juarez and AutoZone finally settled the suit in July 2015.[3]
Although her attorney declined my request for comment, an
AutoZone spokesman told me that "the case was resolved to the
mutual satisfaction of the parties."

## THE GOOD AND BAD OF MATERNITY LEAVE

The experience of Teresa Taylor illustrates how even women who take the briefest of maternity leaves can run into trouble. She would one day become chief operating officer of Qwest Communications International, a telecommunications company. But the birth of Taylor's first son threatened her promising management career at US West, a Denver-based telecom company that was subsequently acquired by Qwest.

Raised in a rural Wisconsin community, Taylor was the first member of her family to attend college. She graduated from the University of Wisconsin–La Crosse in 1985 with a degree in parks and recreation administration, then worked as a sales representative for two other businesses. Three years after she finished college, US West hired her as a product manager.

During her six-week maternity leave in 1993, Taylor heard office gossip that her boss would soon pick someone for a newly created vice presidency in their expanding division. Because she had received positive feedback from him about her performance as a middle manager, "I thought, of course it is going to be my job," she recollected while she sipped tea one windy winter afternoon at the Algonquin Hotel in Manhattan.

Taylor said her supervisor never considered her for vice president. Instead, he tapped one of her peers in their division, a man she didn't respect. "The person who was chosen was a complete idiot," she said bitterly. "Not a performer. A schmoozer."

When her boss called to announce his decision two weeks before Taylor returned to work, she peppered him with questions. "Why is this happening?" she recalled demanding. "Why didn't you talk to me? What's going on? I thought I was next in line."

"I wasn't sure you were coming back," her boss replied. "I had to make a decision."

His remarks infuriated Taylor. She had kept in touch with him every few days by phone despite a colicky baby and little sleep, and she thought he knew she planned to return to work. "I worked so hard not to have this maternity leave be a wrinkle."

Upset by the unwelcome news about the vice president position, Taylor moved fast to recalculate her career trajectory. She phoned another executive, a man who would soon direct a new US West division. "I am coming back in two weeks," she said. "I prefer not to go back to my old job. What do you have going on?"

His response was enthusiastic. "I would love to have you on the new team," he said.

Taylor told her old boss that she was switching divisions because he had not selected her for the VP opening. "It should have been my job," she remembered saying to him. "That was terrible that you didn't think I was coming back." (Years later, he would justify his flawed assumption by saying that he had seen other new mothers decide not to return to work.)

Taylor flourished in her new division. She made presentations in front of the US West board of directors for the first time, and became a vice president within a year. "It was a turning point in my career," she said of her new position.

During one board retreat, Taylor was approached by her former boss. Explaining that the man he had promoted to vice president had left, he confessed he made a big mistake and added, "I need you to come back."

"No way," Taylor retorted. "You missed your time."

The unexpected setback during her maternity leave deepened Taylor's commitment to spelling out her career goals to her superiors, and urging female lieutenants to follow suit. "Make sure your boss knows what you want," she suggested. "If they are not asking you, tell them. Don't assume that they know what you are thinking or what you are doing."

## KOOL-AID CAPER

Irene Rosenfeld, chief executive of the global snacks manufacturer Mondelēz International, isn't easily intimidated. While leading Kraft Foods, then the biggest food company in the United States, she overcame opposition to her $19 billion takeover of Cadbury PLC from the billionaire Warren Buffett, a large Kraft investor. "One has to be willing to do what is right and deal with the consequences," Rosenfeld said when we spoke.

Growing up, she fantasized about becoming president of the United States. "Aspiring to do something important was important to me," explained Rosenfeld, a short woman with cropped brown hair. Athletics honed her competitive skills at a young age. During high school and college, she played basketball despite her small stature because, she explained, "I could wind in and out of people's legs." She stopped playing after breaking her leg in her first year at Cornell University.

Her husband bought her a basketball hoop for her fortieth birthday and mounted it in their driveway. Noticing the hoop, "people would come up and say, 'I didn't know you had sons,'"

Rosenfeld recollected. "I don't," she'd reply. "It's mine." Now in her sixties, the CEO still Rollerblades around the suburban Chicago neighborhood where she lives.

Rosenfeld, who holds a doctorate in marketing and statistics, started her career conducting consumer research for the ad agency Dancer Fitzgerald Sample and worked for General Foods before the company became part of Kraft.

She exhibited her spunk after the birth of her eldest daughter in 1983. At the time, she was one of two group product managers for Kool-Aid, a popular General Foods brand. Their boss, the head of the Kool-Aid business, had just left the company, but his position remained vacant.

Halfway through Rosenfeld's six-week maternity leave, she visited her workplace. She was stunned to see that her fellow product manager had moved his belongings and furniture into her office, which was located closer to the general manager's office than his was. When she confronted him about this switch, he said, "Well, I don't know how this happened."

Skeptical about his explanation, Rosenfeld asked the building's custodian to return her furniture to her office and regained her prime space near the seat of power. The action of her colleague bolstered her view that women must act more assertively in the workplace to avoid similar incidents. "Be prepared to toot your own horn," she advised. "Girls are not socialized to stand up for themselves."

Rosenfeld took that approach again when the top job in the company's Kool-Aid business opened up in 1987. "I went in and said, 'I want it,'" she recalled. Higher-ups granted her request. Once in command of Kool-Aid, she overhauled the brand by marketing it to children using rock-and-roll TV commercials and wooing mothers by making the drink less sweet. In 1988, sales of Kool-Aid grew for the first time in ten years.

## CAREER COUPS

Certain women I met achieved career breakthroughs around the time they became parents. Among them was Penny Herscher, now executive chairman of FirstRain, the business analytics company, and one of the first female chief executives in the U.S. semiconductor industry.

Herscher was head of marketing for Synopsys, a fast-growing maker of design software, when she gave birth to her son in December 1993. He was only four weeks old when the Synopsys CEO asked Herscher to lead a division.

Early in her career, she had realized that she needed experience being responsible for profits and losses in order to reach the corner office, and the position offered by her CEO would be her first with such duties. But his offer came with a catch: she would have to interrupt her six-week maternity leave so she could assist him in revamping the corporate organizational structure. "At week five, I was in the office and I nursed him in the office," she said of her newborn. "It was very shocking at the time."

Even more shocking to her colleagues was the day Herscher breastfed her five-week-old infant in front of Synopsys top management, all of whom were men, during an executive team meeting at headquarters in Mountain View, California. Although she wore a nursing shirt and tried to be discreet, every one of her male peers at the long conference table appeared embarrassed.

"Afterwards, they gave me no end of grief about it," Herscher said. "'You were always a little out there,'" they teased her.

Cheryl Bachelder, CEO of Popeyes Louisiana, made the same sort of stride forward. The day before she went into labor to deliver her daughter Katy in 1991, she landed her first general manager's job when RJR Nabisco put her in charge of its Life Savers division. "I took the media interview six hours after she was born," Bachelder remembered.

Being interviewed while in the hospital with a newborn didn't strike her as strange. "RJR Nabisco was a crazy place," Bachelder said. "Things like that happened all the time."

## WORKING LESS, ADVANCING MORE

Manager moms with an understanding boss can get home for dinner and get ahead, too—even though their jobs often require them to be on call 24/7. That proved true for Melanie Healey after her new supervisor at P&G assigned the new mother multiple daunting tasks to complete in six months. He laid out his marching orders during their initial meeting in her office after she returned from maternity leave.

"No problem," Healey promised him. But, she added, "there is one thing I want you to do." Her boss had a reputation for starting morning meetings before seven o'clock and staying very late at night.

"I am going to get here at eight in the morning. So you can't start a meeting before eight," she recalled saying. "I am going to be at home at six o'clock. So you can't start a meeting after five that doesn't end by five to six, so I can be home by six."

Her boss looked bewildered, but then agreed. He ended his late afternoon meetings at 5:50 and reconvened the next morning at eight. "He never made me feel guilty about it," Healey said. He subsequently joined a company in France, and flew her there several times in an effort to encourage her to come work for him at his new employer.

Healey rejected his overtures because her P&G career was taking off. The company transferred her back to Brazil during the middle of her second maternity leave, a relocation she welcomed because her family lived there, and promoted her shortly after she returned to work.

## PAYOFF FROM MY PAINFUL JOB JUGGLE

Unlike some of the women I interviewed, I did a lousy job of managing my return to the Washington bureau of the *Wall Street Journal* after a three-month leave following the birth of our son Daniel in 1979. At the end of my first day back, a colleague noticed my annoyance while we waited twenty minutes for the bus home. "Well, Joann," he said, "you don't have to be here. You could be home rocking your baby in the rocking chair." I quoted his comments in a first-person essay that I wrote for the paper's editorial page about why I chose to combine motherhood and a career. In those pre-computer days, my piece appeared alongside a drawing of a baby scowling at a typewriter.

"My first week back was the worst," I wrote. "I blew everything out of proportion. The scorecard reads: two stomach-upsets, one anxiety attack, one episode of hysteria, and two fights with my husband." I concluded, "Society still dictates that a working mother must be a lousy mother."[4]

My essay triggered a wave of hostility from men and women. The *Journal* printed a full page of scathing letters to the editor. The letters appeared on a Monday when I already was down in the dumps because I had just stopped breastfeeding our seven-month-old son, a move that occurred sooner than I preferred. A bulging folder atop my desk contained another forty letters that were deemed too nasty to publish.

One letter writer said that Daniel was better off that I worked because I was obviously an unfit mother. Sick to my stomach and sicker at heart, I left work early that day. I tearfully considered quitting, then changed my mind. The venomous reactions from readers intensified my determination to demonstrate I could make working motherhood work.

I sought a better balance between work and family the second time around. Shortly before the birth of our daughter Abra in January 1983 and my four-month maternity leave, I asked for a four-day work schedule at the Washington bureau. Management rejected my proposal because reduced work schedules were rare at the *Journal*.

Thankfully, things changed that fall. A new managing editor and new Washington bureau chief whose wives worked outside the home encouraged me to revive my four-day request. Abra was eight months old and Daniel had just turned four.

The managing editor gave me Fridays off without cutting my

pay or benefits because I was one of the *Journal*'s most experienced female reporters. He also said I could work normal hours the rest of the week and could continue covering my beat, which was organized labor. The schedule worked well. Friday became such a special time for our family that Abra nicknamed it "Mommy Day."

Meanwhile, my bureau chief informed me that the quality and quantity of my stories remained excellent. I even won a promotion to news editor of the *Journal*'s London bureau in January 1987. My four-day schedule ended with my move into management.

Some manager moms I interviewed dialed back their work hours even further. Liz Smith, the Bloomin' Brands CEO, got a three-day-a-week schedule at a division of Kraft after the birth of her eldest son in 1998. Her employer designed a strategy role to accommodate her decreased hours.

Kraft also offered Smith a major promotion to vice president when her son turned one. She took the job, and returned to working full-time.

Sandra "Sandi" Peterson, the highest-ranking woman at Johnson & Johnson, the health products giant, believes women can step off and back on the management track without sacrificing career momentum, despite some research to the contrary. "The idea that your professional life is over if you need to stop working for a while is garbage," said Peterson, who is the mother of two sons.

J&J recruited Peterson in December 2012 partly to turn around its troubled consumer business, whose iconic brands include Tylenol. She came from Bayer AG, where the executive had worked since May 2005 after staying home for seventeen months to care for her ailing husband. He died from lymphoma that spring at the age of fifty-six.

The time that Peterson spent caring for her husband heightened her commitment to assist staffers with pressing family needs. "I am much more likely to say, 'What are we doing to take care of you?'" And, she added, she typically tells those employees, "Go take care of this. The job will be here later."

## SHOWDOWN OVER A
## LONG-DISTANCE COMMUTE

Late one Friday in 1994, Vicki Holt returned home from work around midnight. Holt, who would go on to run two public companies, lived in San Diego at that time with her husband and two children. She took the red-eye flight every Sunday night to St. Louis, where she was a senior aide to the CEO of Monsanto and oversaw a corporate initiative to seek more inspiration from customers. Holt had commuted long-distance for nearly a year, following a California assignment with Monsanto.

She and her husband, Curt, had moved west from St. Louis in 1991 for his job. Curt, who holds a doctorate in molecular biology genetics, worked as a research scientist for Scripps Research Institute in La Jolla, California, near San Diego. He was also the primary parent for the couple's four-year-old son, Matt, and their six-year-old daughter, Lauren, during Holt's weekdays out of town.

Curt was standing in the doorway, looking gaunt and upset, as she entered their house that Friday night. "Lauren is very sick," he said to his wife, "and this is not working anymore."

Suffering from a serious respiratory virus, Lauren had difficulty breathing. Holt rushed her to an emergency room. "They immediately gave her an IV and oxygen and then transported her by ambulance to Children's Hospital in San Diego," the executive said. She slept on a chair during her daughter's three nights in the hospital, which included two days in intensive care.

Holt and her husband debated endlessly about alternatives to her punishing commute. Curt needed to spend an additional five years at Scripps to be eligible for tenure there. "Do I ask Monsanto for a different job here?" Holt recalled musing out loud. She also considered changing employers.

But her husband did not see these as options. "You have better long-term potential," he said, and offered to quit Scripps so their family could move back to St. Louis.

"We cried a lot, both of us," Holt told me. The couple relocated, and Curt eventually obtained a nontenured faculty research position at Washington University. Today, Holt heads Proto Labs.

Other senior businesswomen with children also experienced difficult days during their long-distance commutes. Consider Nancy McKinstry, now chief executive of Wolters Kluwer NV, an international provider of software and information services based in the Netherlands. McKinstry had graduated from the University of Rhode Island with a degree in economics and political science, then spent two years at New England Telephone Co. before she earned an MBA in 1984 and got hired by Booz Allen Hamilton, a major management consultancy in New York.

In 1992, McKinstry joined a Booz client called CCH Inc., a large tax law publisher in suburban Chicago. At the time, she was in her early thirties and the mother of a two-year-old. Her husband, an anesthesiologist, practiced at an orthopedic surgery hospital in New York. "Duplicating that job was not going to be easy," remembered McKinstry, a fast-talking woman who wore a bold, black-and-white print jacket and gold wire-rimmed glasses the day we spoke at a Wolters Kluwer office in Manhattan.

At CCH, McKinstry said, she was the first working mother to commute long-distance. She left for Chicago at six every Tuesday morning, flew home Thursday evenings, and worked in New York on the remaining weekdays. To her surprise, female associates criticized her for abandoning her son. "I don't know how you can leave a child at such a young age," one CCH marketing manager, who was slightly older than her and had no children, chided her over lunch. "I don't know how you can do this."

"I love my son dearly," McKinstry responded. "I have a great husband. I have a great babysitter." The arrangement created a stable home life for her toddler, she explained to the colleague.

The disturbing encounter helped McKinstry recognize the importance of not getting defensive over personal attacks on her private life and business decisions. She said that ambitious women should use such criticism as a teaching moment and try to expand other people's horizons. But at times, "you have to just tune out the noise," she added.

In 2003, the American executive uprooted her husband, son, and daughter to accept an overseas promotion that made her Wolters Kluwer's first female and first non-Dutch CEO. Her husband became a transatlantic commuter, spending two weeks a month at his New York job and caring for their children in Amsterdam during the rest of the month.

## STAY-AT-HOME DADS

Forget clueless Mr. Mom. The father who stays home to care for his children is emerging as an increasingly common and adroit player in the American family. The new model of at-home fatherhood "puts a distinctly masculine stamp on child-rearing and home life," a *Wall Street Journal* colleague wrote in 2013. Her column cited a recent study that concluded that at-home fathers were masculinizing domestic tasks and routines rather than trying to be perfect moms.[5]

Although their ranks remain small, the number of at-home fathers has increased in recent years. There were 211,000 fathers in America in 2014 who cared for about 420,000 children under eighteen while their wives worked outside the home, the U.S. Census Bureau estimated. That's up from 189,000 in 2012.

But highly involved fathers report downsides to the lifestyle. In a 2015 study of 487 heterosexual couples with children conducted by researchers at Georgia State University, men who did at least 60 percent of the child care in a family reported having the lowest-quality sex lives. Yet when men split child care duties equally with their female partners, the couples have more satisfaction with their relationships and their sex lives, the study also found.

At least eight executive women I interviewed married men who reversed traditional parental roles, and all of these women believe the presence of an at-home dad helped them climb the management ladder. The arrangement created bumps as well. Holt's husband, Curt, gave up his academic career to care for their children in 2003. "There weren't a lot of stay-at-home dads," she recalled. "He had to carve his way in [for] stuff going on at school. The roles that he would play were not the same a mom would play."

Mary Dillon, CEO of Ulta Salon Cosmetics & Fragrance Inc., a beauty retailer in Bolingbrook, Illinois, worried about the loss of income when her husband, Terry, became an at-home dad. He quit his job as a drug industry biochemist after the 1993 birth of their daughter Maggie, the second of their four offspring.

When she was pregnant, Dillon had been promoted to a middle management spot at Quaker Oats Co., manufacturer of such well-known products as cooked oatmeal, Rice-A-Roni, and Aunt Jemima pancake mix. The new job included a significant pay increase. She and her husband agreed that her career offered more potential than his, she recollected as we chatted in a midtown Manhattan restaurant. And "he wasn't driven about his work as I was."

Nevertheless, Dillon felt anxious because her pay, even with her raise, wouldn't replace his full-time salary. She had grown up in a modest Chicago household and paid for her schooling—she majored in marketing and Asian studies at the local campus of the University of Illinois—partly by cleaning apartments. Her father had worked as a factory maintenance supervisor, and her homemaker mother raised six children. "I am a first-generation college graduate," Dillon said, grinning broadly.

During her maternity leave in 1993, "I was up all night nursing Maggie. I got panicked a bit about money," Dillon remembered. "I realized, 'Oh, we are in it now. I hope it all works out.'" The couple decided to try the arrangement for a year.

Terry's stint as a full-time father lasted far longer than a year.

Dillon saw her career trajectory accelerate after she gave birth to two more daughters. She was president of Quaker Foods, then a unit of PepsiCo, when McDonald's Corp. tapped her as its global marketing chief in 2005. Five years later, she took the highest post at U.S. Cellular Corp., a wireless carrier, and joined Ulta as CEO in 2013.

Her husband remains an at-home father. "We never had a nanny," Dillon said. "He did it all." But his highly driven wife had trouble tolerating chaotic domestic messes that he allows. "I am so type A that it is hard for me not to always be thinking of the twenty things we have to do right," she admitted. "Men aren't as hung up about keeping things neat and tidy as women. My husband is very happy to leave all the dishes on the table if the kids want to throw the ball outside, and then come back later and clean it up."

That's exactly what happened one summer night in 2000. Their children wanted Terry to play ball with them. "At first, I stayed inside cleaning the kitchen," Dillon recalled. "But after about ten minutes, I asked myself, 'Why am I not outside playing with my kids?' I knew Terry wasn't expecting me to clean the kitchen alone," she continued. "In fact, he would just let it wait until later."

Dillon left the dirty dishes, went outside, and enjoyed playing ball with her family. She and Terry did the dishes later. "I realized that night," she said, "that perhaps it would be better not to be as type A and linear at home as I need to be at work."

Women should let at-home fathers run their household the way they want, Dillon recommended. "As a manager mom, you just have to know when to have a sense of humor and let things go."

## THE LONGEST DAY IS A WORKDAY

Every working mother I met suffered some guilt pangs over their long hours away from their family. But the extent of their guilt antidotes amazed me. Their coping mechanisms went far beyond the popular practice of sharing dinner with their youngsters, then working from home after putting them to bed, or dragging offspring to their office on weekends.

Take Carol Bartz, a former leader of Autodesk and Yahoo. When the youngest of her three children entered kindergarten, Bartz reviewed the school calendar with her daughter and pledged to attend certain key events, such as holiday parties. "Did she totally understand that at five?" Bartz asked. "No. But I did that every year." The executive also placed her commitments to school events on her work calendar, and sternly warned her assistant, "I don't care if the pope comes to audit us. I am going to the Christmas Sing."

Liz Smith, the Bloomin' Brands chief executive, devised a time bank account because she wanted to spend four hours every day with her two young sons. If she missed her goal due to work demands, she replenished the time owed the next week. "Some days, I would cancel my meetings that morning because I was in the hole to them," Smith recalled. "I would spend the morning at home."

## A NANNY'S COFFEE ENEMA

Of course, the best antidote for guilt among manager moms is reliable and high-quality child care. Several women I met made economic sacrifices to pay top dollar for top-quality care. This was the case when P&G assigned Melanie Healey to a plum management role in Caracas, Venezuela, when her children were five and six years old. She said she kept her sanity by initially devoting 100 percent of her salary to setting up an infrastructure to care for them, hiring a nanny, a cook, and a driver.

"There is no better investment than the people who become part of your family when you have a child," agreed Mindy Grossman, chief executive of HSN. She employed the same nanny for her daughter for years, a woman named Lesbia Raez, whom Grossman fondly described as her secret weapon.

In 2000, the New York executive refused to take an attractive offer to command the global apparel business for Nike, the sneaker giant, until she knew that her planned long-distance commute would suit Raez. Nike's headquarters are near Portland, Oregon.

Grossman sat down and discussed the offer with her nanny and her husband, Neil. "Can we make this work?" she remembered asking them. Raez needed to arrive before Neil left for work early in the morning, and to stay overnight with their school-age daughter during his business trips. After the nanny agreed to this schedule, Grossman took the Nike offer.

As working parents everywhere can attest, not every nanny works out well. Stephanie Sonnabend, former CEO of Sonesta International Hotels Corp., a hotel chain, attempted to avoid that scenario by planning ahead. Before she and Gregory Ciccolo married, they bought a home in Brookline, Massachusetts, with a third-floor bedroom and sitting area for a future live-in nanny. Sonnabend was already a Sonesta executive when she gave birth to their daughter in 1987. The couple's son was born in 1989.

Sonnabend's favorite nanny lasted five years. But others displayed weird behavior, and in hindsight, she wished she had fired them sooner. There was one nanny, for instance, "who was really into coffee enemas," she remembered.

Unexpected emergencies represent another source of wrenching stress. Ellen Kullman, DuPont's CEO until October 2015, learned the hard way about the importance of arranging alternative child care arrangements in advance of a crisis. She was a DuPont officer in 2003 when the pregnant nanny for her three school-age children went into premature labor with twins two weeks before the start of the school year. Kullman got the news on a Sunday summer night just before she and her family boarded a flight home after visiting relatives in Missouri.

She had yet to arrange a substitute nanny. "I had nobody to watch the kids," Kullman recollected. "Eighteen hours later, was I going to leave these children home alone?"

Frantically telephoning friends and relatives from the airport, Kullman finally lined up a college student to assist for a few weeks. After that nerve-racking predicament, the executive always made sure that she had three backup plans for unforeseen child care needs.

## BUSINESS TRIP BLUES

Busy executives often travel for work and enjoy it, but business trips can give manager moms the blues. That's how Vicki Holt, the Proto Labs CEO, occasionally felt. During a business trip to China several years ago, Holt remembered calling her home in

Pittsburgh and reaching her teenage son Matt. He was a struggling high school student at the time.

"Why are you always gone?" Matt demanded, close to tears. "Why aren't you here?"

"This is Mom's job," Holt replied. "We can talk anytime."

"No, I want you here and you are not," Matt insisted. After she hung up, Holt said, "I cried and I cried and I cried and I cried."

Even less emotional interactions can make executive mothers unhappy when they're on the road. International business trips mean that Mary Barra, chief of General Motors, sometimes misses watching her teenagers Nick and Rachel play volleyball, soccer, and lacrosse. But, she noted, "they know I make eighty percent of the games." And for crucial sporting events, she added, "I am going to move mountains to be there."

While sleeping in hotels abroad, Barra keeps her phone turned on beside her bed so she can answer calls from Nick or Rachel in the middle of the night. One such conversation lasted an hour. "I don't care if it is one a.m. or five a.m.," Barra said. "Sometimes it is, 'Oh, I forgot you were on a trip.' That's okay."

## WEARING MISMATCHED SHOES

Not surprisingly, most manager moms I interviewed had little time for themselves during the years they raised children and pursued high-octane careers. They frequently gave up hobbies, socializing with friends, separate vacations with their husbands, and workouts at the local gym.

Balancing a demanding career and parenthood is rarely easy

because "there is no such thing as balance," recalled Sally Smith, the mother of two and leader of Buffalo Wild Wings, the restaurant chain. Smith was a midlevel manager when her daughter was born in 1986 and a chief financial officer when her son was born four years later.

As a new mother, Smith grew accustomed to arriving at work feeling distracted and with baby spit-up on her clothes. One morning, she wore mismatched shoes to the office; one was black and the other was blue. Another day, she showed up with both contact lenses in the same eye. "I couldn't figure out why my eye hurt so much," she said.

Nancy McKinstry of Wolters Kluwer urges ambitious manager moms to accept the inevitable trade-offs between their corporate life and their family life. "Otherwise," she warns, "you run the risk of never being happy with anything."

### LEADERSHIP LESSONS FROM
### "MANAGER MOMS ARE NOT ACROBATS"

- Adapt your supervisory style to every staffer, asking newcomers how they wish to be managed—just as you adjusted to each of your children's unique traits.
- Keep your boss informed about your critical parenting needs. Maggie Wilderotter, former executive chairman of Frontier Communications and CEO, persuaded a prior employer to pay for extra child care help while her husband served in the Gulf War. The company offered the same perquisite to three other female vice presidents, even though their husbands weren't soldiers.

- Practice workplace empathy based on your work-life crises. Dorrit Bern, a former CEO of retailer Charming Shoppes, struggled to cope when her firstborn son became sick during infancy and she worked for a different company. At Charming Shoppes, she created its first child care center for headquarters staffers, and hired a nurse in case children got sick there. She describes the center as "the best retention tool I had."
- Organize your household's weekly schedule at regular family meetings, and try to plan the calendar as much as a year in advance so that everyone's needs can be accommodated.
- Bring your children and nanny along on certain business trips.
- Keep a carry-on suitcase packed at all times for unexpected work travel.
- Use practical tactics to ease the stress of being a manager mom. If you start work very early, for instance, you won't feel guilty leaving in time for dinner with your offspring. Sally Smith, CEO of Buffalo Wild Wings, a restaurant chain, suggests, "Buy lots of underwear and socks. You won't have to do the laundry so much."

# 9

# Career Couple Conundrums

Ambitious women often marry equally ambitious men, a combination that can create dangerous roadblocks for women's high-powered careers.

That was true for a number of the business executives I interviewed. These women struggled with thorny career couple problems such as relocation decisions, promotion envy, frequent business travel, and potential conflicts of interest.

Every stressful story I heard stirred strong memories of my own situation. Turn back the clock to the late 1980s. I am deputy bureau chief of the *Wall Street Journal* in London. My husband, Mike, a fellow journalist, has worked there for a news service of Dow Jones & Co., the *Journal's* parent company, since we moved abroad in 1987 when I was promoted into management.

But the longer we live in London, the more anxious Mike becomes about his career prospects. One day he blurts out, "I am tired of being the suitcase to your career moves!"

His complaint surprises me. This isn't how I had envisioned our intertwined lives. We had tried to anticipate the delicate balancing act of being a two-career couple. Before our wedding in 1972, we debated whether a marriage contract might make sense.

"A marriage contract isn't an insurance policy for a happy marriage," Mike pointed out. He gradually came to view a contract as an affirmation of our commitment to each other and a less traditional marriage at a time when some state laws dictated where a wife lived.

We hired a lawyer to draw up a marriage contract in which we declared that we would rotate who took the lead in any relocation. "The right to select a domicile and residence is a joint right to be exercised equally by both parties," the legalistic contract said. "Where they cannot mutually agree on the selection, the choice shall alternate between the parties."

Mike had followed me to San Francisco for my initial job at the *Journal*. In turn, I had trailed him to Evanston, Illinois, in 1973, when he decided to attend graduate school at Northwestern University. He became a Chicago correspondent for *BusinessWeek* several years later. With the next move up to me, I gave him no warning about my tentative acceptance of the *Journal*'s offer of a transfer to its Washington, D.C., bureau in 1979.

I simply telephoned Mike at his office and announced, "I'm going to Washington."

He figured I was taking an out-of-town reporting trip. "Oh, for how long?" he inquired.

"For good," I replied. "Wanna come?" Obviously, I was teasing and we had a more thoughtful discussion before deciding the relocation made sense. I moved to Washington without Mike when I was nearly seven months pregnant with our first child. He thought *BusinessWeek* would probably transfer him, but he was also willing to seek another job. Luckily, the magazine finally relocated my husband to the capital, and he arrived weeks before our son did.

Nearly seven years later, I found out about the *Journal*'s opening in London and Mike enthusiastically encouraged me to raise my hand for the promotion. We had long dreamed of living overseas. But the move disrupted our pattern of alternating career priorities. My husband's subsequent outburst of frustration made me recognize that each partner in a career couple must occasionally act as baggage and weigh down the other person's career. The professional price exacted by such trade-offs was preferable to divorce.

After our stint in London, Mike took a job with Dow Jones in New York. I followed him back to the United States in August 1990 and became a senior journalist in the *Journal*'s New York bureau until I returned to management as deputy management editor in 1992. I wrote about the topic and also supervised a few staffers.

Contemporary two-career couples continue to struggle with figuring out how both partners can get ahead without derailing their relationship. In a major survey of MBA graduates by Harvard Business School, the youngest men described more traditional career expectations than their female counterparts. Half of the millennial men anticipated that their careers would take priority over their spouses' careers, but three-fourths of the millennial women expected their careers would be at least as important as their partners'.

"We do not yet know how these mismatched expectations will ultimately play out," the study's authors cautioned in a *Harvard Business Review* article in December 2014. "But if previous generations are any indication, change won't occur soon."[1]

Yet further progress of women in the upper rungs of U.S. businesses depends heavily on them receiving strong, egalitarian support from their spouses. Sheryl Sandberg, chief operating officer of Facebook, advocates forging a fifty-fifty partnership from the beginning of a relationship. "I don't know of one woman in a leadership position whose life partner is not fully—and I mean fully—supportive of her career," Sandberg wrote in her book, *Lean In.*[2]

## THE UNHAPPY TRAILING SPOUSE

Meg Whitman, chief executive of Hewlett Packard Enterprise since Hewlett-Packard split up in late 2015, learned a harsh lesson about the elusiveness of perfect solutions for career couples. She married Dr. Griffith R. Harsh IV the day after he graduated from medical school in June 1980. Today he is a professor of neurosurgery and director of the Stanford Brain Tumor Center. He joined Stanford in order to trail Whitman to California when the then-fledgling eBay hired her as its leader in 2008.

Most of the couple's career moves during their marriage "have involved a trade-off for either his career or mine," Whitman wrote in *The Power of Many: Values for Success in Business and in Life*, her 2010 book. "Sacrifice is not such a terrible thing when someone you love really wants something," she wrote.[3]

But in 1992, Whitman found it painful to sacrifice her stimu-
lating career with Disney in Los Angeles, where she ran marketing for its consumer products division, the third-biggest unit of
the entertainment giant. "I loved working at Disney," she told me.
"And I think they liked me."

Her husband had been offered an attractive position at Harvard
Medical School and Massachusetts General Hospital in Boston.
"I really did not want to leave Disney, but he really, really, really
wanted to go to Harvard," Whitman said, repeating her words for
emphasis. Unfortunately, Disney lacked a suitable management
opening for her in the Boston area.

"I remember going in to Frank Wells, who was my boss at the
time at Disney, to tell him I was leaving," Whitman said. "I walked
in and I couldn't get the words out of my mouth. I just burst into
tears."

"What's wrong?" Wells asked her.

"I have to move to Boston," Whitman replied. Recounting that
sorrowful episode to me in a Hewlett-Packard conference room,
she scrunched up her face as if ready to burst into tears.

Whitman relocated to Boston without arranging for new employment. Stride Rite, a popular chain of shoe stores, soon chose
her as its head of strategic planning and a member of senior management. "I was pretty happy to be asked to join Stride Rite," she
said. But compared to Disney, "it was a step backward to some
degree," she conceded. "I gave up a lot."

Did Whitman resent making a backward career move so she
could accommodate a move forward for her husband? "I wouldn't
say resentful. I was saddened," she said. "In a perfect world, I
would have stayed in Disney."

Unlike the situation in our household, Whitman and her husband never concocted a grand scheme for alternating whose career took priority. "We used to joke that no sooner did one of us get traction than the other one would get a great idea and sabotage the other's career," she said. "We tried to figure out what the right thing was at that time."

Whitman believes that all career couples must figure out the compromises that suit them. But sometimes, she pointed out, "you have to do things that you do not want to do if you want to stay married."

## WEDDED ONE-UPMANSHIP

Career trade-offs caused strains for Stephanie Sonnabend, the former leader of Sonesta International Hotels, and Gregory Ciccolo, her singer husband, just as their careers were taking off.

Ciccolo was a promising tenor when he abandoned plans to join a small opera company in Europe for six months in 1994. At the time, Sonnabend occupied a powerful new post as executive vice president of Sonesta, one that brought her closer to becoming CEO of the hotel chain. The couple lived with their two children in the Brookline, Massachusetts, home they had bought in 1985, the year they married.

"Both say she requested his sacrifice because she needed to travel more following a Sonesta promotion," I wrote in a 2010 *Journal* article about CEO moms like Sonnabend. Ciccolo stopped singing professionally, opened a small recording studio, and described his disappointment over his trade-offs as "fairly big league." He said he accepted the sacrifice because his wife's job offered greater financial security than his.[4]

When I interviewed Ciccolo for my article, he spoke wistfully about how much he would have enjoyed a career as a world-class opera singer. "I had standing ovations in thirty-five-hundred-seat houses," he said during our conversation. Ciccolo noted that their son Nicholas, born in 1989, "thinks I am a complete jerk because Mom made all the money."

I explored his sacrifice in greater depth with Sonnabend during our conversation for this book. In fall 1993, her husband was in Europe auditioning for singing roles. He telephoned her at home one evening, thrilled to announce that he had been offered a six-month position with a Munich opera company.

"He would have the opportunity to live his dream," Sonnabend said. But she doubted the six-month opportunity made sense for them. "All of a sudden, I burst his bubble," she added. A key issue was the fact that Sonnabend had to travel twice a month for up to ten days, supervising Sonesta hotels in the United States and abroad.

The couple concluded that Ciccolo should reject the Munich offer. "We both realized we didn't want our children to just be raised by the nanny." Sonnabend explained.

"I was sad to disappoint him because we always wanted to help each other fulfill our dreams," she told me. "I was also feeling overwhelmed with working full-time and managing the house with two small children." Sonnabend acknowledged that she made no career trade-offs in return, but she did help finance the recording studio that her husband set up in their home.

The couple currently lives in Florida, where she is a corporate director and executive coach and he does real estate development. He still sings for pleasure.

Their daughter Antonia, a strategic consultant, married a banker in September 2015. Days before their wedding, Sonnabend wrote her a letter that included tips about being part of a two-career couple. "You can do it all, just not all at the same time," she advised Antonia. "It is a pendulum that swings between career, family (and spouse), and self. There is usually only time enough for two of those, so something needs to give."

Paula Rosput Reynolds and her husband, Stephen, experienced an equally difficult juggle of their careers. For years, they were the only chief executives of major U.S. public companies married to each other.

The couple had wed in 2004, when she was running AGL Resources in Atlanta and he was CEO of Puget Energy Inc., a utility holding company in Bellevue, Washington. They squeezed their sunset beach wedding in between board meetings and conference calls about corporate earnings.

"For fourteen months, Mr. Reynolds left his office at noon Friday and flew cross country to join her on weekends," I wrote in a *Journal* article about their unusual blend of ambition and romance. His wife then lived in Atlanta with her teenage son from a previous marriage and her ailing, elderly father.

The directors of Puget Energy worried that their CEO might soon quit and move to Atlanta to live with his wife. As a result, they locked him up with "golden handcuffs," an award of shares that effectively forced him to serve until spring 2008.

The pair finally shared a home after Paula Reynolds switched industries in 2006. She relocated to Seattle to take command of

Safeco, where she earned considerably more money than her husband. Ironically, Safeco directors had considered and rejected him for their CEO spot because they thought he lacked the desired skills.

In my *Journal* story about the couple, both chief executives offered a simple recipe for career couple success. "Honesty, fidelity, and habit," Paula Reynolds recommended. According to Stephen Reynolds, an even-tempered man with a toothy grin like Jimmy Carter's, spouses need to "really like each other and really know each other."[5]

## SCHEDULING WARS

Business travel, increasingly common in today's fast-paced global economy, represents another sticky issue when two-income couples wrangle over whose career is the most important. "Scheduling wars" is what former DuPont CEO Ellen Kullman calls this issue.

She and her husband, Mike, were working as midlevel marketing managers for DuPont after the birth of their eldest child, Maggie, in 1990. They lived in Wilmington, Delaware, but didn't employ a live-in nanny. As Kullman remembered it, they vowed that "we were not going to be both out of town on the same night unless it was an emergency."

Pressing corporate demands, rather than a personal emergency, placed the couple in this awkward situation when Maggie was four, their twin boys were infants, and Mike was in India on a three-week business trip. At the time, Kullman headed a DuPont unit that sold titanium dioxide. Jack Krol, then the company's chief executive, wanted her to make a quick trip to London so she could handle final negotiations on a deal that was reaching its conclusion sooner than expected. He gave her twelve hours to hop on an overseas flight.

Knowing that his last-minute request would mean child care problems for Kullman, Krol offered to see if his wife could care for her three children during her absence. "I will figure it out," Kullman assured him. The family's nanny stayed over the first night, and then Kullman's mother pitched in.

The couple also occasionally disagreed over who could take a routine business trip on a certain date, according to Kullman. "I have to go to Europe then," one spouse would insist.

"What's your reason for going?" the other spouse would reply. In effect, Kullman noted, "we were trying to sell each other on the importance of 'what *I* was doing.'"

Other two-career couples figured out more formal ways to avoid scheduling wars. Liz Smith, chief executive of the restaurant chain Bloomin' Brands, said she escaped such dilemmas while she was a senior Kraft executive and her husband was a partner at a venture capital firm because they had their administrative assistants coordinate their calendars far in advance. "My assistant and his assistant would work overtime on our schedules," Smith recalled. "They became best friends because they managed our lives."

Smith and her husband headed out of town for work so often that they sometimes arranged a catch-up meal at New York's Kennedy Airport. "I was flying out and he was flying in," she said. "We would see each other in passing."

Thanks to their work-coordinated calendars, Smith recollected, "in our worst year there were only three nights out of the whole year that both of us were away." That happened in 2003, and their nanny stayed overnight with their sons, then aged two and five.

## COLLISION OVER CONFLICTS OF INTEREST

Conflicts of interest between personal and work relationships pose the toughest dilemmas for career couples today, because so many married women occupy senior positions in business and politics. Mary Jo White, the highest U.S. securities regulator, epitomizes the problem. A former federal prosecutor, White took charge of the Securities and Exchange Commission in 2013, at a time when her husband, John W. White, was cohead of a practice at Cravath, Swaine & Moore that advised companies about key SEC issues, such as corporate governance and regulatory reporting obligations. He is now chairman of that practice at his law firm, according to the firm's website.

SEC ethics rules require the agency's chairman to steer clear of cases that involve Cravath. As of February 2015, White had recused herself from at least ten probes into Cravath clients, including some that occurred before she joined the commission and at least four that involved her husband, concluded a *New York Times* story based on interviews and a review of federal records.[6]

Nor are conflicts of interest among career couples a new phenomenon. "Such conflicts arise when a man's employer has business or political dealings with his wife's organization or when she works for a competitor or vice versa," I wrote in a 1977 article for the *Wall Street Journal*. Certain employers arranged transfers, sought resignations, or found other suppliers when an individual's job collided with that of a spouse, my front-page story said.[7]

I spoke from firsthand experience. A short sidebar to my article, describing my personal experiences involving this issue, noted that *BusinessWeek* had hired my husband, Mike, earlier that year for its Chicago bureau. Though the rival publications weren't pleased, they decided to trust our professional integrity. Mike attempted to avoid conflicts by requesting a different beat from mine.

The sidebar said that so far we had only once chased the same news story, which concerned the expected appointment of Donald H. Rumsfeld, a former U.S. secretary of defense, as president of G. D. Searle & Co., a health care company. During dinner with friends in Chicago, Mike and I argued because he refused to give me Rumsfeld's phone number, which he hinted he had obtained. One friend, a lawyer, jokingly offered to take our dispute to divorce court.[8]

I later received a tip that Rumsfeld was staying with his mother in suburban Wilmette, outside Chicago, and leaving early Saturday morning for the airport. Figuring that Mike might notice me sneaking out of our home in suburban Evanston at the crack of dawn, we drove together to Wilmette for an hourlong "stakeout" of the Rumsfeld family home. No one emerged or answered the door. Searle's rumored recruitment of Rumsfeld turned out to be true.

In hindsight, the Searle story "was a very painful episode for me," Mike said. "I was under pressure to get some news on this company as well. So we were in direct conflict."

A bigger conflict of interest threatened our marriage in 1984 after Mike sought the organized labor beat at *BusinessWeek*. Unions represented a significant topic for the magazine, and he was tired of writing about agriculture and commodities, his beat at the time. I was happy covering organized labor.

But *BusinessWeek* editors in New York were unhappy to see Mike cover the same beat as I did. He asked me to prevent our conflict of interest by requesting a new beat. My bureau chief refused because he felt uncomfortable about letting a competitor dictate a change in *Journal* assignments.

Anxious to resolve the ticklish situation, Mike proposed that his editors signal their willingness to give him the labor beat without strings. They acquiesced, and my boss ultimately changed his mind. He assigned me to cover housing and urban affairs, a beat with little breaking news. The new assignment didn't disrupt my then-reduced schedule of a four-day week.

Some female corporate leaders I interviewed ran into potential professional conflicts because they and their husbands worked for the same company. Ellen Kullman, for instance, indirectly supervised her husband, who had become DuPont's global director of marketing, after she moved into the company's corner office in 2009. To eliminate any appearance of a conflict, the new CEO never reviewed his compensation and he retired in 2012, a company spokeswoman said.

But a similar arrangement created serious career consequences for Dawn Lepore and her husband, Ken. Her successful stint in upper management at Schwab, the investment brokerage, culminated with her 2004 recruitment to be chief executive of Drugstore.com. As I wrote in the "Getting Ahead Later" chapter, Lepore spent years aiming to be Schwab's chief information officer, a senior position in which she would oversee all of the company's information technology operations.

Yet her success doomed her husband's career at Schwab. A technical developer and systems programmer, he had joined the company in 1983, the same year as his wife. He had risen to a technical management position by 1989, the year Schwab promoted Lepore to a senior vice presidency. He reported to another senior vice president in its technology organization.

"Having us in the same organization was going to limit my advancement," Lepore recalled. "It precluded me from ever becoming CIO." As the highest technology executive, she would oversee every technology staffer. But Schwab policy barred spouses from working for each other, and her husband couldn't change departments because Ken wasn't qualified to work outside of technology.

The couple had a frank discussion and resolved their career conflict amicably. "You are going to have a better career at Schwab than I am, and I am holding you back," Ken told his wife. Lepore agreed, partly because she already earned more money than her husband. "It was clear that I would make a lot more if I kept moving ahead," she said. He left Schwab in December 1989 for a job with Visa, a lateral move where he led a small technical team. She became a Schwab vice chairman in 1999, nearly six years after her ascension to the post of CIO.

Looking back, Lepore regards Ken's resignation from Schwab as the priceless gift of a supportive spouse. "He never resented it," she said. "He has an amazing positive attitude."

## LEADERSHIP LESSONS FROM
## "CAREER COUPLE CONUNDRUMS"

- Examine issues from your spouse's viewpoint and apply that philosophy to managing work colleagues.

- Accept sacrifices involving your spouse and coworkers, but try to make sure those compromises represent a two-way street.
- If you're offered a chance to relocate for a better position, ask your employer to assist your spouse in finding a new job. Take the same initiative when you recruit an out-of-town executive from a two-career household.
- Take a tag-team approach in deciding whose career takes priority. One partner should pursue a professional "surge" for five years before deferring to the other's surge.
- Alternate which spouse chooses the timing and venue for your next relocation. But don't move without a careful assessment of whether the trailing spouse can also land a good new job.
- In a potential conflict of interest, consider how your actions may affect your spouse and devise strategies together to reduce the number of possible land mines.

# 10

# Male Mentors
# Mean Business

Countless women have seen their careers soar thanks to help from a powerful senior executive. But some women paid a price for their close relationship with a male mentor.

One such woman was Melissa Dyrdahl, chief executive of Ella Health, a health care start-up for women, until November 2015. She saw her career take off after Bruce R. Chizen, a former boss, hired her in 1994 to join Adobe Systems, the software maker, as a senior marketing manager. The two had developed a strong rapport at Claris, their former employer, and Dyrdahl assisted him in running a small new division of Adobe.

"He knew exactly what he was getting from an employee standpoint," Dyrdahl remembered. Chizen became her unofficial career coach at Adobe, offering insights about ways to excel in the male-dominated technology industry. Having a boss as a mentor helped Dyrdahl to get the respect she felt that she deserved, she said when we spoke. She saw that when professional challenges arose, Chizen and other senior Adobe men "always came in with an answer."

Because the two knew each other so well, "I'm brutally honest with her," Chizen said in a *Wall Street Journal* article that I wrote about executive mentors.[1] He also acted as Dyrdahl's sponsor, an influential individual who opens the door of a promotion elevator and pushes a protégé through. During his climb to top management at Adobe, he brought along Dyrdahl and other valued members of his team.

"I had someone who was highly respected, a more senior leader, making sure my name got put on the table," Dyrdahl told me. With Chizen's support, Adobe appointed her global vice president of marketing in 1998 and then advanced her to a senior vice presidency before elevating Chizen from president to CEO in late 2000.

Once they both had reached the executive suite, Chizen and Dyrdahl occasionally drove to and from Adobe headquarters in San Jose together because they and their spouses lived near each other in suburban Los Altos. "We socialized together," Dyrdahl recalled. "I know his kids. My husband has remodeled their house." But as a result of these ties, the two high-profile executives encountered unexpected repercussions.

One day, a human resources staffer at Adobe who was friends with Chizen and Dyrdahl strode into her office. "I just need to tell you, because nobody is going to tell you," she said. "There's people who think there's something going on with you and Bruce."

The office gossip shocked Dyrdahl. Her jaw dropped, and "I was reeling," she recollected. It suddenly dawned on her that she and Chizen now occupied a much more visible stage at the office. She quickly assured the human resources staffer that their relationship was purely professional. "I don't want people to think I slept my way to the top," Dyrdahl told her HR colleague.

Driving home with Chizen soon after, Dyrdahl told him that coworkers wrongly perceived him as being something more than her supervisor and mentor. "They are only going to think badly of me," she said. "Lots of things that we take for granted and we don't think twice about, I can't do anymore."

Chizen understood and accepted dramatic adjustments. They stopped driving together or going out for drinks unless a third person was present. "Never sat next to him in a meeting again," Dyrdahl said. "I told him, 'Unless there is no other chair, do not sit next to me.'"

Even today, suspicions about an illicit affair sometimes arise when a male executive mentors or sponsors a female subordinate. For this reason, most senior-level men hesitate "to have one-on-one contact with a potential protégé who happened to be a younger woman," said Sylvia Ann Hewlett in her 2013 book, (Forget a Mentor) Find a Sponsor: The New Way to Fast-Track Your Career. Her observations reflected research by the Center for Talent Innovation, a New York think tank that she heads and that studies issues in the workplace.

This reluctance, Hewlett wrote, explains "why men are so much more likely to sponsor other men, inadvertently perpetuating the old boy's club." A 2010 study by her think tank found that men are 46 percent more likely to have sponsors than women. "Up-and-coming females tend to conclude that sponsorship, sexually fraught as it might be, is something they don't actually *need*," she said in her book.

Hewlett considers that a dangerous assumption. Mentors build a woman's self-esteem and serve as an empathetic sounding board, but sponsors expend valuable chips on a woman's behalf and provide air cover so she can take risks. "Sponsors, not mentors, put you on the path to power and influence by affecting three things: pay raises, high-profile assignments, and promotions," she wrote.[2]

Other researchers support Hewlett's argument. More than half of senior executive women said having a higher-level sponsor is extremely important, yet women have less access to senior male staffers who could assist with their careers, concluded a 2015 study by LeanIn.Org, founded by Sheryl Sandberg, and McKinsey. The research tracked women's progress at 118 North American companies.[3]

A handful of corporate programs designate workplace advocates for managerial women. At least nine big businesses have set up sponsorship initiatives that match promising female leaders with sponsors or teach such women how to attract a sponsor, I wrote in an advice column on careers published on WSJ.com in 2011. American Express Co., for example, launched its "Pathways to Sponsorship" program that year for twenty-one female senior vice presidents at the major financial services company.[4]

By the end of 2014, 25 percent of those initial participants had been promoted and 45 percent had made strategic lateral moves, an American Express spokeswoman told me. The company has also expanded its sponsorship effort to cover a wider range of managerial levels.

Yet formal mentoring and sponsorship programs remain far

out of reach for most professional women. Only 30 percent of all American professionals have access to such programs, and there is a smaller proportion of women than men within that group, according to a 2014 survey of 1,005 adults by Edward Jones, a financial services firm. Just 18 percent of the women allowed to participate in these programs actually do, the poll showed, compared with 21 percent of the men.

## MEN ON WOMEN'S SIDE

Male mentors and sponsors played crucial parts in the careers of numerous corporate executives I interviewed. "At the end of the day, men still hold most of the power," suggested Sandra "Sandi" Peterson, the group worldwide chairman of Johnson & Johnson. "So you better have male mentors."

But as is evident from Dyrdahl's experience, women must make sure that their relationships with higher-level men don't raise eyebrows among coworkers. To further refute false rumors about any romantic entanglement with Chizen, she stopped her habit of flying alone with him on commercial flights for business travel.

In Dyrdahl's view, things haven't improved for women since she left Adobe in late 2006. These days, she encourages women to take steps that clarify their ties with a male mentor so the relationship cannot be misconstrued by colleagues. "You give up your power when you wittingly or unwittingly put yourself in situations where people perceive you as having an affair and getting something because of your sex," she pointed out. "I felt I had to work twice as hard because I was blond and attractive."

Male mentors significantly influenced the careers of several other executive women by serving as their leadership role models. Among them was Nancy McKinstry, now chief executive of Wolters Kluwer, an international provider of software and information services. She began her career in 1980 by becoming an assistant manager for New England Telephone in Boston.

"Your first job is so instrumental, you sort of need to have somebody tell you how to navigate it," McKinstry recalled when we talked. "Nothing prepares you for your first real business job."

Her boss, Jimmy Dolan, coached her about navigating New England Telephone's office politics. Thanks to a rigid corporate hierarchy, staffers were assigned to numerical job levels, starting with Level One for lowly positions like hers. "I never met a Level Seven," McKinstry said. "You knew exactly where people stood because levels were so critical."

But she didn't realize that the elaborate pecking order would affect her informal interactions with associates. One morning, McKinstry said hello to a Level Three employee whom she didn't know well as she and the man crossed paths in front of an office elevator.

The man ignored McKinstry's greeting. "I was stunned," she remembered. "I thought, 'Oh my God, what did I do wrong?'" She turned to her manager for advice.

"This is kind of how it all works," Dolan replied, and patiently described the behavior expected of staffers. For instance, "very rarely would a Level Three talk to a Level One unless you were at a meeting talking about a specific thing," McKinstry said. "I had never experienced that."

Even more important, McKinstry noticed that Dolan dealt with employees at all levels in exactly the same manner. "He treated everyone with respect," she added. Dolan exemplified how a good boss behaved, she said, and helped her recognize that supervisors who treated subordinates poorly "got much less out of them, and they were generally not well liked."

For Maggie Wilderotter, a mentor's willingness to pinpoint shortcomings benefited her career, which culminated with her selection to be leader of Frontier Communications, the telecommunications company. Such feedback proved useful, she told me, because "I am a strong personality."

The day we met, Wilderotter sat in a high-backed leather chair at the head of the long boardroom table at Frontier headquarters in Stamford, Connecticut, occasionally glancing out the window at the frozen gray pond and bare trees behind the building. We spoke shortly before Wilderotter stepped down as CEO in spring 2015, after running Frontier for more than a decade. She remained the company's executive chairman, a full-time role that includes overseeing the new chief, until spring 2016.

Wilderotter, who is thirteen months younger than her sister Denise Morrison, the head of Campbell Soup, grew up in Elberon, New Jersey, with two other sisters. Their father, Dennis Sullivan, was an AT&T executive who explained to his daughters about setting profit margin targets while they were still in grade school and encouraged them to cultivate high goals for themselves, according to a 2007 *Wall Street Journal* article about how all four girls became executives.

Wilderotter was raising money for community causes during ninth grade when she got summoned to the principal's office to take a phone call from the White House. She had invited President

Richard Nixon to attend a local benefit for Vietnam veterans, and a Nixon aide was calling to say the president couldn't accept her invitation. "Isn't he at least going to pay for the dinner tickets I sent?" Wilderotter asked the aide. Nixon's check arrived the next week.[5]

Despite her father's lofty expectations, Wilderotter didn't aim for the corner office at a young age. "I was going to be either an actress or a radio announcer," she recollected during our chat.

Wilderotter got a degree in economics from College of the Holy Cross, then accepted an accounting position at Cable Data, a small software company in California. By age twenty-seven, she was in charge of her employer's regional operations and she held fourteen different jobs during her dozen years there.

Wilderotter was thirty-four in 1989 when she left Cable Data for McCaw Cellular Communications Inc., a cell phone company that hired her as its highest-ranking woman and president of its western region, based in Sacramento, California. The four other regional presidents were men. "That was a big breakthrough in my career," she said.

A few years later, Wilderotter received an especially worthwhile critique of her interpersonal style from Jim Barksdale, the second-highest executive at McCaw as well as her boss and mentor. Barksdale confronted her during a flight they took together after he saw her clash with the regional president of the Pacific Northwest unit over a significant business decision.

"You know he is right and he is wrong. But sometimes, it is just okay," Barksdale told Wilderotter. "You can give on this one, Maggie," he went on, citing her region's stronger results. "Just give on it."

Wilderotter backed down. "The lesson was not about being

right or wrong, but about team play," she said to me. She and her fellow regional president grew to be close friends and colleagues. "If you can build strong relationships with peers that you work with, they have your back, too," Wilderotter continued. "Because our markets were contiguous, we started to do more things together where we could get more power and better results collectively for both of us."

The lessons Wilderotter acquired from her McCaw mentor accelerated her career momentum. AT&T Wireless acquired McCaw Cellular in 1994 and made Wilderotter its executive vice president of national operations. In 1996, Wilderotter assumed the CEO spot at Wink Communications, a small start-up in which Microsoft owned a minority stake. Wink's initial public offering in 1999 marked one of the first times a woman had taken a U.S. technology company public, Wilderotter recalled.

## THANKS TO MALE SPONSORS, YOU CAN SOAR

The best sponsors are willing to stick their necks out and do their best to ensure that a protégé lands a better job. That was true for Mary Barra years before her 2014 ascent to chief executive of General Motors. She told me that internal sponsors endorsed her for so-called stretch assignments because they recognized her passionate commitment to get results.

In 1997, some male vice presidents for whom Barra had worked lobbied privately on her behalf after they heard that Chief Executive Jack Smith and Harry Pearce, vice chairman of the automaker, wanted someone with operational experience to be their executive assistant. GM typically reserved that role for rising

young stars, offering them a chance to acquire a broader perspective of the auto business through dealings with the top brass.

At the time, Barra was thirty-five years old and a first-rung executive at GM's Tech Center in Warren, Michigan. She led a team
that oversaw production processes and launches at assembly
plants building midsize cars. But she didn't know that her sponsors had urged Smith and Pearce to pick her as a top aide. So when
a human resources staffer left her a message about a job interview
for the coveted position, she suspected that some associates were
playing a prank on her.

"I am like, 'Ha, ha, ha,'" Barra remembered thinking to herself.
"Who is playing a joke on me?" She confirmed the call's legitimacy
with her boss, and Smith and Pearce did indeed select Barra for
the position, which she held until 1999.

Working alongside GM's highest two executives turned into a
pivotal assignment. "I thought it would be a great learning experience, and it was," Barra told me. "I was able to learn about GM
on a global basis." Partly based on what she learned from this role,
she won her first corporate vice presidency in 2008.

During our conversation, Barra recommended that ambitious
women find bosses willing to take chances and sponsor them because they recognize their hard work. And "if you are not working for somebody you respect as your leader," she added, "then I
would look to find a new position."

## A POWERFUL SISTERHOOD

Managerial women eager to succeed need more than high-level
male supporters. They also need high-level female allies and advo-

cates. But finding such fans can be a challenge, given the continu-
ally thin ranks of women in the upper ranks of business.

Certain executives interviewed for this book found a prominent woman outside their workplace to serve as their mentor. For
Clara Shih, CEO of Hearsay Social, the social media advisory firm,
that woman was Sheryl Sandberg, the current chief operating officer at Facebook.

"You can't go around asking people, 'Will you be my mentor?'"
Shih noted during our chat in a small conference room at the San
Francisco headquarters of Hearsay Social, the firm that she cofounded in 2009 at the age of twenty-seven. A large photograph
of Hearsay Social employees had greeted me in the tiny foyer of
its warehouse-style offices, where all staffers wore T-shirts, and
exposed silver cooling-and-heating ducts snaked around the ceil-
ings like oversize serpents.

Shih, heavily pregnant, was expecting her first child in two
weeks. She felt unsure about accepting Hearsay Social's four-
month maternity leave because, as she put it, running a start-up
"is fun." (She went back to work full-time three months after her
son's birth.)

Shih thinks that women can rely on an outside mentor to gain
insights about starting a business or landing a better job as long
as the women making the request already do interesting things.
"Be passionate," she advised. "Naturally, people will want to spend
time with you."

Shih immigrated to the United States from Hong Kong with
her family at the age of four and was raised in Chicago. Her father,
an electrical engineer and inventor, taught her to program before
her eighth birthday, and she kept programming throughout high
school.

Shih majored in computer science at Stanford, completing her first of two Stanford degrees in 2004 with a 4.0 grade point average, higher than any other student completing a computer science major that year. Her first professional job after college was as a Microsoft software engineer. She stayed a year, finished graduate school, and was then hired as a strategy analyst for Google, the Internet search giant where Sandberg was vice president of global online sales and operations. Though the women attended a few meetings together, Shih said, "it was never one-on-one."

The women finally came to know each other well after Shih's 2006 arrival at her next employer, Salesforce.com Inc., a company that makes software used by salespeople to keep tabs on current and prospective clients. Shih soon devised the first business application for Facebook. In 2008, while in charge of social media strategy for Salesforce.com, Shih invited Sandberg to speak at a company conference attended by thousands. The two bonded, Shih remembered, and Sandberg mentored the younger woman as she contemplated creating Hearsay Social.

"Talked through career decisions," Shih recollected in her rapid-fire way. "Leaving Salesforce. Starting the company." Sandberg endorsed its debut, and introduced Shih to the principals at Sequoia Capital, an influential venture capital firm. Sequoia ultimately poured $33 million into Hearsay Social, and is still the company's single biggest investor. As things turned out, Shih and her fellow founder launched the firm the year that Shih's first book, *The Facebook Era*, appeared.

When Sandberg decided to leave the board of Starbucks, she put Shih's name on her list of possible successors there and Starbucks named Shih a director in December 2011, when she was just twenty-nine. "She has just been a great friend," Shih said.

In her book, *Lean In*, Sandberg cited Shih as "a superb example" of why women eager to find a mentor must first cultivate a professional relationship based on an earned and reciprocal connection. "We have sent the wrong message to young women," Sandberg wrote. "We need to stop telling them, 'Get a mentor and you will excel.' Instead, we need to tell them, 'Excel and you will get a mentor.'"[6]

Virginia "Ginni" Rometty followed that approach at IBM. She was already a star senior executive when her boss, Chief Executive Samuel Palmisano, asked Maggie Wilderotter to informally mentor her. The two women met about four times for a year. Then came the announcement in October 2011 that Rometty would soon be the first female leader of the century-old technology giant.

Rometty feels proud that she had multiple mentors during her management career, even though all of her high-level IBM guides were men. "You should look to learn from many people," Rometty said when we talked in an executive dining room at company headquarters in Armonk, a woodsy suburb of New York. The long wall just outside that dining room was lined with formal portraits in tall gold-leaf frames that showcased every man who had led IBM before her.

"It is a mistake to connect yourself only with one person, one style, one lesson," Rometty explained. She sounded hoarse from a lingering cold that day as she nursed a cup of tea, a beverage she consumes several times a day. "I encourage people to have a wide network of people they learn from and develop relationships where you learn both ways."

Rometty took her own advice almost from the start. A computer science and electrical engineering major at Northwestern University, she worked briefly for General Motors and joined IBM as a systems engineer in 1981. Over the years, she dealt with corporate clients across a range of industries. Rometty caught the attention of top management after she successfully integrated the consulting arm of PricewaterhouseCoopers LLP, which IBM had bought in 2002 for $3.5 billion. In 2009, she took charge of IBM's sales force. She moved up again the following year.

Wilderotter said she was asked to coach Rometty "on being a better executive," and so encouraged her to work more closely with Wall Street, big banks, and key customers whom she didn't know, according to a *Wall Street Journal* profile of Rometty that I coauthored. Rometty sought Wilderotter's ideas about other internal assignments she could take on in order to keep growing.[7]

The two women already knew each other because Frontier was a major IBM client. During the time Wilderotter mentored her, the executives liked to get together for salads at an Italian restaurant near Greenwich, Connecticut, "a small place where it was not too loud and easy to talk," Rometty recalled.

She appreciated the fact that Wilderotter was a good listener who shared sage advice. "What Maggie does better than anybody I know is network," Rometty said. "It is a very good recommendation to remember to prioritize that."

## PAYING IT FORWARD

A number of business leaders I spoke with "pay it forward" by trying to guide and propel the careers of their junior female associates. Sandi Peterson, for instance, has passionately committed herself to this task at Johnson & Johnson since 2012, when she took charge of the consumer unit that makes Tylenol and other iconic products along with global manufacturing operations.

By June 2015, women comprised about 31 percent of the company's vice presidents worldwide. "We are going to make sure we have 50 percent women in leadership roles by the time we are all done," Peterson vowed during our conversation at Johnson & Johnson's global strategic design office, housed in a converted factory with exposed white brick walls on Manhattan's Lower East Side. "That is part of what I do, because I want to have a positive impact on women's lives," she said, creasing her forehead as she arched her eyebrows for emphasis.

Peterson's game plan? Pressing other high-powered women to champion lower-level ones. "You need to actively sponsor other women to make them successful," she implores fellow female executives. "Don't wait for the guys to do it."

In taking this stance, Peterson stresses that sponsorship represents a key aspect of their team-building duties "and by the way, you are responsible for making sure the people who work for you also do that."

Peterson acknowledges that she came of age during a very different era. When McKinsey hired her as a management consultant in 1987, she recollected, some female peers regarded her as weird because unlike most of them, she had a young child. "Women didn't support each other," she said. "They pulled up the ladder."

But women managers who work extra hard to counsel other employees can also run risks, such as by providing too much mentoring. As I reported in a 2013 career advice column for WSJ.com, about one in three participants in ELI Group's Leadership Lab for Women get more than two dozen requests annually to mentor lower-level colleagues. Such women often ignore their own networking needs and lack time to network upward in ways that might win them sponsors.[8]

Of course, part of being a boss requires coaching men as well as women. Mentoring a man created headaches for Teresa Taylor, the former chief operating officer of Qwest Communications. While an executive vice president around 2006, she frequently traveled to distant business conventions with her sales chief, a younger man who, unlike Taylor, was not married.

Qwest colleagues attending the same conference observed the two of them enter the hotel, go up in the elevator, and dine together. Upon Taylor's return from one trip with the sales chief, a human resources staffer warned that there was office buzz over a possible romance.

"Well, you are in the same hotel together, you use the same car at the hotel, you leave for the airport together," the HR official said when she met with Taylor. "They saw you having a drink before the dinner."

Though offended by the malicious scuttlebutt, Taylor kept her cool. "Also, I am thinking, 'Who is watching me so much anyway?'" she said. "That's irritating." She nevertheless changed her behavior and no longer shared a car from the airport with her sales chief, nor had drinks alone with him at conferences. But the pair took business trips together for the two years she held the job of executive vice president, and she continued to advise him informally about issues such as how to make better presentations.

Taylor urged women who now travel with male mentees to be highly vigilant about not stoking the office rumor mill. "It is not going to go away," she cautioned. "Manage it accordingly."

## LEADERSHIP LESSONS FROM
## "MALE MENTORS MEAN BUSINESS"

- Look for mentors and sponsors where your professional relationship will benefit both of you. Liz Smith, leader of the restaurant chain Bloomin' Brands, used to be a top deputy of Avon CEO Andrea Jung. The two women became role models for each other, Smith says.

- Being chosen as a protégé takes time and multiple small steps. Consider asking potential sponsors how you can inspire their trust and make them look good.

- At the outset, figure out the personal interests that you share with a mentor and what you hope to get out of being mentored.

- Model your managerial behavior on positive examples set by your mentors. Watching how male mentors operate can give you insights about how to convey authority and get your voice heard during meetings. Ask female mentors with children about strategies they used to combine parenthood with a career.

- Enlist sponsors' help in seeking a promotion even though you may not feel ready for the promotion. Sponsors can give you "a realistic but aspirational set of things to go after," notes Clara Shih, CEO of Hearsay Social.

- To avoid misperceptions about being romantically involved with

a male informal advisor, try to meet in public settings during
work hours, and avoid joint business trips.

- When you become a mentor or sponsor, give lower-level
  staffers frank feedback because being respected counts more
  than being liked. Sandi Peterson, the highest-level woman
  at Johnson & Johnson, received this advice from a McKinsey
  boss and mentor when she struggled over how to ask some
  underperformers to leave.

# 11

## Managing Men Well

Women keen to get ahead must learn to manage men well, especially those who don't want to be managed by women.

Many business leaders I met ultimately won respect from male lieutenants and customers, mainly because they figured out how to cope with sex-role stereotypes. But they often hit speed bumps along the way.

Consider the mid-career dilemma that Cathie Black faced long before she became president of Hearst Magazines. It is fall 1983 and she is flying high, literally. As the thirty-seven-year-old new president of *USA Today*, she is the only passenger aboard a Gulfstream corporate jet en route from New York to the newspaper's headquarters in Rosslyn, Virginia, just across the Potomac River from Washington. "I am pinching myself, thinking, 'I am Dorothy from Oz,'" Black told me. "I had never been on a corporate aircraft."

Al Neuharth, the irascible newspaper baron who ran Gannett, had launched *USA Today* the previous year with the hope of creating a national circulation daily. That day, he assembled its top editors in the headquarters executive dining room to announce Black's appointment as the newspaper's third president and first female leader.

Joe Welty, the top-ranking advertising executive at *USA Today*, pulled Black aside just before she entered the dining room. The red-faced, heavyset man was sweating anxiously. "Oh, by the way, I had dinner with Al last night and I don't report to you," Welty whispered to her.

His comment flabbergasted Black, who had assumed that all key *USA Today* executives would report to her. Yet she had never confirmed that arrangement in writing. She smiled, but inwardly fumed. "Not only did I want to kill Welty, I wanted to kill Neuharth," she recalled. In hindsight, she suspects that Welty resisted reporting to her because he had never worked for a woman before and she was relatively young.

Over the next few months, Welty repeatedly tried to play petty games of one-upmanship with Black and undercut her authority, she said in her 2007 memoir, *Basic Black: The Essential Guide for Getting Ahead in Work (and in Life)*. "He'd call meetings and deliberately not tell me about them," she wrote. When she excluded him from a *USA Today* meeting, "he'd show up and stand in the doorway, arms folded, as if demonstrating to those assembled that he was still in charge."[1]

Black finally complained to Neuharth, citing employees' confusion over who was really the boss of *USA Today*. "This is an unworkable situation," she remembered telling him in a letter. "It is not fair to me." Neuharth settled the matter by transferring Welty to a senior executive position at Gannett.

Nowadays, executive women managers rarely face openly hostile resistance from their male deputies. Yet their career progress continues to be slowed as a result of less obvious sex-role stereotypes, which "manifest themselves in all kinds of subtle and not-so-subtle ways," said Robin J. Ely, a Harvard Business School professor who specializes in gender issues.

This harsh new reality, known as "second-generation" gender bias, involves "powerful yet often invisible barriers to women's advancement that arise from cultural beliefs about gender, as well as workplace structures, practices, and patterns of interaction that inadvertently favor men," said Deborah M. Kolb in the 2015 book she coauthored, *Negotiating at Work: Turn Small Wins into Big Gains.*[2]

Men's flawed assumptions about gender roles made Clara Shih, the leader of Hearsay Social, a victim of mistaken identity in 2011. A venture capital firm with a stake in Hearsay Social organized a summit at a Silicon Valley hotel for Shih and about 150 other chief executives of companies in which it had invested. The only female CEO in attendance, she wore a badge showing her name and her employer but no title.

Shih spent an hour during the registration period fielding questions from various male chiefs who approached her. Some wanted her to fetch them bottled water. Others asked for directions to the men's room. "I don't know," she replied to that question, without explaining why.

Shih initially had trouble understanding why those CEOs didn't recognize her as their peer. After the fifth such request, Shih recollected, "it dawned on me that they thought I was part of the events staff." But she chose not to get upset over being unfairly stereotyped, reminding herself that she fully deserved to be at the event.

During the opening session of the conference, participants assembled in a large meeting room and introduced themselves. When Shih stood, conference organizers displayed a slide showing Hearsay Social's logo and the figure $18 million—the amount of money that her start-up had raised since 2009. Many of the clueless male CEOs later apologized for their demeaning demands and they now regularly fetch Shih a bottle of water whenever they see her at industry conferences.

The double bind that can trap women leaders represents another example of second-generation bias. As I explained in the chapter "Getting Ahead Sooner," research shows that women are expected to act stereotypically feminine by being collaborative, caring, and helpful rather than exhibit such typically masculine traits as decisiveness, taking charge, and assertiveness. Women in authority who act conventionally feminine get viewed as "too emotional to make tough decisions and too soft to be strong leaders," Herminia Ibarra, Robin J. Ely, and Deborah M. Kolb wrote in *Harvard Business Review* in 2013.[3]

On the other hand, work colleagues describe women as bossy more often than they describe men that way, and bossy women are less likely to be promoted, concluded a 2014 study of 201 male and female managers by the Center for Creative Leadership in Greensboro, North Carolina. "It is tempting to encourage women to be more like men in order to create more women leaders," the study's authors said. But "when it comes to being bossy, being more like men is not likely to get women very far."[4]

Such findings match the real-world experience of several

women I interviewed. As a female executive, "you are damned if you do and doomed if you don't," noted Sara Mathew, a former head of Dun & Bradstreet, the leading business credit ratings firm. She believes that a woman is damned for being too aggressive and seen as inconsequential if she never speaks. "You can never pick the exact spot in between [where] you want to be," she said.

## EARLY VICTORIES SUPERVISING MEN

Anne Mulcahy walked the fine line between collaboration and decisiveness when she managed men for the first time at Xerox, the giant copier and printer company that she eventually led.

In 1981, five years after joining Xerox as a sales representative, Mulcahy was named the company's sales manager for Maine, long among its worst-performing regions, as I described earlier. Then in her late twenties, she inherited a team of about nine older salesmen. "I don't think there was anyone under forty," she recalled.

Mulcahy had achieved the promotion after six unsuccessful attempts to ascend into Xerox management, and she frankly admitted these multiple setbacks to her new male colleagues. She said she told them "that everyone was capable of raising their game and performing better."

In an attempt to make the longtime employees feel comfortable with their young female boss, Mulcahy made a herculean effort to work alongside her team members. "I busted my ass," she remembered. "I traveled with them. I made all the calls." She also got to know the representatives personally, visiting some of them and their families at home. "All of a sudden, you are not that manager from Boston anymore," she said. "You are somebody who cares about their lives." By Mulcahy's second year on the job, Maine was one of Xerox's top three regions.

Looking back, Mulcahy thinks that those efforts profoundly shaped her leadership style. "I wanted to walk away from every single job leaving a group of people that felt it was a great experience," she said. "It is what actually has been the major driver of my entire career."

But I wondered whether Xerox staffers liked working for Mulcahy when she eliminated their jobs or cut their budgets. "*Like* is probably not a great word," she agreed. "You have to make tough decisions. But you make them personally. You communicate personally."

## THE POWER OF SMALL WINS

Challis Lowe, a former top human resources executive at three big companies, tried a different tactic to deal with a skeptical male subordinate early in her management career. In the mid-1970s, when she was in her late twenties and the first black female officer of Continental Bank, she took charge of a group of personal bankers that included a white man in his fifties who had trained her. After more than two decades at Continental, the man yearned to be a bank officer.

"He had never dreamed he would work for a woman, and certainly not an African American woman," Lowe recollected. "He just really choked on it. He had a physical, almost visceral reaction when I asked him to do something." He responded to her work requests with a grimace that implied his unspoken words might be, "How dare you think you can tell me what to do!"

Lowe finally summoned the man to her office. Seated opposite her desk, he struck a pose of indifference. "He was sitting with his shoulders squared" and his hands clasped between his legs, she said. She offered to help him obtain an officer's title.

"You would do that?" he asked, unclenching his hands.

"You have been at the bank a long time," Lowe told the banker. "The work you do is really excellent." But, she added, "the role that you have been cast in isn't at the officer level." She gave him responsibility for supervising a team, and he immediately altered his behavior toward her. Helping him clearly "was more important to him than any resistance he had about working for me."

When the bank promoted the man to an officer's position about a year later, "he gave me a hug," Lowe recalled. She gleaned a critical lesson from this encounter, and urges current women bosses to go out of their way when dubious male lieutenants need support. "If they see you being in their corner, the walls go down," she said.

Ann Moore also scored a minor early victory involving gender bias and lower-level men during a long career climb that culminated with her appointment in 2002 as the first female chief executive of Time Inc., publisher of such marquee titles as *Time*, *Fortune*, and *Sports Illustrated*. In the 1980s, while associate publisher of *Sports Illustrated*, Moore cohosted a corporate event for advertising clients. Company planners chose a Connecticut golf club as the event venue because the head of Time Inc. was a member.

But the club excluded women from indoor events. "They said I could stand out on the patio," Moore recalled. "I didn't go."

In response, she restricted a perk for her division's executives and salespeople, most of whom were men. *Sports Illustrated* stopped covering the cost of their dues at clubs that discriminated. When it comes to sex bias, Moore suggested, "you don't just sit there and whine about it. You do something about it so somebody else doesn't have to stand on the patio."

## THE MALE MYSTIQUE ABOUT TOP FEMALE BOSSES

Given the rarity of women in the executive suite, women often discover it's even harder to manage men once they have reached upper management. Consider Mary Dillon, who landed her first corner office at U.S. Cellular in 2010 and now runs Ulta, the beauty retailer.

Dillon had earned kudos during her five years as global chief marketing officer of McDonald's, the fast-food giant that spent billions of dollars a year on advertising. One of her notable accomplishments was using consumer feedback to broaden the chain's appeal to families. But when U.S. Cellular, a wireless carrier, recruited her from McDonald's, Dillon knew nothing about selling cell phones, lacked a technology background, and had never directed an all-male management team.

Imagine you're following Dillon during her first week as chief executive. She strides into a conference room at U.S. Cellular headquarters in the Chicago suburb of Rosemont, Illinois, where her four senior lieutenants await her. All are men, and she is their first female boss.

The long, narrow room contains an oval, dark table surrounded by more than a dozen black chairs. Two of Dillon's new deputies sit on either side of the table, their arms crossed, their postures displaying skepticism. They have left a chair vacant for her at the head of the table. "Instead," she remembered, "I sat in one of the seats on the long side of the table." Her choice of chairs reflected her belief in the power of collaboration rather than traditional command and control. "Even the nonverbal aspects of it are important," she said.

Sitting along one side of the conference table wasn't the only way that Dillon signaled her preferred approach. She decided to brighten the conference room, which struck her as very dark. "One of the first things I did was go over and open the shades to let in some light," she said. The seemingly small gesture offered an additional hint of how she would change things at U.S. Cellular.

Dillon then told her lieutenants that she wanted "everybody's expertise coming together to get to the best answers," she recalled. "I am not going to be an expert on technology. What I can do is focus on the guest experience," she explained. "Not any one of us has all the answers."

Nevertheless, Dillon now realizes that she made an early mistake in managing her top team. She wishes that she also had been clearer about her intention to make hard decisions. Sometimes, she said, men regard women with her kind of collaborative style as not being decisive enough.

Dillon tweaked her leadership techniques over the next few months, based on advice from the man who ran human resources for U.S. Cellular. "I understand how you want to lead, but you sometimes need to be more direct and more decisive," the HR official recommended during a meeting in the CEO's office. He encouraged her to pick her best shots, set clearer expectations for her staffers, and be more visibly decisive.

"It was a really good 'aha' for me," Dillon said. "It was probably one of the most helpful pieces of feedback that I had. I probably would have benefited from that earlier in my career."

In 2012, Dillon made a controversial call by deciding to sell certain U.S. Cellular assets, including customers and airwave licenses in the company's home market of Chicago. The deal enabled U.S. Cellular to exit its weaker markets and focus on stronger ones. But "this clearly was not a decision that was popular or easy," Dillon said, and "it was not supported by all of my leaders."

She sees her experience at U.S. Cellular as highly relevant for other managerial women. Make sure that male subordinates view you as you both decisive and collaborative, she advised. "You can't be one or the other. You have to be both."

## CURSED OVER PRICE CHANGES

A tense confrontation with a male lieutenant tested the mettle of Brenda Barnes during her first weeks as chief operating officer of Sara Lee in 2004. The company, a major producer of baked goods and other popular foods, then had annual sales of about $20 billion. Before coming to Sara Lee, Barnes had run Pepsi-Cola North America, a beverage business owned by PepsiCo Inc., and subsequently spent seven years at home with her three children.

Barnes, the first woman to hold the No. 2 spot at Sara Lee, initially managed a team of eight men and one woman. They included a European executive who had never before worked for a woman, and he argued loudly with Barnes during a staff discussion of her proposed overhaul of pricing strategy to improve profit margins.

"I don't know what you are talking about in pricing with these fucking pricing changes," the European said in front of the entire group. "I am not going to do it."

"Well, you had better figure it out," Barnes responded sharply. Afterward, she privately chewed out the executive for being disrespectful. "He never did repeat that kind of behavior, and became a strong leader on pricing and other changes we made," she told me.

Barnes doubted that the executive would have so brazenly cursed out a male supervisor. And if he had done so, she continued, "he would have been fired on the spot."

## "MEN CRY IN MY OFFICE"

Other executive women, such as Anne Stevens, a former chief of Carpenter Technology, a company that develops and manufactures specialty alloys, tapped their empathy skills in order to manage men well. Men "are more likely to be open and share a weakness or a concern with a woman boss than they are with a male boss," Stevens said when we talked at the Algonquin Hotel. "I've had men cry in my office," added Stevens, a fearless individual who has driven race cars and flown in a fighter jet.

She encountered this situation while a senior executive for Ford Motor Co. A nursing school dropout, Stevens was already the mother of two young children and had turned thirty by the time she received a degree in mechanical and materials engineering from Drexel University. She spent a decade at the company then called Exxon Corp. before going to Ford as a business planner in 1990.

By 2004, Stevens was the company's group vice president for Canada, Mexico, and South America. Around that time, a divorced father on her executive team started crying in her office after she chided him for missing a work deadline.

"Number one, I am disappointed in myself," the man admitted. "Number two, I don't want to disappoint you. Number three, I am in overload with my personal situation." He said that he had trouble arriving on time for her early meetings because he needed to drop off his children at school.

Stevens sought to ease his distress. "Sit down, this isn't a big deal," she reassured him. "Instead of starting a meeting at eight, I can start a meeting at ten."

The man's performance soon improved. Stevens was not surprised. "Sometimes when you are under stress, it is hard to be at your best," she observed.

And her empathetic leadership abilities paid off. Ford later promoted Stevens to chief operating officer for the Americas, making her the highest-ranked woman in the U.S. automotive industry at that time. Carpenter recruited her to be its CEO in November 2006.

## DON'T KILL THE NARROW-MINDED CUSTOMER

Recalcitrant male customers created equally ticklish issues for a number of women executives. But such attitudes didn't daunt

Denise Morrison, the chief executive of Campbell Soup, who knew by about age twelve that she wanted to someday lead a business. She and Maggie Wilderotter of Frontier grew up to be the first sisters to command Fortune 500 concerns.

Encouraged by her parents to aim high, Morrison decided to become a baton twirler in her high school marching band after she failed to make the cheerleading team. And although she didn't walk gracefully, she addressed her shortcoming in methodical fashion. "Denise worked to correct the problem by taking long walks," a *Wall Street Journal* colleague wrote in a 2007 piece about the Sullivan family. "She became captain of the team and the first twirler in her school to perform with a fire-lit baton," the article said.[5]

"In my household, you could not say 'I can't,'" Morrison recollected on the wintry afternoon that we chatted in a forty-fifth-floor hotel room with a panoramic view of snowy Central Park in Manhattan. "My parents would say, 'That is not in the dictionary.' I saw no barriers," she went on. "When I was going out into the job market looking for a job, I set my standards pretty high."

Morrison graduated magna cum laude from Boston College, where she earned a degree in economics and psychology. She began her career in the paper products division of Procter & Gamble. As the sole saleswoman in that division's Boston office, she sold everything from Pampers diapers to Charmin toilet paper and Bounty paper towels.

"I do remember getting some odd looks from some grocery managers," Morrison said. "I remember one of them asking me if I worked for L'eggs," a producer of women's pantyhose.

"With these legs, are you kidding me?" she shot back, alluding to her less than model-thin limbs.

Morrison hoped to serve her largely male customers by depending on her listening skills. "To influence somebody, you really have to listen to their point of view," she said. "Then explain if you have a different point of view."

Morrison tried this strategy in the late 1970s, while in her mid-twenties and a P&G sales manager. She entered the Boston office of an influential buyer at a grocery wholesaler, a middle-aged man whom she was meeting for the first time. He controlled millions of dollars of P&G purchases, and, she recalled, "was known to be extremely abrupt."

The executive turned around in his desk chair as Morrison took a seat. "I don't do business with women," he bluntly declared.

Morrison needed a calm retort. "I am not going to allow him to upset me," she remembers thinking to herself.

"Well, I work for Procter & Gamble and I do eleven million dollars of business with you," she replied as she described her employer's annual sales to this customer in a steady, even tone. "If you want to do business with Procter & Gamble, you are going to need to do business with me."

Apparently impressed, "he went right into our business conversation as if nothing had happened," Morrison told me. "I was amazed." She now suspects that he tested her in an effort to have her win his respect. The volume of P&G goods bought by that wholesaler increased to about $15 million over three years, and "I exceeded plan each year he was my customer," she reported.

A P&G women's network that Morrison cofounded helped hone her ability to combat sex-role stereotypes among male customers. The network consisted of six sales managers from different divisions who dined together at a local restaurant about once a month. "I remember a discussion about being aggressive in your ideas, but not in your demeanor," she said. The group reached that conclusion after realizing that "women are held to a different standard," she recollected. "Being aggressive is not always considered a good thing for them."

Morrison, who moved into Campbell's highest job in 2011 after working for four other food manufacturers, still uses the same low-key approach today. Women should frame information "in a way that you are convincing someone to do something that they might never have thought of," she said.

## A SPILLED DIET COKE

Another veteran CEO who has spent decades dealing with men's uncertainty about her role is Penny Herscher of FirstRain, the business analytics firm. "When it comes to managing men, I've developed all kinds of techniques to establish the fact that I am the executive," Herscher told me. "Because I am blond, I have frequently been taken for the secretary."

That occurred during her command of Simplex Solutions Inc., a California start-up that made software for the design of semiconductors. She had become the leader of Simplex at age thirty-six in 1996, when the company employed just a few engineers. By early 2000, Herscher was preparing to take Simplex public.

A group of investment bankers gathered in a conference room at its Sunnyvale headquarters because they wanted to be picked as advisors during the company's initial public offering. But they didn't know Herscher or Simplex.

As Herscher walked into the room, a male banker seated at one end of the conference table knocked over a Diet Coke. "Without missing a beat, the banker turned to me and said, 'Sweetie, can you clean that up?'" Herscher wrote on *The Grassy Road*, her blog. She grabbed a paper towel from the kitchen, cleaned up his mess, and washed her hands. She then reached out her hand to the banker "and with a big smile said, 'Hello, my name is Penny. I am the CEO.'"

Herscher still takes extra steps to avoid similar awkward encounters nowadays. The day before we talked in March 2015, she had conferred with a potential customer for FirstRain, a delegation that included three men whom she had never met. When they entered the room, Herscher had three male colleagues by her side. Shaking hands with the male visitors, she said, "Hello, I am Penny. I am the CEO."

## LEADERSHIP LESSONS FROM "MANAGING MEN WELL"

- View yourself as a confident leader, and your male lieutenants will do so, too. "If you don't consider yourself important," notes Adele Gulfo, chief strategy officer at Mylan NV, a maker of generic drugs, "no one is going to consider yourself important."

- Help men you supervise to succeed and they'll root for your success in return. This is a win-win approach because "their success is your success and vice versa," notes Ilene Gordon, Ingredion's CEO. "People respond very well to that."

- Deal with subtle forms of gender bias such as ignored marching orders by getting to personally know each man who you oversee and using data to defuse a tense situation.
- Encourage recalcitrant men to look at the world through your eyes and solicit their ideas about what they would do in your situation. Treat them with respect even if they disrespect you.
- Establish clear objectives that emphasize your collective shared goals, and never ask male lieutenants to carry out tasks that you wouldn't do. "The power of all of us together will be very compelling," Mary Dillon told her all-male team during her first week as chief executive of U.S. Cellular.
- Signal your willingness to collaborate with male colleagues by where you sit during meetings and how empathetically you listen to them.
- Seek further guidance from formal leadership development training, your professional network, or an executive coach.

# 12

# Spotlight on Executive Presence

You convey an aura of leadership if you know the part, act the part, and look the part. Executive presence is a combination of confidence, authenticity, and projecting a distinct personal brand.

Strong competence and ability matter the most. But smaller and less obvious things, such as the way a woman speaks, can dramatically affect how she is regarded in the workplace. Women often lack executive presence because they have a weak hand-shake, gesture a lot, slouch, or speak tentatively with too many qualifiers. Corporate leaders I met typically spent many years developing their executive presence because they recognized its particular relevance for women. Some, such as Nancy McKinstry, kept refining the image they projected even after they reached the corner office.

McKinstry was the first woman and the first American to become chief executive of Wolters Kluwer, an international provider of software and information services headquartered in the Netherlands. Weeks after her 2003 promotion, she unveiled plans to slash 8 percent of the company's workforce as part of a corporate restructuring.

When McKinstry held a news conference in 2004 to review her progress with these plans, she expected that press coverage would focus on her remarks about the company's financial outlook. Instead, a columnist at the *Financial Times,* a major British newspaper, mocked her for wearing a sky-blue suit that matched the uniforms worn by KLM flight attendants, adding that the correspondent half-expected her "to point out the emergency exits as she addressed journalists."[1]

McKinstry, who had spent more than a decade in the upper echelons of corporate America, was taken aback by the newspaper's discussion of her attire rather than her push to adapt Wolters Kluwer to the rapidly changing digital world. "I am living with this business that is undergoing a huge transformation," she remembered thinking. "Why are we talking about this?"

In McKinstry's opinion, a leader with solid executive presence knows how to communicate a clear strategic vision. "What you wear doesn't create executive presence," she insisted. But as a high-profile woman in the public limelight, she understood that she had to pay attention to what she wore because appearance is a key element of executive presence.

If McKinstry had been a male CEO, the *Financial Times* columnist probably wouldn't have written, "'Oh, he is wearing a dark suit like a KLM pilot,'" she pointed out. "You have to be conscious that you are going to be judged and looked at differently because you are a female executive," she added. "Work around it."

Nowadays, McKinstry regularly reviews photos from her latest twice-a-year meeting with investment analysts in order to make sure that she doesn't don the identical outfit for the next session. She believes that her wardrobe planning helps outsiders to concentrate on her role as the top boss of Wolters Kluwer.

Other women also resented being evaluated based on such superficial details as their attire rather than the more substantive "gravitas," which involves qualities such as grace under fire. A journalist once criticized Mary Barra, CEO of General Motors, for wearing an expensive brand of shoes. "That's really not that important," Barra said. "Judge me on the results."

The idealized notion of executive presence "gets misused a lot," suggested Anne Mulcahy, the former chief of Xerox. "Women really do have to be comfortable in their own skins."

Still, appearance does influence how executives are viewed, and "women are much more likely to be pilloried on the basis of it, whatever they do," said Sylvia Hewlett in her 2014 book, *Executive Presence: The Missing Link Between Merit and Success.* The same danger looms when women try to display gravitas, Hewlett wrote. A woman "who is decisive, assertive, and willing to hold her ground risks being perceived as a bitch, or noncooperative," she cautioned.

Hewlett's observation reflected a 2012 survey of nearly four thousand U.S. professionals, including 268 senior executives, by the Center for Talent Innovation, the New York think tank that she manages. Thirty-one percent of those polled said that being "too bossy" undermines a woman's executive presence, but the same percentage said being "too passive" undermines it as well.[2]

Employers ranging from Intel to American Express and Morgan Stanley have introduced internal programs to enhance the development of executive presence among their female staffers. Intel, a maker of computer chips, created a "Command Presence" workshop for rising female technical stars in 2010 because the manufacturer believed that they needed extra help selling ideas to colleagues. Participants in the four-hour session practiced presenting effectively through a simulated meeting with an executive audience, I said in a 2011 career advice column for WSJ.com.[3]

The quarterly workshop, conducted by senior Intel women, had reached more than four hundred staffers by late 2015. They learned to communicate as leaders, command respect from leaders, and defend their ideas, said Diane M. Bryant, a senior Intel executive. The company now offers the seminar in locations worldwide.

American Express, the financial services giant, began a similar executive presence workshop in late 2012. Research by the Center for Talent Innovation showed "that when it comes to high-level promotions, managers are often more critical about whether women fit the right image," said Valerie Grillo, chief diversity officer at American Express. "Although we conduct workshops for men and women, our executive presence work has typically been centered on providing women with the skills they need to succeed," she continued. The workshops teach women about central aspects of executive presence: projecting gravitas, communication skills, and personal appearance.

## APPEARANCE MATTERS

"Always dress like you are going to the president's office."

Beth Mooney, chief executive of KeyCorp, a big U.S. bank,

regularly recites that maxim to women interested in enhancing their executive presence. "One thing you control," she noted, "is, do you look the part?"

Mooney learned that lesson the hard way early in her career. Hired as a $14,000-a-year management trainee by Republic Bank of Dallas in 1979, she won the title of vice president within a few years. One day in 1985, while working in the real estate department, Mooney unexpectedly found herself summoned to the office of the bank president, an impressive space outfitted with extensive wood paneling.

"I had on a rather colorful outfit," Mooney recollected. She wore a red, yellow, and black dress accented by stark bold lines that resembled a Mondrian painting. Seated behind his desk, the president asked Mooney why the bank might have to write off $10 million on a commercial real estate loan that she had handled.

"You had to be there to understand the logic," Mooney replied. Her offhand comment didn't amuse him.

The president, known for his dry wit, peered over his glasses as Mooney rose to leave. "My, we're colorful today," he said.

"You have to know that every now and then, color is a good thing," Mooney explained.

"Well," the president retorted, "color has its place."

Mooney left his office annoyed that she had been wearing a dress that was obviously unsuitable in a financial institution with a conservative Southern culture. "Why do I have this outfit on?" she recalled fretting. "What was I thinking?"

Her supervisor, the head of the real estate department, promptly called Mooney into his office. She figured that he would fire her over the looming $10 million charge and her poor choice of clothing.

Mooney figured wrong. "You made the loan," her boss said. "What I am going to judge you on is what you do from this point forward to work this loan out."

Mooney tossed her colorful dress into a Goodwill bin and battled hard to recover nearly $5 million for the bank. She came to appreciate that an ambitious leader with executive presence must accept responsibility for fixing a problem because "people never want to hear an excuse." Make things right even if you didn't cause the problem, she advised. And clearly, you shouldn't compound a professional problem with inappropriate attire. Impressed by her performance, the bank promoted Mooney to senior vice president in 1986, the following year.

## TALL TALES

For aspiring businesswomen, height shouldn't make a difference. But it does, because height helps to signal executive presence.

Being tall has long benefited men in upper management. Male chief executives of Fortune 500 companies are, on average, just under six feet, compared with five foot nine for the average American man, according to a poll of such companies by Malcolm Gladwell for his 2005 book, *Blink: The Power of Thinking Without Thinking.*[4]

Not surprisingly, more than a dozen women leaders I interviewed stand at least five foot seven. The average height for American women is five foot four. Experienced CEOs such as Meg

Whitman, Penny Herscher, and Dorrit Bern are five ten. Cheryl Bachelder, chief of Popeyes Louisiana Kitchen Inc., a fast-food restaurant chain, said that her six-foot height, along with her low voice, connotes strength and credibility. "My presence and my voice give my words impact," she added.

Taller women frequently took steps to further enlarge their stature. At five foot seven, Melissa Dyrdahl disliked looking up at men as her career progressed and so always wore heels to work once she entered senior management at Adobe. The extra inches put her eyeball to eyeball with most male coworkers. "If I am look-ing them in the eye, they have to take me more seriously," ob-served Dyrdahl, who later led Ella Health.

But why must women still don heels nowadays before they're taken seriously as business bosses? "There's a lot about physical presence and structure and posture that conveys a lot to men," Dyrdahl replied.

Carol Bartz, a former leader of Autodesk and Yahoo, exhibited the importance of powerful posture for women when we talked in the glass-roofed conservatory filled with oversize plants at her mansion in a San Francisco suburb. She wore a V-neck white shirt and black capri pants that afternoon.

"You spread your feet, put your 'bitch wings' on," said Bartz, who is five foot eight, as she jumped up, placed her arms on her hips, and assumed a wide stance. "You take up space. Men all stand around like this."

Shorter women can also exhibit executive presence by focusing on other attributes that express their authority and confidence. Being short never bothered Nancy McKinstry, who is just five foot one. "I think like a tall person," she said.

## A *VOGUE* AFICIONADO WINS FANS AMONG
## SPORTS JOCKS

Many rising stars polish their executive presence with expensive assistance, such as a coach, voice lessons, training for presentations, and improvisational acting classes. But some of these options, such as using an executive coach, can be time consuming.

Mindy Grossman, chief executive of HSN, the shopping service, previously led the global apparel business for Nike, the sneaker giant. For several of her six years at the company, she was counseled by leadership coach David Dotlich about executive presence and related issues.

Grossman joined Nike, headquartered near Portland, Oregon, in 2000, after presiding over the Polo Jeans unit of Ralph Lauren Corp. and spending the rest of her management career in the fashion apparel business on the East Coast. She persuaded Nike to retain Dotlich because "this was like going from the farm leagues to the major leagues," Grossman said. In her view, executive presence means commanding respect and identifying how a person is perceived.

But at first, some male Nike executives perceived Grossman negatively because she was an outsider and the only woman in senior management, Dotlich recalled. They believed that a pushy New York woman with a passion for both *Vogue* magazine and swift action would never fit in at a sports-minded company in the laid-back Northwest. She also lacked footwear industry experience. For all of these reasons, Dotlich observed, Grossman was "something odd and unusual in the middle of the culture."

In addition, many of the male executives disliked the way

Grossman challenged her peers during meetings, according to her coach. "When I first joined, I didn't take enough time to recognize that I needed to have inside credibility," Grossman told me. "It was critical to develop influence skills." Dotlich suggested that she act less brash, direct, and publicly confrontational to better fit into the Nike culture.

Grossman decided to offer her associates tools to deal with her fast processing of information and rapid decision-making style. "Look, if you can say it in ten minutes, don't take thirty minutes to say it," she remembered telling her colleagues. "Just tell me where are we, where are we going, how are we going to get there."

Grossman also started letting team members speak before she weighed in, "so as not to sway the room with an initial assessment," she continued. "It allowed people to open up more and for us to get more diversity of thought."

Though Grossman adjusted her executive presence at Nike, she never turned into a sports jock. "The greatest power that you can have as a leader is true self-awareness," she said. "Being true to yourself is so important." For example, she wore her four-inch heels to work every day because "I loved being the fashionista."

Grossman gradually won over associates through her business expertise and compassion, Dotlich recollected. "She had found her own style and presence." Her fashion background and deep ties with retailers helped Nike revitalize its stagnant apparel division and grow the unit into a nearly $4-billion-a-year business.[5]

To better understand what it takes to coach women about executive presence, I watched a live session in which BPI Group, a major management consultancy, trained a promising U.S. vice president of a global energy giant. The executive is one of the twenty-five highest women at the company worldwide. Her employer had paid for six months of the face-to-face training because she repeated herself so much during meetings that colleagues had stopped paying attention, recalled Mary Herrmann, a BPI managing director. "It showed up as a lack of confidence," she said.

The session in April 2015 took place in Chicago near the end of the executive's training. As I watched via Skype, Herrmann and a fellow coach reminded the woman to prepare better before she spoke, to listen harder, and to ask good questions at meetings.

"I don't need to spend so much time talking," the executive agreed. Previously, she added, "I wasn't paying attention as much as I could." The energy giant subsequently saw evidence of the woman's improved executive presence, Herrmann reported, because she was participating substantively "rather than talking to talk."

## WOMEN TEACH WOMEN ABOUT PRESENCE

Once women land in the executive suite, they occasionally criticize other women when their unacceptable attire detracts from their executive presence. "Some even send subordinates home or to a store to fix a wardrobe mistake," I wrote in a 2013 career advice column for WSJ.com. "High-level women say their younger counterparts must look the part if they want to advance, according to nearly two dozen leadership coaches, image consultants, and women managers."[6]

A confrontation between women over workplace clothing might sound trivial, yet it can prove uncomfortable. Paula Rosput Reynolds, a former chief of Safeco and AGL Resources, had such an encounter about a decade ago with an executive woman who displayed too much cleavage.

"Here is the deal. You are a very attractive woman," Reynolds told her lieutenant. But "the men on your team joke about what you are wearing, how much cleavage was showing here today." The executive began to wear less revealing blouses, though "every so often, she regressed," Reynolds recollected. "She will always be a more flamboyant dresser than I might be."

Penny Herscher, executive chairman and prior chief executive of FirstRain, the business analytics firm, sometimes tells female entrepreneurs that they should pay closer attention to how they dress, talk, and sit. During our 2015 interview in a conference room at FirstRain headquarters in San Mateo, California, Herscher acted out what she considered an authoritative seated position. "My elbows are on the table," she said. "My hands are gripped together in front of me. My body is over the table, I am leaning over. Women don't tend to sit forward like that."

A week earlier, a first-time entrepreneur in her thirties had sat upright at the same table, described her planned tech start-up, and requested Herscher's guidance about pitching venture capitalists to invest in her business. The woman wore jeans, a white camisole, and a black sweater. "She kept opening and closing her notebook," Herscher recalled. "And putting the pen on the elastic of her notebook. She just couldn't sit still."

The FirstRain leader chided the woman for looking nervous and childlike, then urged her to stop fiddling and wear a monochromatic dress to every business meeting. Herscher also advised that she study photographs of Sheryl Sandberg, the author of *Lean In* and chief operating officer of Facebook, because "she is in a monochromatic dress in every single one of them." The next time the aspiring entrepreneur visited FirstRain, she wore a dress in a single color.

"You need to establish your professional authority," Herscher told me. "You are going to be the only woman in the room half the time."

## GAINING GRAVITAS GRADUALLY

Gravitas, which combines qualities that help a person project serious competence, represents the most critical element of executive presence. Yet it's a behavior that may be the hardest to achieve.

Unless you exhibit gravitas, Hewlett wrote in her book, "you simply won't be perceived as a leader, no matter what your title or level of authority, no matter how well you dress or speak." Senior leaders surveyed by her Center for Talent Innovation described gravitas as consisting of six key traits: confidence under fire, decisiveness, integrity, emotional intelligence, reputation, and vision.[7]

For Teresa Taylor, a former chief operating officer of Qwest Communications, her effort to develop gravitas paralleled much of her upward climb at US West, the Denver-based telecom company that Qwest later acquired.

In the mid-1990s, for example, Taylor sought to exhibit gravitas during a meeting that she and fellow company vice presidents attended. "Can someone take notes?" one man asked. In response, most of the other men looked at Taylor, the only woman VP in the room.

Wanting the men to regard her as a serious decision maker rather than a stereotypical female nurturer, she ignored their stares. "I just waited, waited, and waited," Taylor remembered. "It seemed forever. I am sure it was only seconds." Finally, a male vice president started taking notes.

Taylor, who never forgot that awkward silence, now encourages other executive women to refuse to take notes or hand out documents during meetings. "Sit there and wait for that uncomfortable moment," she recommended. "Be bold about that."

As Taylor's ability to project gravitas increased, she also tried hard to maintain a "game face" at the office. "When you are in a leadership role, that is what people expect of you," she wrote in her 2013 book, *The Balance Myth: Rethinking Work-Life Success*.[8]

But maintaining an image of strength, another element of executive presence, proved particularly arduous for Taylor at one point in 2002, when she was an executive vice president of Qwest. She said she hated her stressful job so much that she often shed tears in the "cry room," her nickname for the women's restroom across the hall from her fifty-second-floor office. "I was miserable. I was going to quit," she recalled.

Women in senior management were so scarce at Qwest that none stumbled across Taylor in tears in the bathroom. "I didn't want anyone to see me cry," she said. "Who wants to go home and say, 'I saw my boss cry today'?" Her negative attitude toward work shifted soon after Qwest recruited a new CEO in June 2002, and in 2008, the company elevated her to its second in command.

## PENALTY FOR POWERPOINTS

Communicating effectively during formal presentations is another crucial element of executive presence. A woman's communication style must demonstrate composure, clarity, and credibility, noted Mary Herrmann, the executive coach, because "there are nuances that get in the way for women."

Ginni Rometty, the first woman to lead IBM, has paid attention to this issue for years. Near the end of our chat at the company's headquarters, she gingerly removed a folded yellow sheet of paper from a clear plastic folder. The paper was covered with her handwritten notes, scrawled in fading pencil, for a lecture about leadership lessons that she had given to new IBM executives at least a decade ago.

Among other things, Rometty told me, "I wrote down, 'Communications is a science, not an art.' I believe that. As an example, I never use a chart. Never use an overhead. Nothing."

Rometty stopped relying on flip charts or PowerPoint slides for IBM presentations twenty years ago because those communication aids detracted from her executive presence. Skipping props "is a sign of respect to the audience that you are dealing with. That improves your ability to communicate and connect with them," she argued. "It is my job to be able to tell a story in a way you will remember," she went on. "People will remember how you made them feel."

At the same time, Rometty made sure that she always knew her stuff. "I had a career of being an expert in this to being an expert in that," she said. She thinks executive presence emerges from "this idea that you become an expert."

## OWNING THE ROOM

But being knowledgeable failed to quell the intense jitters that almost incapacitated Diane M. Bryant at Intel moments before she spoke to hundreds of high-tech executives at a San Francisco conference in 2005. Then a general manager for a unit of the big semiconductor company, she had never addressed such a large audience. "I was very, very nervous," recalled Bryant, now an executive vice president of Intel. "I was shaking."

Waiting backstage to be introduced, "I was frantically flipping through my notes thinking, 'I don't know this. I don't know this,'" Bryant said. A top Intel leader stood nearby. "He could see I was falling apart," Bryant went on. "He grabbed my arm and he shook me and he said, 'There is no one out there who knows your material better than you.'"

The executive continued with his pep talk for Bryant. "Put down your notes and go out there and make it happen," he insisted. "Don't let your voice give it away. Don't quiver." Bolstered by his words, Bryant realized that she really did know her stuff.

She walked onto the stage, began talking, and paid close attention to how she sounded. When her voice started to falter, "I paused, swallowed, breathed, and regained control," Bryant said. "With the senior Intel leader in the audience, I was determined to show him that I listened," she added. "I wouldn't say it was a superb performance. But it was far better than it would have been without the pointed lecture on the power of 'self-talk.'"

For Bryant, the larger lesson from that nerve-racking experience was that women leaders must double their efforts to exude executive presence. Otherwise, she pointed out, "nobody wants to follow you."

## LEADERSHIP LESSONS FROM
## "SPOTLIGHT ON EXECUTIVE PRESENCE"

- Dress, talk, and act in ways that match the next job you seek as well as the high-level executives you want to impress.

- Don't behave in an overly emotional manner, because everything you do gets magnified and affects others' initial impressions of you. Being cool, calm, and collected requires "having the presence to be thoughtful and professional," recommends Anne Mulcahy, a former Xerox CEO.
- Rather than quickly announce how you want to settle an issue, allow a thorough staff discussion within set time limits. Teresa Taylor, formerly chief operating officer of Qwest Communications, recalls that she sometimes "damaged the flow of my own information because I was coming off too quick." She corrected the problem by telling subordinates how much time she had to discuss their concerns.
- Make sure that your body language reinforces the impression of strength that you want to project by sitting forward at a conference table, spreading out your papers, straightening your shoulders, and using broad gestures.
- Wear heels, stand tall, never apologize unnecessarily, and fill your mind with memories of important work experiences where you displayed confidence. "Don't talk in a little, tiny voice. Don't 'um' and 'er,'" says Penny Herscher, executive chairman and prior CEO of FirstRain. At the same time, adds Pat Russo, a former CEO of Lucent Technologies and Alcatel-Lucent, don't act in a way that implies you have all the answers.
- Object diplomatically when a male colleague steals credit for your ideas. Your viewpoints are more likely to be heeded if you sit in the middle of a conference table because you can look to the right and the left as well as project your voice better, says Cathie Black, a former president of Hearst Magazines.

- Don't get noticed for the wrong reasons, such as excessive cleavage or noisy metal jewelry. Presenting yourself professionally makes a difference. If you are not crisply dressed, and "you are standing next to the guy in the crisp suit, you don't stand a chance," warns Denise Morrison, CEO of Campbell Soup. "People are human. They are going to respond to packaging."

# 13

# Beating Board Bias

Serving on the board of a public company can propel your management career because the unique experience fortifies leadership skills and visibility.

Elected by investors to monitor management, boards are dominated by outside members with no ties to management. Yet women still occupy few seats in the typical corporate boardroom. In 2015, they comprised 13.3 percent of board members at companies in the Russell 3000 Index, which tracks the share prices of the three thousand largest publicly traded companies. That proportion was virtually unchanged from 13.2 percent in 2014 and up slightly from 11 percent in 2011, according to Institutional Shareholder Services, a firm that advises investors about corporate elections for directors and shareholder proposals.

When it comes to female directors, the slow progress isn't for lack of trying. In early 1997, for instance, Janet M. Clarke sought to become the first woman on the board of a big chemical

company. She was forty-four years old and a senior vice president at R. R. Donnelley & Sons Inc., a printing firm where she
had previously overseen a $300-million-a-year manufacturing
operation.

Clarke interviewed for the directorship at the chemical company's headquarters in Westchester, New York. She met with the
three men on the board's nominating and governance committee, some dressed in tuxedos for an imminent black-tie affair. The
seventy-two-year-old chairman of the committee and his two colleagues sat on one side of a table, facing her.

"Do you plan to have children?" the committee head asked
Clarke.

His inquiry infuriated her. "In the back of my mind, I am thinking, 'His question is completely wrong, it's illegal,'" Clarke said
during our chat at a midtown Manhattan restaurant. "I wanted
to say, 'That's a terrible question to ask me. It's an insulting question.'" Always a fast talker, the ruddy-faced executive spoke faster
than usual while recounting her tense interview. "He's a jerk, he is
a total jerk," she recalled telling herself, "but I need to get beyond
this first question."

"I'm going to be a step-grandmother in the fall," Clarke replied.
"Should I bring him or her to a board meeting?"

Ignoring her cheeky response, the committee chairman posed
his second question. "What does your husband do?"

Clarke turned flippant again. "What does your wife do?" she
countered.

"I am not married," he said. At this point, the board interview
abruptly ended, and Clarke marched into the office of the chief
executive, a man she already knew. Being the first woman on the

board "is not going to be a good fit for me," she told him. "Check with the guys. I think they felt the same about me."

Clarke later became managing director of global database marketing for Citibank and has been a director of six public companies. At Cox Communications Inc., the big cable TV operator, she sought to behave like one of the guys in the otherwise all-male boardroom and sprinkled her comments during their meetings with references to football plays. She already had a background in sports; she had helped create the women's ice hockey team at Princeton University, her alma mater.

Many women business leaders started knocking on boardroom doors years ago and were eventually successful. Maggie Wilderotter, former executive chairman and CEO of Frontier Communications, obtained her first corporate directorship in 1983 at age twenty-eight and since then has been the first woman on most of the twenty-four boards of public companies where she has served. She remains the sole female director at the latest, a biotech firm called Juno Therapeutics Inc., which selected her in November 2014. When such boards take a bathroom break, Wilderotter noted, "there's never a line to the ladies' room."

Gender diversity on boards is a good deal for investors. Between 2004 and 2008, big companies with at least three female directors produced significantly better financial results than those with none, according to a 2011 study by Catalyst, the nonprofit research group.[1] Similarly, a 2014 review of 140 studies in a variety of countries by researchers at Lehigh University and Syracuse University revealed that women's presence in corporate boardrooms positively affected financial performance.

Sizable representation of women on boards affects the success of women CEOs, too. For a study of Fortune 500 companies published in 2015, two Utah State University researchers looked at return on assets, a financial measure that's widely used by investors. Their sample included seventeen firms that had appointed female leaders. "Firms with a woman CEO and multiple women board members tend to perform better than firms with a woman CEO and few or no women on the board," the researchers said. "It is clear that board diversity is critical."[2]

Not surprisingly, companies led by women frequently populate their own boardrooms with multiple women. About 54 percent of the sixty-seven concerns in the Standard & Poor's 1500 Index with a female CEO had at least three female directors as of fall 2014, according to an analysis that I commissioned for a *Wall Street Journal* story I wrote on the topic. That was true for only 15.5 percent of those companies run by a man, reported corporate governance researchers at MSCI Inc., a provider of stock indexes.[3]

Several women chief executives I interviewed for this book typify this practice of gender diversity. At HSN, the retailer known for its home-shopping network, Mindy Grossman has another three women beside her, plus six men on its board. Among others are Gracia Martore at TEGNA, the broadcasting and digital company that Gannett spun off in 2015, and Meg Whitman at Hewlett Packard Enterprise, the company she has led since the 2015 breakup of Hewlett-Packard.

An emerging mini-industry aims to widen the female makeup of U.S. boards. There are databases of qualified candidates, board coaches, recruiters who specialize in finding potential members, how-to books, and training programs. OnBoard Bootcamp, a one-day seminar that costs $1,500, is typical. About five hundred women completed the seminar between about 2002 and 2015, though no more than 15 percent of participants subsequently won business board seats, estimated Susan Stautberg, the seminar's cofounder.

## SHOT HEARD AROUND THE WORLD

Scoring a spot on the board of a powerful industry group opened doors for Maggie Wilderotter as both an executive and a corporate director. She became a board member of the National Cable Television Association (NCTA) in 1987 after waging a campaign that was very different from a conventional job search.

At the time, Wilderotter was vice president of sales at Cable Data, a small software company that catered to cable TV operators. She wanted a seat on the NCTA board because its board members led businesses that were potential Cable Data customers. But the first time she ran for a board seat, she lost.

For her next try, Wilderotter called or wrote two thousand industry suppliers who belonged to the association, soliciting their support. She promised to represent their interests and to issue a newsletter after every board meeting. Nobody at the NCTA knew about her strategy, but it worked. "I got the board seat," she remembered. "It was a little bit like the shot heard around the world."

Wilderotter's fellow board members already worked in corner offices, and a year later, they passed a resolution stating "that you had to be a CEO in order to be on the board," she continued. "But they grandfathered me."

Thanks to ties Wilderotter fostered with cable industry leaders on the trade group board, Cable Data increased its U.S. market share to 85 percent from about 50 percent, she said. In 1989, she quit Cable Data to become the highest-ranking woman at McCaw Cellular, a cell phone company. She knew Craig McCaw, the company's chief executive, from their NCTA board membership and today, she added, "Craig and I are still absolutely great friends."

In 1996, Wilderotter took the No. 1 job at Wink Communications, a small start-up. She raised more than $200 million privately through her business relationships, tapping certain investors who had been on the association board with her. When Wink made its initial public offering in 1999, the action represented one of the first times that a woman had taken a U.S. technology company public.

Wilderotter soon found herself wooed for board openings at small public companies, based on her NCTA board connections with those businesses' key executives. Her record as a corporate director offered a stepping-stone to the big leagues, such as Xerox, the giant copier and printing company. Wilderotter had become good friends with Glenn Britt, another influential industry player on the trade group board. He was in charge of Time Warner Cable Inc. and a Xerox director when he persuaded Xerox CEO Anne Mulcahy that Wilderotter should join them in 2006.

Looking back, Wilderotter sees a larger lesson from her failed initial pursuit of the NCTA board seat. "Everyone's career has ups and downs," she observed. "It is kind of how you work through them that really matters."

## A SISTER'S PROTRACTED PUSH

Denise Morrison, now CEO of Campbell Soup, had a tougher time amassing experience on the boards of public companies than did Maggie Wilderotter, her younger sister. Morrison was a U.S. vice president for Nestlé SA, a major food company, in 1994 when she joined the board of Leadership California, a nonprofit organization for young women.

But eight years elapsed before Morrison got her first corporate directorship. Her father, Dennis Sullivan, a former AT&T executive, "encouraged her to doggedly promote skills that qualified her for a corporate board seat," I wrote in a career column for WSJ.com.[4] So, Morrison traveled to New York to lobby recruiters about recommending her to board clients. By then, she was a vice president of Kraft Foods, in charge of a $1-billion-a-year business unit.

Recruiters resisted Morrison's efforts, explaining that boards preferred to pick active CEOs. But she persisted, citing her full responsibility for her unit's financial results and her supervision of a sizable staff. "What's the difference between that and being CEO of a small company?" she challenged one recruiter. "He couldn't answer my question," she told me.

Six months later, a recruiter whom Morrison didn't know at a search firm she had visited approached her about being the first female director of Ballard Power Systems Inc., a Canadian maker of fuel cell products. "Sometimes, the way it works is your résumé gets into their database," she said. "They were looking for a sales and marketing skill set." She accepted the Ballard seat in 2002 and moved up to the board of a major business when she was picked as a director of Goodyear Tire & Rubber Co. in 2005, six years before Campbell promoted her to its CEO post.

Morrison now wishes that she had used a more effective strategy during her initial drive for a company directorship. "I did it the hard way," she admitted. "If I was more savvy, I could have networked better [by] getting somebody to open a door for me. I didn't do that."

Nevertheless, many contemporary executive women continue to feel excluded from corporate boards because they haven't achieved a sufficiently lofty position at their workplace to merit being chosen. "You need to spend time thinking about why you should get picked," Morrison suggested. And don't forget, she said, that "you always know somebody who knows somebody who can open a door for you."

## A MEMORABLE F-16 FLIGHT BY A BOARDROOM NEWBIE

Corporate boards greatly value collegiality, and that can be good and bad news for women with high aspirations. Female newcomers rarely fit in quickly in a boardroom, especially when they represent a significant minority. Women directors also frequently say little during their first year, making their colleagues slow to acknowledge their credibility and expertise.

Anne Stevens is an exception. "I didn't realize you didn't just jump in and get engaged," recollected Stevens, a former CEO of Carpenter Technology. She demonstrated that she had the right stuff soon after her debut as a corporate director, thanks to an unusual flight in a fighter aircraft built by Lockheed Martin Corp., the largest military contractor in the United States.

Trained as an engineer and hired by Ford in 1990, Stevens was vice president of North American vehicle operations for the automaker by 2002. A recruiter contacted another Ford executive about going on the Lockheed board as its second female member. The woman, a marketing and sales specialist, proposed Stevens instead because Lockheed preferred an operating executive.

Stevens was chosen, and dined with Lockheed's vice president of human resources at a restaurant in Bethesda, Maryland, weeks before her inaugural board meeting that October. In discussing Lockheed aircraft, the executive described his test flight in its F-16 Fighting Falcon. "That's real exciting!" Stevens exclaimed.

"Would you like to go up in an F-16?" the Lockheed executive asked, pointing out that other board members had spurned his invitation. Stevens said she jumped at the chance for the flight because she had driven race cars and was fascinated by the fighter aircraft's technology.

The day before her flight in spring 2003, she passed a physical exam and underwent training to cope with an emergency in the two-seat jet. "You have to learn to eject in case something happens," Stevens explained. "Because if the pilot has a heart attack, you are up there" and must eject.

She took a seat behind the pilot as the F-16 prepared to ascend. "Do you want to do a performance takeoff?" he asked.

Stevens agreed. "It is when you kind of go straight up like that," but those aboard are upside down, she told me, waving her right palm high in the air.

"We did loops, we did rolls," Stevens said in describing the flight, and the pilot even let her take over the controls for about fifteen minutes. As they flew, g-forces—the force of gravity inside the aircraft—started to intensify. During a rocket launch, astronauts normally undergo a maximum of 3 g's, which equals three times the force of gravity that humans are exposed to on earth. High levels of g-forces can harm the body and at 9 g's, most people black out or vomit.

The pilot pulled 5 g's. "You want to go for nine?" he asked Stevens.

"Sure," she replied. The pilot later said that he had never seen a woman passenger sustain 9 g's during an F-16 test flight. Stevens suffered no ill effects. In fact, "I loved it," she said. And "after I came down, two other board members went up." When those men showed up at the next board meeting, they told her, "We took the flight, but we couldn't do nine g's. You are the only one who could do nine g's."

Stevens believes that her performance aboard the F-16 bolstered her standing in Lockheed's boardroom, especially because some male members were military veterans who had flown fighter jets during war battles. "They saw me as a risk taker," she said. "Courageous and technically competent in a traditionally male activity. More adrenaline-seeking than expected."

Speaking broadly, Stevens encouraged novice female directors to cultivate a reputation as a valued contributor by sharing relevant business experiences with other board members and getting to know them as individuals. To that end, she arranged breakfasts and dinners with her Lockheed board associates right after she arrived. "The guys were really great," she said.

## MEN TO THE RESCUE

Janet M. Clarke also thought highly of nearly all the men on the board of Gateway Inc., a maker of personal computers that named her its first female board member in 2005. She took a spot vacated by Ted Waitt, the company's founder. But she clashed early on with an older male director, who began yelling at her during one of her first board dinners, held in a private room of a California hotel.

"Janet, I am very angry. You're a friend of Don Rumsfeld," the director said, referring to the then U.S. secretary of defense. "Nobody can be friendly with him. You must be a Republican conservative. That's a lousy party."

Clarke indeed was a Republican and a friend of Rumsfeld's, with whom she had served on the board of Princeton University, their alma mater. But she decided to ignore the attack. "If you fight back, you will go down to the gutter with the person who is attacking you," she told me. "As a woman, you can't win by fighting."

The director berated Clarke for nearly ten minutes. She said she coped by drinking as much wine as she could. Afterward, three Gateway board members came up to her as she waited for an elevator to her hotel room. "Are you okay? How are you feeling?" they asked. Clarke replied that she had lived through worse treatment. One man hugged her. "This is just a terrible thing," he said. "Just let me know if you need to be comforted."

The next morning, Clarke and fellow Gateway directors assembled for their board meeting. "The guy who had reamed me out comes running over to me," she recalled.

"I am so, so sorry. I was way out of line. I have new medication and it doesn't go with my drinking," he confessed to Clarke. "It way screwed me up. I know I said some things I shouldn't have said to you."

Clarke accepted his apology but doesn't regret that she stayed silent during his tirade. If she had spoken up so early in her tenure, "I would have been thought of as a scrappy board member," she said. "Civility isn't always the case in the boardroom. And you just have to make sure you handle it."

## FROM BOARDROOM TO CORNER OFFICE

Vicki Holt leveraged a seat on a corporate board to land a berth in a corner office, an increasingly popular practice. Since 2011, men who were outside directors have moved into the CEO spot at such businesses as DuPont, Mattel Inc., International Flavors & Fragrances Inc., and Newell Rubbermaid Inc. "Companies often do so because boards are quicker to fire poorly performing leaders but don't have a potential internal successor ready to advance," I wrote in a WSJ.com article in April 2015. My piece appeared after Christopher Sinclair, a Mattel director turned acting chief executive, ascended to the position of permanent head of the big toy maker.[5]

At first, Holt refused to assume command of Spartech, a maker of plastic packaging products. Fellow board members had sounded her out about being the company's leader in 2007, only two years after the neophyte director had taken her place on the Spartech board. She then was a senior vice president at PPG Industries, where she oversaw a complex, global operation. "I was in the middle of so many things," Holt remembered. "I wasn't done at PPG yet."

Spartech directors approached Holt again in summer 2010, after they had lost confidence in their chief, the man they had hired less than three years earlier. "We are suddenly losing a lot of customers," she recollected. "We are losing a lot of key employees. Our margins are dropping pretty dramatically," she continued. "Something is really wrong."

Holt took Spartech's renewed offer partly because she recognized that she never would attain the No. 1 job at PPG. She also figured that her tenure on Spartech's board would give her a running head start as its chief. "I don't have to learn who the board members are," she said. "I generally know the company because I had been on the board for a while."

Spartech announced Holt's appointment in September 2010, the day the company reported a swing to a loss in its latest fiscal quarter due to a sharp increase in bad debt, higher raw materials costs, and delays in plant consolidation. The new chief executive uncovered far deeper problems than she had known about as an outside board member.

Holt's plan was to revive Spartech over three to five years. "You don't have three to five years," fellow board members warned. "You just have to go faster." She rose to the challenge, replacing 30 percent of her management team within 120 days. She recruited people she trusted "that could drive the change that needed to happen," she observed. "It was very gut-wrenching."

Operating profit gradually improved, but Spartech's recovery had not advanced as far as Holt would have liked before PolyOne Corp. agreed to acquire the company. Less than a year after the deal closed in March 2013, she moved into her present job as CEO of Proto Labs, a medium-size manufacturer of custom-made product prototypes and parts.

I asked Holt whether executive women on corporate boards should follow her path to reach the pinnacle at that company. In response, she said that whether a director gets selected for a senior management job depends on "how you act on the board." A woman must also build her personal reputation as a leader, based on "the experiences you've had outside the boardroom that make you a qualified candidate."

## BOARD WOMEN LEND A HELPING HAND

Some executive women I interviewed garnered professional benefits from the extensive presence of women in their employer's boardroom. This group included Beth Mooney of KeyCorp, a major regional bank. Women held more than a third of its directorships in 2010, when Mooney and a male colleague emerged as the front-runners to be the company's next chief executive. The proportion of women was even higher among the outside directors, who controlled CEO succession planning.

With a diverse board, "gender is not on the table," and so no member voiced concerns about whether a woman should run Key-Corp for the first time, recalled Kris Manos, a director since 2009. That's also why she and female board associates felt comfortable critiquing Mooney during their lengthy, separate interviews with her during the internal horse race.

Their main concern was that "we weren't seeing 'the real Beth' in board meetings," Manos said. "She didn't always show emotional intensity. She was very prepared, but not necessarily very passionate." Directors also didn't know how Mooney, a veteran banker who had worked for KeyCorp since 2006, would handle an unexpected and difficult situation.

Mooney acted very formally for her board presentations because "I felt it was my job to be as prepared and buttoned up as I could be," she told me. In addition, the baby boomer executive said, "I grew up in a period and time and place where I never dreamed I would be in a boardroom." The negative feedback from directors gave her permission to display her true personality during their interactions. "I had the opportunity to be more forthcoming, more genuine, and more down-to-earth," she continued.

Mooney moved into the corner office in May 2011, and the promotion made her the first woman to lead one of the country's twenty largest banks. And KeyCorp directors weren't unique in choosing a woman for a high-level job. Researchers have uncovered a significant relationship between women in the boardroom and the future ranks of women in senior management. Fortune 500 companies where 30 percent of their directors were female in 2001 on average had 45 percent more women corporate officers by 2006 than those with no female directors, according to a 2008 research report by Catalyst.

## A MIXED PICTURE

How quickly will U.S. corporate boardrooms reach gender parity? The picture is unclear. In recent years, the number of men-only boards has shrunk. About 9 percent of 842 big businesses lacked any female directors in late 2015, down from about 11 percent of 867 such companies a year earlier, according to 2020 Women on Boards, an advocacy group.

But there are also negative signs. The pace of women joining boards has slowed after years of brisk growth, though it isn't obvious why. Women comprised 31 percent of new outside directors disclosed by S&P 500 companies as of mid-2015, an increase of just one percentage point over 2014, according to a study by Spencer Stuart, an executive recruitment firm. A related survey by the firm found that the proportion of boards giving priority to the recruitment of women had slipped to 58 percent in 2015 from 71 percent the previous year.

Meanwhile, a deep split over the issue has emerged between men and women on corporate boards. Sixty-three percent of female directors describe board gender diversity "as a very important attribute, compared to only 35 percent of male directors," said PwC US, a professional services firm, in a report about its 2015 survey of 783 public company directors. And 74 percent of female directors "very much" agree that gender diversity on a board leads to enhanced company performance, compared to just 31 percent of male directors.[6]

The ultimate secret weapon may be women like Kathleen Ligocki, CEO of Agility Fuel Systems, a developer and maker of natural gas fuel systems for heavy-duty vehicles. She also was the first female leader of Tower Automotive, a major supplier of vehicle parts. Ligocki, who serves on the board of Lear Corp., belongs to an elite cadre of women with corporate board experience whom businesses actively court to join their boards.

"I get asked a lot of times," Ligocki said. But rather than accept an additional seat, she advocates on behalf of other women who seek to be corporate directors. "I have a group of five women that I know are amazing women," she explained. "I work hard to get them on a board," introducing them to important recruiters and CEOs.

Ligocki, hired by Agility Fuel in December 2015, won her new job partly based on her long-standing ties with its previous chief executive and two outside directors. You never know when networking "is going to pay off," she pointed out. That's why executive women with board experience "should be active in opening doors for other women," Ligocki urged. "Once those newcomers arrive in boardrooms," she added, "they are going to prove themselves."

## LEADERSHIP LESSONS FROM "BEATING BOARD BIAS"

- Find colleagues, suppliers, customers, and executives of target companies and ask them to promote your board candidacy. You also need to be considered a hot prospect by executive recruiters, whom boards often use to fill openings. "Make sure that people know you are interested," suggests Vicki Holt, CEO of Proto Labs.
- Develop specialized board talents that are in high demand, such as expertise in cybersecurity and digital commerce. Once you acquire such skills, you should then "cast a wide net to find the right match," says Denise Morrison, leader of Campbell Soup. "This isn't like interviewing for a job."

- Anticipate repeated turndowns before you win your first public company directorship. "You have to be okay with a lot of 'nos' to get to a 'yes,'" says Kathleen Ligocki, CEO of Agility Fuel Systems and a former head of Tower Automotive.
- Showcase your expertise by speaking at prominent industry conferences, picking ones where you could meet the CEO of a target company.
- Make sure that a board wooing you isn't merely looking for a token woman member, sometimes dubbed a "golden skirt."
- Prepare a customized biography that lists your leadership skills and nonprofit board experience along with preferred companies. But don't expect rapid results after your name appears in a database of prospective directors. Women are wrong to wait "for someone to ask us to dance. And we think if nobody asks us, then that's the problem," Ligocki contends. "Target who you want."
- Display formal behavior during board interviews. Janet M. Clarke, who has been a director of seven public companies, often witnesses overly casual behavior when she screens female board candidates. "Flipping of hair, of course," she reports. "Crossing and uncrossing your legs. Women kicking their shoes off under the table."

# 14

# Will the Glass Ceiling
# Ever Shatter?

One evening in the late 1990s, Carol Bartz attended a University
of Wisconsin dinner for alumni like her who ran companies in the
San Francisco Bay area. She had been chief executive of Autodesk,
a maker of design software, for several years.

Bartz brought her husband, Bill, to the event, which was held
at a San Francisco hotel. During the cocktail hour, they met a CEO
and his wife. "The guy doesn't want to talk to me, he just wants to
talk to Bill," Bartz recollected.

Bill, a vice president at Sun Microsystems Inc., a computer
maker, tried to set things straight. "I didn't go to the University
of Wisconsin," he told the male CEO. Though Bill's statement implied that he wasn't a corporate chief, his clue fell on inattentive
ears. "We get to the table and we go around and introduce our-
selves," Bartz continued. When her turn came, she announced her
name, title, and employer.

The man who had snubbed her five minutes before appeared astonished. "You are Carol Bartz?" he demanded in a loud voice.

For countless women business leaders I met, put-downs due to mistaken identity have been a common annoyance for years. And the problem persists today. Nancy McKinstry, an American who runs Wolters Kluwer, an international provider of software and information services headquartered in the Netherlands, was subject to just such a snub in November 2014. That month, she became the second woman to join the European Round Table of Industrialists, or ERT, a prestigious group of CEOs of big European businesses. McKinstry took a front-row seat for a picture of ERT members after she attended her first Round Table meeting in Munich. But the photographer tried to remove her from his shot, indicating that he would photograph wives of members separately.

"She's on the council," insisted the organization's chairman, who was sitting beside McKinstry. She laughed at the photographer's unintentional gaffe. "You have to have a sense of humor about this," McKinstry told me.

Such cases of mistaken identity typify what is called "unconscious bias"—hidden beliefs about the capabilities of women that arise from widespread implicit preferences for certain groups. Unconscious biases cause barriers that can impede the advancement of individuals because the hidden beliefs frequently influence critical workplace decisions. Yet, you can learn to recognize concealed attitudes and limit their impact on behavior, research shows. Employers that train staffers to recognize and combat unconscious bias may one day help close the gender gap, a breakthrough that would have enormous positive repercussions for our economy and our society.

In upper corporate management, however, that day is likely far off. At the current pace, more than a century will elapse before companies achieve gender equality at their highest echelons, concluded a 2015 study by LeanIn.Org, a nonprofit organization formed by Sheryl Sandberg, chief operating officer of Facebook, and McKinsey, the management consultancy.

For the study, researchers tracked the progress of women at 118 North American companies and surveyed nearly thirty thousand men and women. They found that only 43 percent of women yearn to be a top executive, far below 53 percent of men. Twenty-five percent of women believe that "their gender has hindered their progression, a perception that intensifies once women reach senior levels." And women comprise just 17 percent of occupants of the executive suite.[1]

The broader American public also has a pessimistic outlook about women's prospects for getting ahead in the corporate workplace. Men will continue to hold more top business positions in the future, predicted 53 percent of 1,835 American adults surveyed in November 2014 by the Pew Research Center. A key reason cited by respondents for the continuing scarcity of women in upper-level roles was the fact that women must do more than their male counterparts to prove themselves. And nearly two-thirds of women polled said their gender faces some discrimination in society today.

It is no wonder that women still go to court to battle alleged sex bias. In September 2015, Ellen Pao stepped away from a protracted legal contest that highlighted sexism in Silicon Valley by not appealing the trial loss to her former employer, Kleiner Perkins Caufield & Byers. Pao had worked for the venture capital firm between 2005 and 2012.

Other women are waging court fights against tech industry heavyweights, including Microsoft and Twitter Inc., the social media service. The lawsuit against Microsoft, filed the same month that Pao abandoned her legal battle, alleged the software maker paid its female technical professionals less money and promoted them less frequently than it did their male counterparts. Microsoft has said it would review the lawsuit. The litigation against Twitter, brought in March 2015, claimed that the company "creates a glass ceiling for women that cannot be explained or justified by any reasonable business purpose." Twitter, which has said that it wants women to account for 25 percent of its leadership roles by the end of 2016, denied that the company has a glass ceiling.

The suit put that powerful metaphor back in the spotlight. The term had showed up in print for the first time in a 1984 *Adweek* article about magazine editor Gay Bryant. "Women have reached a certain point—I call it the glass ceiling," Bryant told *Adweek*. "They're in the top of middle management, and they're stopping and getting stuck."[2]

These days, a number of companies are trying to dismantle the glass ceiling by doing more than simply paying lip service to gender diversity. Pacesetters include Rockwell Automation Inc., the maker of computer equipment; Salesforce.com, the business-software company; and Intel, the maker of computer chips.

Rockwell organized what it dubbed "change inclusion teams," many of which were run by white men. Teams devised tactics to reduce gender bias, such as discouraging "old boys' network" socializing at the bar after company conferences. As part of a "women's surge" initiative at Salesforce.com, managers must consider women candidates when filling positions at the level of vice president and above.

In 2015, Intel pledged $300 million to increase workforce diversity. The company hopes to achieve what it calls "full representation" of women and underrepresented minorities in its U.S. workforce by 2020. Intel offers employees up to $4,000 apiece, double the usual referral bonus, if they assist the company in meeting this goal by proposing female and minority prospects.

## CONFRONTING UNCONSCIOUS BIAS

We favor certain types of people based on our upbringing, experience, and values because we need bias to survive, I pointed out in a 2014 *Wall Street Journal* article about unconscious bias. Our brains naturally use bias to detect differences and danger. "Left unchecked on the job, though, unconscious bias can affect hiring, assignments, promotions, evaluations, and dismissals," I wrote.[3]

Certain companies made a decision to train staffers about unconscious bias attitudes, determined by the Implicit Association Test, a widely used measure of hidden stereotypes created in 1994. With this test, even people with egalitarian beliefs about gender often stereotype people based on their sex. By 2019, 50 percent of large U.S. employers with diversity programs may offer training programs aimed at overcoming these biases, predicted Margaret Regan, a diversity consultant.

Under orders from Linda Hudson, then chief executive of BAE Systems, all middle managers and executives at the major U.S. defense contractor completed a two-hour class about unconscious bias by the end of 2013. During one such BAE class that I observed for my *Journal* story, the trainer encouraged participants to identify where bias had crept into their thought processes rather than blame them for the anemic numbers of senior-level women and minorities.

Numerous other employers, such as Google, Intel, VMware Inc., Pfizer Inc., and Dow Chemical Co., have also encouraged workers to try to detect their hidden biases. At Microsoft, annual training on this issue is mandatory company-wide. Facebook took an even bolder step. In July 2015, the social network inaugurated a public website to display video presentations from its own course about managing unconscious bias.

One presentation described "performance bias," which involves how women are judged by standards that differ from those used to judge men. Members of a dominant group, such as men, are assessed by what is seen as their expected potential to handle a job, while members of less dominant groups, such as women, are judged by their prior accomplishments.

The company's training program "helps people recognize how bias can affect them, and gives them tools to interrupt and correct for bias when they see it in the workplace," Sheryl Sandberg said in a blog post unveiling Facebook's unusual website. "Studies show that job applicants with 'black sounding names' are less likely to get callbacks than those with 'white sounding names,'" she went on. "And applicants called Jennifer are likely to be offered a lower salary than applicants called John."

But heightened awareness of unconscious bias doesn't always suffice. Companies see quicker improvement when they combine training with such measures as mandates that slates of candidates include diverse prospects. Thanks to prodding by Hudson, a woman or a person of color began to take part in interview panels for potential middle managers and executives at BAE. The hiring panels previously tended to select white males.

Largely as a result of these changes, the number of women and people of color in BAE senior management climbed nearly 10 percent between May 2011 and May 2013. Since then, the company has mostly maintained that rate of gain, "with some additional small increases for women and a slight decrease for people of color," a BAE spokesman told me in December 2015.

As part of its expanded diversity effort, more than one thousand first-line supervisors and midlevel managers have taken a course called "The Inclusion Advantage." The three-hour course goes beyond raising awareness about unconscious bias by focusing on how managers can help create a more diverse workforce, the BAE spokesman said.

Businesses keen to lessen the negative impact of unconscious bias can also turn to computer algorithms designed to reduce gender and racial discrimination. An app called Textio, for example, discourages the use of words in job listings such as "rock star" because they may unintentionally attract more male applicants, two of my *Wall Street Journal* colleagues wrote in 2015. The Gap-Jumpers app enables employers to test the abilities of job seekers without knowing their gender or race. Hiring managers conduct online "blind" auditions, "where candidates compete anonymously to solve problems related to the job."[4]

## WOMEN'S ISSUES BECOME MEN'S ISSUES, TOO

Another seismic shift in the workplace could further accelerate the ascension of women into the executive suite. Companies have long considered women's advancement as women's problem. Now some are teaching men to be more involved in solving that problem.

In fall 2014, about sixty male bosses from Cardinal Health Inc., a health care services concern, and four other big employers finished a six-month program organized by Catalyst, the nonprofit research group. The men learned to bolster women's prospects partly by organizing informal alliances with male colleagues. Programs like Catalyst's "reflect research that suggests men carry considerable clout but fear being called out for helping women to move ahead," I wrote in a *Wall Street Journal* article about the trend.[5]

Men featured in my article included Mike Kaufmann, chief financial officer of Cardinal and head of the company's networking group for women. The group had only a handful of inactive male members when he took charge. Kaufmann urged his male associates to join; his efforts bore fruit. By December 2015, the group boasted about 270 men and the proportion of women at the senior vice president level and above stood at 27 percent—up from about 23 percent in 2011, a Cardinal spokeswoman reported.

Yet "this whole notion of involving men is still relatively new," said Carole Watkins, Cardinal's chief human resources officer. "We have to build it deep into the culture," she went on. "Culture change is hard. It takes time."

A leadership consultancy called White Men as Full Diversity Partners LLC assisted with the Catalyst program. During 2014, the firm advised seventeen Fortune 500 companies about increasing men's role in advancing women. That compares with only six such companies in 2006. The firm coaches men to foster a more inclusive work culture by scrutinizing their mind-sets, understanding their privileged status, and altering their behavior.

Bill Proudman, a cofounder of White Men as Full Diversity Partners, elaborated about the merits of his firm's approach. "Men intervening and engaging with other men helps to create more equitable policies and behavior that not only benefit women," he explained to me. "They also benefit men." He thinks that a work culture changes after a company trains a critical mass of staffers. "It creates pull rather than push," Proudman said, and thus eases men's fears about women usurping their jobs.

Anne-Marie Slaughter agrees that a broader focus for gender diversity efforts is essential. "Advancing women means breaking free of a new set of stereotypes and assumptions, not only for women, but also for men," said Slaughter, a former dean at Princeton University's Woodrow Wilson School, in her 2015 book, *Unfinished Business: Women, Men, Work, Family*.[6] The book evolved from Slaughter's 2012 article in the *Atlantic*, titled "Why Women Still Can't Have It All." The widely read piece described her decision to return to her husband and two sons in Princeton and resume teaching after working in Washington for Hillary Clinton, then U.S. secretary of state.

An equally profound change is emerging as employers heed demands from a new breed of working fathers. Some men tap flexible-workplace policies originally intended for working mothers, while others revamp their career goals so they can spend more time with their family.

The youthful millennial generation, which dominates today's workforce, exemplifies this upswing in expectations about work-life balance. A study by the Boston College Center for Work &

Family, cited in a *Wall Street Journal* story that I coauthored, noticed that most fathers, especially those under forty, are departing from the traditional "breadwinner" role and see themselves
as responsible for the emotional and financial needs of their
children. Companies are beginning to realize that future leaders
of both genders will refuse promotions or otherwise curb their
ambitions unless they receive greater support for their parental
responsibilities, added Brad Harrington, head of the Center for
Work & Family.[7]

Slaughter agrees about this idea, too. "Most of the pervasive
gender inequalities in our society—for both men and women—
cannot be fixed unless men have the same range of choices with
respect to mixing caregiving and breadwinning that women do,"
she argued in her book.[8]

Yet young fathers often find it difficult to persuade employers that they will work as hard once they assert a desire to actively care for their children. The conflict between the desire to
be a good employee and a good parent or partner "is the essence
of the new male mystique," said Ellen Galinsky, president of the
Families and Work Institute, a New York think tank, in a 2011
report about rising work-family conflicts among men. And more
than 90 percent of men and women canvassed for the Lean In and
McKinsey study reported fears that stopping work for six months
or more for a family matter would hurt their position at work.

Consider the paternity leave taken by my son, Daniel, in 2013.
He was a senior Democratic staffer in the Minnesota House of
Representatives when he received two months off with full pay
after the birth of his son and his wife's return to work that year.
Daniel worried that his parental break might harm his career.

Caring for his newborn while trying to stay connected to the fast-paced world of government and politics worsened his anxiety about being away from work. Rather than detach himself completely, he attended weekly staff meetings by phone—and muted his side of a conference call if his baby suddenly cried.

The larger world also regarded Daniel as an oddity during his paternity leave. With his son in an infant carrier, he sometimes walked around an indoor mall near their home on weekdays. He never encountered another young father like him on those mall visits. Nor did store salesclerks realize that he was an at-home parent. "How nice! You're giving Mommy the afternoon off!" the salesclerks usually gushed.

## ARDENT ADVOCATES IN THE CORNER OFFICE

Forceful actions by chief executives can improve the status of women in their workforce. That's certainly been true for many female CEOs. Both General Motors and IBM, which are run by Mary Barra and Ginni Rometty, respectively, earned spots on the 2015 list of "Top 50 Companies for Executive Women" assembled by the National Association for Female Executives. The professional group picks businesses with the best record of advancing women. The proportion of women among the highest-paid executives at the fifty winners in 2015 was 40 percent, up from 35 percent the year before.

A small but growing number of male corporate leaders are becoming visible role models and powerful innovators. Mark Zuckerberg, CEO and founder of Facebook, enhanced the social acceptability of new fathers taking significant time off when he announced that he would embark on a two-month paternity leave after his daughter was born in fall 2015. "Studies show that when working parents have time to be with their newborns, outcomes are better for the children and families," Zuckerberg wrote on his Facebook page. A week later, the company decided to extend its parental leave policy of four paid months for U.S. staffers to full-time employees worldwide.

The most committed CEOs have a personal passion about placing more women into senior roles, according to Joanna Barsh, a director emeritus of McKinsey and a veteran researcher on the subject of women in the workplace. Such business leaders "make the goal clear and specific, and they tell everyone about it," Barsh wrote in a report about a 2012 study of sixty U.S. companies that she codirected for McKinsey. "When a CEO is the chief advocate and storyteller, more people believe that gender diversity matters," the report said. That's important, the report continued, because "it is simply harder for women to get into the right networks of powerful executives and to cultivate sponsor relationships."[9]

One of the male chiefs who personifies Barsh's archetype is Carl T. Camden, the longtime leader of Kelly Services Inc., a company that provides staffing services. Camden has made his greatest mark by promoting the idea that the company should consider unexpected internal and external candidates for management jobs. He pointed out, for instance, that the woman in charge of one of its fast-growing units was once an engineer for General Motors.

"There is no reason you have to fill positions with people who have spent their time on a linear career path," Camden told me.

He himself epitomizes this philosophy. He had been a college professor, copresident of an advertising agency, and a bank marketing executive before Kelly Services hired him in 1995 as a senior vice president. He landed in the corner office in 2006.

As of 2008, only two of the eleven senior officers at Kelly Services were women. Camden remembered being surprised by its thin ranks of women in upper management, since women comprised a majority of the fresh college graduates that the company recruited for entry-level professional posts.

Camden sought to fix the gender imbalance in the Kelly Services executive suite through a variety of tactics. He has been chairman of the Talent Deployment Forum at Kelly Services, which hastens the development of female leaders, since its launch in 2008. The forum, now called Leadership in Action, makes sure that women are being prepared for highly visible roles, pushes for diverse applicant pools, and encourages staffers to pursue management positions that they otherwise might not have considered. Camden also personally sponsors high-potential women and minorities within the company.

Women now occupy six of the thirteen highest spots at Kelly Services, representing about 46 percent. "Over the course of time, you should end up with near majority or majority female in the senior officer corps," Camden said. But he refuses to take much credit for women's progress at his employer. "It's not one person's job," he added. "It has to be every person's job."

Yet at many other workplaces, most lower-level staffers remain dubious about the extent of commitment to this issue at the top. Seventy-five percent of companies studied by Lean In and McKinsey named gender diversity as a priority of the chief executive, yet less than half of employees said the issue was high on their own CEO's priority list.[10]

## BEING ACCOUNTABLE COUNTS

This mismatch on the importance of gender diversity may reflect a lack of management accountability. "A lot of people are going through the motions," without investing adequate money and organizational resources, suggested Gracia Martore, chief executive of TEGNA, the broadcasting and digital media company that remained after the spin-off of Gannett's publishing arm in 2015.

At TEGNA, Martore said, the progress of women "is something you can measure and we hold people accountable for." She links compensation packages of TEGNA managers to how well they recruit and advance women, just as she did while leading Gannett before the split. As of December 2015, women at TEGNA had won 41 percent of the promotions at the middle manager level and higher as well as 47 percent of all promotions company-wide that year.

Other big businesses, such as Time Warner Inc., the media conglomerate, pay executives bonuses based somewhat on their success in promoting diversity. At Johnson & Johnson, the health products giant, the 2015 payout of bonuses for top managers was partly influenced by diversity measurements, such as the number of women hired in the past year.

Establishing specific goals for gender diversity also appears to make a difference in improving a company's track record, even if those goals aren't directly linked to pay. That's another conclusion from the Lean In and McKinsey study, which included some companies that McKinsey had studied in 2012. "Firms with established targets in 2012 outpaced those that didn't set goals when it came to bulking up the share of women in senior management," a *Wall Street Journal* colleague reported.[11]

The finding didn't surprise me. After all, remember that cliché? What gets measured is what gets done.

# 15

# Male Champions of Women

Looking back at the fifty-two business leaders I interviewed for this book, I realize they frequently shared qualities that hastened their ascent to the pinnacles of power.

They displayed tremendous confidence, calculated risk taking, and a stubborn refusal to admit defeat when career obstacles loomed. Pat Russo relied on such traits during her first stint as a chief executive. When she joined Lucent Technologies in 2002, the troubled telecom equipment maker had lost so much money that "we were unscrewing every other lightbulb. We stopped cutting the lawn," she told me. "It was all about survival because the only alternative was to go bankrupt."

Russo tapped her inner resilience to weather Lucent's stormy times. "You fall back, you get back up," she explained. "I would go home and I would say to myself, 'Tomorrow the sun will come up.' You know what? It always did." The extensive job cuts that Russo ordered helped rescue Lucent from the brink of bankruptcy.

Many of the executives I met proved their professional prowess time and again by completing difficult assignments and producing enviable results. Some became glass-ceiling crackers after they pursued a zigzag path to upper management. They transformed painful episodes of sexual harassment, bad bosses, and biased male associates into building blocks for their empathetic management style. The most effective leaders never forgot how to walk in the shoes of their subordinates.

The women often coped with significant personal setbacks, too. Several found themselves fired amid hostile press coverage. Others struggled with working-mother guilt. A handful became seriously ill, sometimes in part due to their passionate commitment to a high-pressured post.

A number of women also benefited from influential male champions. These men fought hard to improve the workplace success of the second sex. In 2011, Doug Conant ended 142 years of male occupants in the corner office at Campbell Soup, the largest soup company in the United States, when he handed the keys to his protégé, Denise Morrison.

Another champion was Dennis Sullivan, the highly demanding father of Morrison and Maggie Wilderotter, the first sisters to take charge of Fortune 500 companies. A third is Ed Zimmerman, a technology industry attorney who took an unusual pledge against gender bias in front of more than six hundred people at an industry conference in 2014. He vowed not to join any conference panel with four or more speakers unless at least one was a woman, and refused to attend business dinners or lunches for ten or more people if women weren't on the guest list.

## THE CATALYST OF A CATALYST DINNER

Conant became a fierce proponent of women's advancement late in his career. An "aha" moment radically altered his perspective not long after his 2001 debut as CEO of Campbell, where he enjoyed wearing suspenders and a tie emblazoned with Campbell soup cans.

In March 2002, Conant attended an awards dinner for businesses with impressive gains in developing and promoting women. Campbell wasn't among those honored that night by Catalyst, the nonprofit research group, even though he believed that his employer embraced diversity. During a conversation about opportunities for women with a female executive he met on the dais of a Waldorf-Astoria hotel ballroom in Manhattan, Conant happened to mention his fifteen-year-old daughter.

"I would encourage you to think about this in terms of your daughter," the executive suggested to Conant. "Don't you want her to have all the opportunities available to men when she has an opportunity to go into the workforce?"

Conant had never considered the future through the eyes of Sarah, his youngest child. He suddenly worried that her gender might crimp her chances to excel in a career. "That night I realized, 'Wow. I have missed something,'" he told me. "I missed that the opportunities were not available to talented women who had the capacity to contribute in extraordinary ways," he said.

That night, Conant continued, "I committed myself to someday being able to celebrate our progress at Campbell" and win a Catalyst award. He asked Catalyst researchers to assess the company's diversity efforts, especially those involving women. "Unfortunately, we were in the dark ages," Conant remembered.

About 80 percent of Campbell customers were women, yet "they are not represented in your company," Catalyst concluded, according to Conant. The researchers observed that "the way diversity is embraced in your company is not best practice. It is poor practice."

Conant took strong remedial action. Immediately after getting Catalyst's report, he recalled, "I put diversity at the top of my staff-meeting agendas." He insisted on diverse slates of candidates for management openings, and women quickly turned up on virtually every slate. He hired Campbell's first head of diversity and inclusion. The company launched a website to showcase achievements of its high-performing women. And "we increased the presence of women at all levels of the organization," he said.

At the highest level, Conant recruited another three women for his management team; it had previously consisted of a single woman and a dozen men. But his aggressive push on behalf of women bothered some male Campbell executives, who felt less valued by their chief. He tried to reassure them without backing down on his commitment to women. "If you perform," Conant told those men, "there will be opportunities."

Denise Morrison was one of Conant's picks for the senior leadership spots. She had worked for him at Nabisco Holdings Corp., where Conant ran the foods unit before he went to Campbell. As her boss for nearly all of her Nabisco tenure, he also had been Morrison's informal mentor. Conant once pulled her aside to chide her for being "so results-driven and so transaction-oriented that I wasn't taking time to build relationships," Morrison said in a 2012 interview with the *Wall Street Journal*. By building trusted

relationships, "you'll get more done," Conant counseled his lieutenant. "You'll have more influence."[1]

Morrison previously had failed to realize "how important it
was to take time at work to build relationships that weren't one
hundred percent business-related," she told me. "I made immediate adjustments to my style," taking time to get to know people.
The changes "helped me increase my effectiveness," Morrison
said. "I now pass this advice on to younger women."

Morrison joined Campbell in 2003 and initially assumed the
new global position of chief customer officer because the company needed somebody who could deal with customers on a global
scale. She said she told Conant that she yearned to run a bigger
business, and he assured her that was a strong possibility as long
as she continued to perform well.

Two years later, Morrison became president of Campbell USA,
an operational role where she introduced a line of healthy soups
and marketed more aggressively to women. She next led North
America, a highly complex unit. "She took all the challenging
assignments and made them work," Conant recollected. In fall
2010, Campbell elevated Morrison to chief operating officer and
announced that she would be the CEO's eventual successor.

That same year, the company finally won a Catalyst award. The
proportion of Campbell women in executive jobs had increased
from 21 percent in 2005 to 25 percent in 2009, Catalyst said.
Conant remains an outspoken proponent of women's advancement. He was among the seven men and women chosen in 2014
as the initial "Champions of Change" by the Thirty Percent Coalition, a U.S. advocacy group whose goal is for women to hold
30 percent of public company board seats.

"Women are half the population. They ought to be half of the executive population in the workplace," Conant insisted. "This is going to take another generation of leadership." In his view, men should take more responsibility for achieving gender equity, such as by mentoring high-potential women. "You need a personal commitment that transcends the ordinary," he explained.

Conant, who is a coauthor of a book about leadership, stresses this point during his speeches by saying, "If it is to be, it is up to me." The maxim was written by William H. Johnson, an African American who became a prominent twentieth-century painter despite racial prejudice and only a grade school education. "I live that," Conant noted.

Not surprisingly, Conant has also acted as an advocate for his daughter, who turned twenty-nine in December 2015. He introduced Sarah to successful working mothers, such as a partner at McKinsey, the management consultancy. The partner helped Sarah land a McKinsey summer internship during college. Since 2011, Sarah has been executive director of the Rumsfeld Foundation, formed by former U.S. secretary of defense Donald Rumsfeld and his wife, Joyce, who are her great-uncle and great-aunt.

Sarah likes the fact that she was the catalyst behind her father's 2002 decision to press harder for gender diversity on the job. "I am really heartened by all he went on to do for women at Campbell," she told me. "Not just talking about their hiring and advancement, but making actual changes on behalf of women."

## WHAT'S YOUR NEXT FEAT AFTER BEING A CEO?

Dennis Sullivan, a Korean War veteran whose two eldest daughters became chiefs of major public companies, probably never pictured himself as a male champion of women. He expected to have at least one son rather than four daughters. So, the AT&T executive shared "everything he knew about business with his girls, including talking to them, while they were still in grade school, about setting profit-margin goals," a *Wall Street Journal* colleague wrote in her 2007 story about the Sullivan sisters.[2]

Morrison credits her father with whetting her appetite for a business career at a very young age. "He talked excitedly about business and how the road would open up for women and he wanted us to be ready for it," she said when we spoke. "I just knew I wanted to be a part of it."

Sullivan took Denise and Maggie to his office years before taking your daughters to work came into vogue. He usually didn't return home until seven o'clock. Though they had already eaten dinner and finished their homework, the older sisters sat with him during his weeknight meals.

"We would have dinner table discussions every night about what he worked on," Wilderotter recalled. Occasionally, Sullivan acted out an amusing meeting. His colorful tales "really brought his business world to life—and it also took the mystery out of it," she went on. The nightly discussions with their father, begun when Maggie was seven and Denise was eight, lasted through their high school years.

To justify the purchase of new bicycles, Sullivan required his eldest daughters to prepare a business plan and contribute allowance money toward their cost. They also had to convince him "that we could accept the responsibility and take care of the 'asset,'" Morrison recollected.

Similarly, Sullivan taught his oldest girls about marketing after giving them a pink Princess Trimline phone with a touch tone, a trial product that he oversaw. Thanks to such chats, Wilderotter said, marketing "is in my DNA."

Sullivan never stopped insisting that his daughters aim high as they approached adulthood. "He would always ask us for our goals. Then, he would add one or more for good measure," Morrison remembered. "He was a really good balance of tough and nice."

In a 2013 career column that I wrote for WSJ.com, Wilderotter said her father urged her to seek tough assignments, get profit-and-loss duties early in her management career, and deliver results. When I interviewed Sullivan for that column, he revealed the best career advice that he had offered his daughters: "Always have a plan."

Morrison heeded his words during the years she spent pursuing her childhood dream of running a company. She created a chart monitoring her career progress when she joined Nestlé as a U.S. sales planning manager in 1984. The chart described her tenure in each job, how much money she was responsible for, the number of people she supervised, her accomplishments, and her skill gaps.[3]

Decades later, Morrison phoned her father to announce that Campbell had chosen her as its next chief executive. "So what's your next goal?" he asked.

"To build a great company," she replied.

## "MANELS" ARE UNMANLY

Ed Zimmerman typifies the contemporary version of male champions of women. The forty-something lawyer is a mover and shaker in the testosterone-laden world of venture capitalists. He uses social media to trumpet his views about the importance of gender diversity. In particular, he's an outspoken opponent of "manels," men-only panels of experts at conferences and other business events.

Zimmerman chairs the tech group for Lowenstein Sandler LLP, a national law firm. He represents small and growing tech firms and venture funds that invest in them. He had quietly fought all-male tech gatherings long before he decided—on the spur of the moment—to make his public pledge during a New York conference that he led in the spring of 2014.

Tech industry executives increase their visibility through panel appearances, and high-profile people are more likely to be tapped for jobs, Zimmerman told me. Excluding women from these panels robs them of chances to do business deals, too, he said, adding, "Opportunities emerge because you are proximate to interesting people."

Zimmerman drew broader attention to his pledge by describing it in an online column that he occasionally wrote for *The Accelerators*, a WSJ.com blog. "Make a true and good-faith effort to have meaningful representation on these panels," he wrote on August 8, 2014. "Otherwise I'm out." And don't invite me to a sizable business dinner, lunch, or drinks outing unless you include women, he continued.

But Zimmerman's gender diversity stance made him a pariah among certain event organizers and stirred criticism that he was discriminating against men. In the spring of 2015, a tech industry group that Zimmerman had previously addressed invited him to speak again at its annual conference. He emailed the group a link to his pledge and offered to help find qualified female speakers for his conference panel.

"The organization went silent on me," Zimmerman remembered. "The failure to reply to that email was related directly to the pledge." The withdrawn speaking engagement was the latest in a series of conferences and other business events that canceled their invitations after he unveiled his diversity commitment.

On the other hand, Zimmerman sees some signs of progress as a result of his pledge. Women have landed speaking engagements that they otherwise wouldn't have gotten, he said. A Silicon Valley venture capitalist cited Zimmerman's vow when he sought his assistance in lining up female investors. Other venture capitalists have called him for advice about "how to recruit great female investors to come work at their fund," he recollected.

Some small tech firms with all-male boards are paying attention because Zimmerman is outside counsel for their directors. The chief executive of one such firm invited him to a 2014 event for his senior team. "I said I'd only go if the event included women, and I told the CEO that he needed to do a better job on diversity more generally," Zimmerman remembered. Taken aback at first, the company leader then altered the event's guest list and committed himself to seeking his first female director during a subsequent board meeting.

Meanwhile, outrage over "manels" is spreading. Saara Särmä, a Finnish feminist scholar and artist, used the Tumblr blogging platform to publicly shame the organizers of events with only men as experts via a blog that she created in February 2015. Her widely viewed blog, which is called *Congrats! You Have an All-Male Panel!* has posted hundreds of photos of all-male panels in various countries. One especially ironic photo displayed a six-man panel at the Global Summit of Women in Paris in June 2014. The summit, held since 1990, aims to dramatically expand women's economic opportunities around the world.

Academics, proponents of arms control, and others have organized their own drives to end the exclusion of women from professional events. Owen Barder, head of Europe at the Center for Global Development, a U.S. nonprofit, encourages men to publicly promise that they won't participate in conference panels that do not include at least one woman. The names of more than four hundred men taking this pledge appeared on Barder's website as of late December 2015.

Zimmerman prefers to educate tech industry colleagues about gender diversity rather than shame them with embarrassing online photos. "I care about the issue, and it is important," he emphasized. "I am trying to walk the line between being pushy and being a jerk. Because if I am a jerk, no one will listen to me."

Zimmerman has a teenage daughter who may influence his further activism. She held him accountable "on these types of issues since long before my pledge," he recalled. If he has a chance to make her even prouder of having a feminist father, he said, "you can bet I will lean into that opportunity!"

## LOOKING AHEAD

We need more good guys like Doug Conant, Dennis Sullivan, and Ed Zimmerman to join forces with women. As husbands, fathers, uncles, brothers, or sons, men have a vested self-interest in seeing women succeed in the executive suite. Numerous studies have shown that businesses tilted toward gender parity perform better, gain critical competitive advantages, and increase their market value. "Equality is not a zero-sum game," observed Sheryl Sandberg, Facebook's chief operating officer, in a 2015 opinion piece that she cowrote for the *New York Times.* "More profits mean more rewards and promotions to go around."[4]

For the same reason, we need more good women like Mary Barra at General Motors, Gracia Martore at TEGNA, Linda Hudson at BAE Systems, Sandi Peterson at Johnson & Johnson, and many other female executives I got to know. Their career trajectories plus their efforts on behalf of other women provide a clear road map. These female leaders highlighted the need for everything from transparent tracking of gender progress to management accountability and company-wide training about unconscious bias.

Some of the best advice came from Carol Bartz, the former CEO of Autodesk and Yahoo. Whether you turn to higher-level men or women, "find your allies and don't get sucked into bad behavior," she urged ambitious women. And "don't make everything a mountain," she continued. "Find the passes."

My young granddaughter, Isabel, can't envision mountains blocking her adult ambitions. At age four and a half, she told me that she hopes to make her living as a doctor, actor, princess, and bus driver. I approved her career choices, but pointed out that women weren't allowed to drive buses years ago.

"Why not?" Isabel asked, perplexed.

"Because people thought women couldn't drive buses," I replied. I yearn for the day when my tale about barring female bus drivers sounds completely far-fetched because no one remembers rampant sex bias in the American workplace.

Betty Spence shares my dream. In March 2015, the president of the National Association for Female Executives gazed out at the crowd in a huge Manhattan banquet hall, the setting for its annual awards luncheon for outstanding companies. Nearly every guest was a woman executive. "The women to come will fill a room a hundred times this size when we are gone," Spence declared. The crowd roared its approval. So did I.

# ACKNOWLEDGMENTS

Becoming a published author takes months of hard work. But for me, *Earning It* was a true labor of love.

For starters, I got an incredibly detailed look at the careers and lives of fifty-two corporate executive women—including ones in command of the biggest U.S. businesses. I am extremely grateful for their willingness to share their stories of how they got ahead and to give back to the next generation of business leaders.

Writing this book also allowed me to give back to my daughter, Abra. That was my intent in a 2008 essay I wrote for WSJ.com that proved the launchpad for *Earning It*. My first-person piece described how too many women assume they will enjoy equal status and opportunity on the job because they were too young to remember the barriers that their mothers and other older women had battled.

At that point, Abra had been in the labor force for only three years. But she already wondered whether discrimination ex-plained why most assistants at her nonprofit employer were female. I am grateful to Abra for inspiring me to pursue this book.

I drew inspiration as well from her older brother, Dan, a feminist-minded father whose 2013 decision to take paternity leave made him a pacesetter in his office. In turn, I hope he and his wife, Rachel, an equally hard-working attorney, can inspire their daughter, Isabel, to always aim high.

My parents, Betty and Irv Lublin, were always my biggest boosters. I started making up stories at age four, before I learned to write. My mother served as my scribe, jotting down my tales that I illustrated. I later came to greatly admire her ability to teach full-time while mothering four youngsters aged four to sixteen years old.

As *Earning It* began to take shape, I was fortunate to find a skilled editor, Constance Rosenblum. She deftly polished my prose. I also appreciate the considerable help and support I received from my literary agent, Karen Gantz, and my publisher, Hollis Heimbouch.

I owe my biggest debt of gratitude to my husband, Mike. He's far more than my longtime love and life partner. He was my tireless soul mate every step of the way on this lengthy project. He read and critiqued so many drafts that he began to quote memorized portions aloud! He also was my ever-present "tech" support.

I recently thanked Mike for all of his help with the book. "My pleasure," he replied. Being married to him has been my pleasure.

# INTERVIEWED EXECUTIVE WOMEN

Cheryl A. Bachelder, chief executive of Popeyes Louisiana Kitchen Inc.*

Brenda Barnes, former CEO of Sara Lee Corp.*

Mary Barra, CEO of General Motors Co.*

Carol Bartz, former CEO of Yahoo Inc. and Autodesk Inc.*

Charlotte Beers, former CEO of Ogilvy & Mather Worldwide

Dorrit J. Bern, former CEO of Charming Shoppes Inc.*

Cathie Black, former president of Hearst Magazines

Diane M. Bryant, an executive vice president of Intel Corp.

Janet M. Clarke, a former managing director of Citigroup Inc.

Mary Dillon, CEO of Ulta Salon, Cosmetics & Fragrance Inc. and former CEO of U.S. Cellular Corp.*

Janet Dolan, former CEO of Tennant Co.*

Dina Dublon, former chief financial officer of J.P. Morgan Chase & Co.

Melissa Dyrdahl, former CEO of Ella Health Inc. and a former senior vice president of Adobe Systems Inc.

Carly Fiorina, former CEO of Hewlett-Packard Co.*

Ilene Gordon, CEO of Ingredion Inc.*

Mindy Grossman, CEO of HSN Inc.*

Adele Gulfo, an executive vice president of Mylan NV

Melanie Healey, former vice chairman of Procter & Gamble Co.

Penny Herscher, executive chairman and prior CEO of FirstRain Inc. and former CEO of Simplex Solutions Inc.*

Victoria Holt, CEO of Proto Labs Inc. and former CEO of Spartech Corp.*

Linda Hudson, former CEO of BAE Systems Inc.

Andrea Jung, former CEO of Avon Products Inc.*

Ellen Kullman, former CEO of DuPont Co.*

Geraldine Laybourne, former CEO of Oxygen Media LLC

Shelly Lazarus, former CEO of Ogilvy & Mather Worldwide

Dawn Lepore, former CEO of Drugstore.com*

Kathleen Ligocki, CEO of Agility Fuel Systems Inc. and former CEO of Harvest Power Inc. and Tower Automotive Inc.*

Challis Lowe, former highest human resources officer at Beneficial Corp., Ryder System Inc., and Dollar General Corp.

Gracia Martore, CEO of TEGNA Inc. and former CEO of Gannett Co.*

Sara Mathew, former CEO of Dun & Bradstreet Corp.*

Helen McCluskey, former CEO of Warnaco Group Inc.*

Nancy McKinstry, CEO of Wolters Kluwer NV*

Beth Mooney, CEO of KeyCorp*

Ann Moore, former CEO of Time Inc.

Denise Morrison, CEO of Campbell Soup Co.*

Anne Mulcahy, former CEO of Xerox Corp.*

Sandra Peterson, group worldwide chairman of Johnson & Johnson

Abbe Raven, former CEO of A+E Networks

Paula R. Reynolds, former CEO of Safeco Corp. and AGL Resources Inc.*

Janet Robinson, former CEO of New York Times Co.*

Virginia Rometty, CEO of International Business Machines Corp.*

Irene Rosenfeld, CEO of Mondelēz International Inc. and former CEO of Kraft Foods Inc.*

Pat Russo, former CEO of Alcatel-Lucent SA and Lucent Technologies Inc.*

Clara Shih, CEO of Hearsay Social Inc.

Liz Smith, CEO of Bloomin' Brands Inc.*

Robin Smith, chairman and former CEO of Publishers Clearing House

Sally J. Smith, CEO of Buffalo Wild Wings Inc.*

Stephanie Sonnabend, former CEO of Sonesta International Hotels Corp.*

Anne Stevens, former CEO of Carpenter Technology Corp.*

Teresa Taylor, former chief operating officer of Qwest Communications International Inc.

Meg Whitman, CEO of Hewlett Packard Enterprise Co. and former CEO of Hewlett-Packard Co.*

Maggie Wilderotter, former executive chairman and CEO of Frontier Communications Corp.*

Total: Thirty-four of the fifty-two women—or 65 percent—are a current or past CEO of a public company. Asterisks denote who they are.

# NOTES

## INTRODUCTION

1. Joann S. Lublin, "Remember the Barriers," *WSJ.com*, August 5, 2008, http://www.wsj.com/articles/SB121794061558213255.
2. Joann S. Lublin, "In Britain, Two Women May Lead but Sexism Rules," *Wall Street Journal*, March 13, 1987.

## CHAPTER 1: WORKING WOMEN HAVE COME A LONG WAY

1. Catalyst, *Historical List of Women CEOs of the Fortune Lists: 1972–2014* (New York: Catalyst, 2014).
2. Pat Wachsler, "Women-Led Companies Perform Three Times Better Than the S&P 500," *Fortune.com*, March 3, 2015, http://fortune.com/2015/03/03/women-led-companies-perform-three-times-better-than-the-sp-500/.
3. Vivian Hunt, Dennis Layton, and Sara Prince, "Diversity Matters," McKinsey & Co., November 24, 2014.
4. Ibid.
5. David Wessel, "The Positive Economics of 'Leaning In,'" *Wall Street Journal*, April 4, 2013.
6. Patricia A. Milligan, Brian Levine, Linda Chen, and Katie Edkins, "When Women Thrive, Businesses Thrive," Mercer, November 2014.
7. Joann S. Lublin, "Discrimination Against Women in Newsrooms: Fact or Fantasy?" *Journalism Quarterly* 49, no. 2 (1972): 359–61.
8. Joann S. Lublin, "Remember the Barriers," *WSJ.com*, August 5, 2008, http://www.wsj.com/articles/SB121794061558213255.
9. Nadya A. Fouad, "Leaning In, but Getting Pushed Back (and Out)," research presented at the annual convention of the American Psychological Association in Washington, D.C., August 9, 2014.
10. Colleen McCain Nelson, "Poll: Most Women See Bias in the Workplace," *Wall Street Journal*, April 12, 2013.

11. Sheryl Sandberg, *Lean In: Women, Work, and the Will to Lead* (New York: Knopf, 2013), 8.
12. Sue Shellenbarger, "The XX Factor: What's Holding Women Back?" *Wall Street Journal*, May 7, 2012.

CHAPTER 3: GETTING PICKED: BLOOM WHERE YOU ARE PLANTED
1. Anne Doyle, *Powering Up! How America's Women Achievers Become Leaders* (Bloomington, IN: Xlibris, 2011), 278.

CHAPTER 4: SEXUAL HARASSMENT NEVER VANISHED
1. Carly Fiorina, *Tough Choices: A Memoir* (New York: Portfolio, 2006), 33.
2. Ibid., 34.
3. Joann S. Lublin, "Employers Act to Curb Sex Harassing on Job; Lawsuits, Fines Feared," *Wall Street Journal*, April 24, 1981.
4. Lauren Weber, "Retailer Paid Large Awards to Plaintiffs," *Wall Street Journal*, June 10, 2015.
5. Jeff Elder, "Accuser in Kleiner Perkins Case Testifies of Sex Discrimination," *Wall Street Journal*, March 10, 2015.
6. Jennifer L. Berdahl, "The Sexual Harassment of Uppity Women," *Journal of Applied Psychology* 92, no. 2 (2007): 434.
7. Adam Bryant, "Fitting In, and Rising to the Top," *New York Times*, September 21, 2009.
8. Joann S. Lublin, "Bringing Hidden Biases into the Light," *Wall Street Journal*, January 9, 2014.
9. Marshall Heyman, "In Charge; In Wonderland," *Wall Street Journal*, February 8, 2012.

CHAPTER 5: THE PAIN OF THE PAY PINCH
1. John Bussey, "Gender Wage Gap Reflects the 'Ask' Gap," *Wall Street Journal*, October 10, 2014.
2. Rachel Feintzeig and Rachel Emma Silverman, "Careers: Haggle Over Salary? It's Not Allowed," *Wall Street Journal*, May 27, 2015.
3. Cathie Black, *Basic Black: The Essential Guide for Getting Ahead at Work (and in Life)* (New York: Crown Business, 2007), 211.
4. Deborah M. Kolb, with Jessica L. Porter, *Negotiating at Work: Turn Small Wins into Big Gains* (San Francisco: Jossey-Bass, 2015), 10.
5. Joann S. Lublin, "How One Black Woman Lands Her Top Jobs: Risks and Networking," *Wall Street Journal*, March 4, 2003.
6. Ibid.
7. Stefania Albanesi, Claudia Olivetti, and Maria José Prados, "Gender and Dynamic Agency: Theory and Evidence on the Compensation of Top Executives," *Federal Reserve Bank of New York Staff Reports*, no. 718, March 2015.

CHAPTER 6: GETTING AHEAD SOONER

1. Michelle K. Ryan and S. Alexander Haslam, "The Glass Cliff: Evidence That Women Are Over-Represented in Precarious Leadership Positions," *British Journal of Management* 16, no. 2 (June 2005): 81.

2. Sarah Ellison, "P&G Chief's Turnaround Recipe: Find Out What Women Want," *Wall Street Journal*, June 1, 2005.


CHAPTER 7: GETTING AHEAD LATER

1. Sue Shellenbarger, "Sue Shellenbarger Answers Readers' Questions," *Wall Street Journal*, December 11, 2013.

2. Cheryl Bachelder, *Dare to Serve: How to Drive Superior Results by Serving Others* (San Francisco: Berrett-Koehler, 2015), 13.

3. Julie Jargon, "At Popeyes, Recipe for a Turnaround," *Wall Street Journal*, March 9, 2014.

4. Bachelder, *Dare to Serve*, 85 and 86.

5. Meg Whitman, *The Power of Many: Values for Success in Business and in Life* (New York: Crown, 2010), 159 and 163.

6. Ibid., 161.

7. Shelly Banjo, "HSN Enjoys a Mobile-Shopping Rebirth in the Digital Era," *Wall Street Journal*, July 4, 2013.

8. Ibid.


CHAPTER 8: MANAGER MOMS ARE NOT ACROBATS

1. Sandberg, *Lean In*, 113.

2. Joann S. Lublin, "The Corner Office, and a Family," *Wall Street Journal*, October 17, 2010.

3. Tom Spiggle, "What You Should Know About AutoZone's $185 Million Pregnancy Discrimination Case," *Huffington Post*, July 31, 2015, http://www.huffingtonpost.com/tom-spiggle/why-corporate-america-sho_b_7913226.html.

4. Joann S. Lublin, "What Should a Mother Do About Her Career? Juggling Job and Junior," *Wall Street Journal*, March 21, 1980.

5. Sue Shellenbarger, "At-Home Dads Make Parenting More of a Guy Thing," *Wall Street Journal*, January 22, 2013.


CHAPTER 9: CAREER COUPLE CONUNDRUMS

1. Robin J. Ely, Pamela Stone, and Colleen Ammerman, "Rethink What You 'Know' About High-Achieving Women," *Harvard Business Review* 92, no. 12 (December 2014): 108.

2. Sandberg, *Lean In*, 110.

3. Whitman, *The Power of Many*, 218 and 134.

4. Lublin, "The Corner Office, and a Family."

5. Joann S. Lublin, "CEOs Juggle Love, Power," *Wall Street Journal*, March 7, 2006.

6. Peter Eavis and Ben Protess, "She Runs S.E.C. He's a Lawyer. Recusals and Headaches Ensue," *New York Times*, February 24, 2015.

7. Joann S. Lublin, "Careers in Collision: Working Couples Find an Increasing Chance of Conflicts in Jobs," *Wall Street Journal*, November 18, 1977.

8. "Here's Firsthand Story of a Reporter's Conflict," *Wall Street Journal*, November 18, 1977.

## CHAPTER 10: MALE MENTORS MEAN BUSINESS

1. Joann S. Lublin, "Even Top Executives Could Use Mentors to Aid Careers," *Wall Street Journal*, July 1, 2003.

2. Sylvia Ann Hewlett, *(Forget a Mentor) Find a Sponsor: The New Way to Fast-Track Your Career* (Boston: Harvard Business Review Press, 2013), 22 and 139–40.

3. Liz Rappaport, "Networking Isn't Always Easy. But It Is Crucial," *Wall Street Journal*, September 30, 2015.

4. Joann S. Lublin, "Career Gold: A Word from Your Sponsor," *WSJ.com*, June 9, 2011, http://www.wsj.com/articles/SB10001424052702304259304576375812178030014.

5. Carol Hymowitz, "Raising Women to Be Leaders," *Wall Street Journal*, February 12, 2007.

6. Sandberg, *Lean In*, 68.

7. Spencer E. Ante and Joann S. Lublin, "IBM's Rometty Kept on Rising," *Wall Street Journal*, October 27, 2011.

8. Joann S. Lublin, "When Women Mentor Too Much," *WSJ.com*, October 11, 2013, http://www.wsj.com/articles/SB1000142405270230338200457912927377505 5280.

## CHAPTER 11: MANAGING MEN WELL

1. Black, *Basic Black*, 243.

2. Kolb, *Negotiating at Work*, xxviii.

3. Herminia Ibarra, Robin J. Ely, and Deborah M. Kolb, "Women Rising: The Unseen Barriers," *Harvard Business Review* 91 (September 2013): 65.

4. Cathleen Clerkin, Christine A. Crumbacher, Julia Fernando, and William A. Gentry, "Bossy: What's Gender Got to Do With It?" White Paper from the Center for Creative Leadership, February 2015.

5. Carol Hymowitz, "Raising Women to Be Leaders," *Wall Street Journal*, February 12, 2007.

## CHAPTER 12: SPOTLIGHT ON EXECUTIVE PRESENCE

1. "Observer: Flying High," *Financial Times*, August 11, 2004.

2. Sylvia Ann Hewlett, *Executive Presence: The Missing Link Between Merit and Success* (New York: HarperCollins, 2014), 132 and 139–41.
3. Joann S. Lublin, "How to Look and Act Like a Leader," *WSJ.com*, August 12, 2011, http://www.wsj.com/articles/SB100014240531119041406045764983 80000356032.
4. Malcolm Gladwell, *Blink: The Power of Thinking Without Thinking* (New York: Little, Brown, 2005), 86–87.
5. Stephanie Kang, "Nike Apparel Chief Leaves for IAC," *Wall Street Journal*, April 18, 2006.
6. Joann S. Lublin, "From the Boss: Lessons in What Not to Wear," *WSJ.com*, November 14, 2013, http://www.wsj.com/articles/SB1000142405270230328 9904579197811450356286.
7. Hewlett, *Executive Presence*, 16.
8. Teresa A. Taylor, *The Balance Myth: Rethinking Work-Life Success* (Austin, TX: Greenleaf Book Group Press, 2013), 70.

CHAPTER 13: BEATING BOARD BIAS
1. Joann S. Lublin, "Female CEOs Make Room for Female Directors," *Wall Street Journal*, November 12, 2014.
2. Alison Cook and Christy Glass, "Diversity Begets Diversity? The Effects of Board Composition on the Appointment and Success of Women CEOs," *Social Science Research* 53 (2015): 143 and 144.
3. Lublin, "Female CEOs Make Room for Female Directors."
4. Joann S. Lublin, "How High-Achieving Parents Raise Star Scions," *WSJ.com*, January 18, 2013, http://www.wsj.com/articles/SB10001424127887323468 604578248242767407084.
5. Joann S. Lublin, "From the Board to a Corner Office," *WSJ.com*, April 6, 2015, http://www.wsj.com/articles/from-the-board-to-a-corner-office-1428374984.
6. "Governing for the Long Term: Looking Down the Road with an Eye on the Rear-View Mirror," PwC US, October 2015, 10.

CHAPTER 14: WILL THE GLASS CEILING EVER SHATTER?
1. Nikki Waller and Joann S. Lublin, "What's Holding Women Back," *Wall Street Journal*, September 30, 2015.
2. Ben Zimmer, "The Phrase 'Glass Ceiling' Stretches Back Decades," *WSJ.com*, April 3, 2015, http://www.wsj.com/articles/the-phrase-glass-ceiling-stretch es-back-decades-1428089010.
3. Joann S. Lublin, "Bringing Hidden Biases Into the Light," *Wall Street Journal*, January 9, 2014.
4. Rachel Emma Silverman and Lindsay Gellman, "Apps Take on Workplace Bias," *Wall Street Journal*, September 30, 2015.

5. Joann S. Lublin, "Men Pitch In to Boost Women at Work," *Wall Street Journal*, March 10, 2015.
6. Anne-Marie Slaughter, *Unfinished Business: Women, Men, Work, Family* (New York: Random House, 2015), xxii.
7. Lauren Weber and Joann S. Lublin, "The Daddy Juggle: Work. Life, Family and Chaos," *Wall Street Journal*, June 14, 2014.
8. Slaughter, *Unfinished Business*, 127.
9. Joanna Barsh and Lareina Yee, "Unlocking the Full Potential of Women at Work," McKinsey & Co., 2012, 6 and 9.
10. Waller and Lublin, "What's Holding Women Back."
11. Rachel Feintzeig, "More Companies Say Targets Are the Key to Diversity," *Wall Street Journal*, September 30, 2015.

## CHAPTER 15: MALE CHAMPIONS OF WOMEN

1. Laura Landro, "Born to Be the Boss," *Wall Street Journal*, May 7, 2012.
2. Carol Hymowitz, "Raising Women to Be Leaders," *Wall Street Journal*, February 12, 2007.
3. Lublin, "How High-Achieving Parents Raise Star Scions."
4. Sheryl Sandberg and Adam Grant, "How Men Can Succeed," *New York Times*, March 8, 2015.

# SELECTED BIBLIOGRAPHY

Bachelder, Cheryl. *Dare to Serve: How to Drive Superior Results by Serving Others.* San Francisco: Berrett-Koehler, 2015.

Black, Cathie. *Basic Black: The Essential Guide for Getting Ahead at Work (and in Life).* New York: Crown Business, 2007.

Calderon, Nancy, and Susan Stautberg. *Women on Board: Insider Secrets to Getting on a Board and Succeeding as a Director.* West Palm Beach, FL: Quotation Media, 2014.

Colby, Laura. *Road to Power: How GM's Mary Barra Shattered the Glass Ceiling.* Hoboken, NJ: Wiley, 2015.

Doyle, Anne. *Powering Up! How America's Women Achievers Become Leaders.* Bloomington, IN: Xlibris, 2011.

Fiorina, Carly. *Tough Choices: A Memoir.* New York: Portfolio, 2006.

Hewlett, Sylvia Ann. *Executive Presence: The Missing Link Between Merit and Success.* New York: HarperCollins, 2014.

———. *(Forget a Mentor) Find a Sponsor: The New Way to Fast-Track Your Career.* Boston: Harvard Business Review Press, 2013.

Kolb, Deborah M., with Jessica L. Porter. *Negotiating at Work: Turn Small Wins into Big Gains.* San Francisco: Jossey-Bass, 2015.

McLaughlin, Debora J. *Running in High Heels: How to Lead with Influence, Impact & Ingenuity.* Bloomington, IN: Balboa Press, 2014.

Myers, Henry, ed. *Women at Work: How They're Reshaping America.* Princeton, NJ: Dow Jones Books, 1979.

Ross, Howard J. *Reinventing Diversity: Transforming Organizational Community to Strengthen People, Purpose, and Performance.* Lanham, MD: Rowman & Littlefield, 2011.

Sandberg, Sheryl. *Lean In: Women, Work, and the Will to Lead.* New York: Knopf, 2013.

Slaughter, Anne-Marie. *Unfinished Business: Women, Men, Work, Family.* New York: Random House, 2015.

Taylor, Teresa A. *The Balance Myth: Rethinking Work-Life Success.* Austin, TX: Greenleaf Book Group Press, 2013.

Vanderkam, Laura. *I Know How She Does It: How Successful Women Make the Most of Their Time.* New York: Portfolio/Penguin, 2015.

Whitman, Meg. *The Power of Many: Values for Success in Business and in Life.* New York: Crown, 2010.

# INDEX

1-800-FLOWERS, 127
2020 Women on Boards, 240

A&E, 32
A+E Networks, 32, 33, 35, 41, 114
Abra (author's daughter), 144, 145
*Accelerators, The*, 266
Accenture, 135
accountability, 256–57
Adobe Systems Inc., 52, 59, 77, 173–74, 177, 214
*Adweek*, 246
Agility Fuel Systems Inc., 27, 28, 56, 103, 132, 240, 241, 242
AGL Resources Inc., 82, 98, 165, 217
Alcatel-Lucent SA, 9, 119, 223
Allied Department Stores, 71
all-male panels, 267–68
Altoids, 100, 105
American Apparel Inc., 62
American Express Co., 176, 210–11
appearance:
    clothing, 209, 211–13, 217–18, 224
    executive presence, 208–24
    height, 213–14, 223
    posture and body language, 214, 218, 223, 242
Apple Inc., 50, 51, 101

Ascension Health, 91, 93–96
Association of Executive Search Consultants, 94
AT&T Corp., 9, 60–61, 179, 231, 264
AT&T Wireless, 181
at-home dads, 149–51, 253
*Atlantic*, 251
Aunt Jemima, 150
Autodesk Inc., 7–8, 20, 49, 78, 152, 214, 243, 269
AutoZone Inc., 136
Avon Products Inc., 39, 43–44, 46, 59, 101, 189

Babcock, Linda, 82–83, 88
Bachelder, Cheryl A., 123–26, 128, 131, 142, 214
Bachelder, Katy, 142
bad bosses, lessons from, 49–50
BAE Systems Inc., 20, 41, 68–69, 247–49, 269
BAE Systems PLC, 20
*Balance Myth, The: Rethinking Work-Life Success* (Taylor), 220
Ballard Power Systems Inc., 231
banks, 10, 24–26, 36, 65, 196–97, 211–13, 238, 239
Barder, Owen, 268
Barksdale, Jim, 180

Barnes, Brenda, 69–70, 83–84, 96, 200–201

Barra, Mary, 4, 8, 54–56, 84, 155, 181–82, 210, 253, 269

Barsh, Joanna, 254

Bartz, Bill, 243

Bartz, Carol, 7–8, 20–21, 49, 78, 152, 214, 243–44, 269

*Basic Black: The Essential Guide for Getting Ahead in Work (and in Life)* (Black), 85, 192

Bayer AG, 145

Beers, Charlotte, 73–77

BeingGirl.com, 113

Beneficial Corp., 89, 90–91

Berdahl, Jennifer L., 63–64

Bern, Dorrit J., 71–73, 77, 98, 157, 214

Black, Cathie, 18, 84–88, 191–92, 223

*Blink: The Power of Thinking Without Thinking* (Gladwell), 213

Bloomin' Brands Inc., 29, 99, 145, 152, 167, 189

Bloomingdale's, 43–46

blooming where you are planted, 43–59

considering promotions, 45–48, 50–52, 189

leadership lessons on, 58–59

boards, 225–42

leadership lessons on, 241–42

Bonefish Grill, 29

Bon Marché, 71

Booz Allen Hamilton, 147

Boston College Center for Work & Family, 251–52

*Boston Globe*, 106

BPI Group, 216–17

breastfeeding, 141–42

Britt, Glenn, 230

Bryant, Diane M., 52–54, 79–80, 211, 221–22

Bryant, Gay, 246

Buffalo Wild Wings Inc., 36, 156, 157

Buffett, Warren, 139

Business and Professional Women's Foundation, 4

business leaders, women as, 4–5, 7, 11, 15, 19, 26, 101, 102, 135, 161, 170, 186–87, 194, 227–28, 244

business trips, *see* travel, for work

*BusinessWeek*, 23, 159, 160, 169–70

Cable Data, 180, 229–30

Cadbury PLC, 139

Callard & Bowser, 100–101, 103–5

Camden, Carl T., 254–55

Campbell Soup Co., 9–10, 22, 179, 203, 205, 224, 231, 232, 241, 259, 260–63

Cardinal Health Inc., 250

career breakthroughs, 141–42

career couples, 158–72

Carpenter Technology Corp., 114, 201, 202, 232

Catalyst, 3–4, 19, 227, 239, 250, 260–61, 262

CCH Inc., 147–48

Center for Creative Leadership, 194

Center for Gender in Organizations, 88

Center for Global Development, 268

Center for Talent Innovation, 175, 210, 211, 219

Center for Work & Family, 252

Charles Schwab Corp., 117–19, 170–71

Charming Shoppes Inc., 71, 77, 98, 157

Chemical Bank, 65–67

child care, 149, 152–54, 156, 157, 167, 252

*see also* parenthood

Chizen, Bruce R., 52, 173–75, 177

Christensen, Kathryn, 13

Ciccolo, Gregory, 153, 163–65
Cincinnati Bell, 117
Citibank, 227
Civil Rights Act of 1964, 16
Claris Corp., 50–52, 173
Clarke, Janet M., 225–27, 235–36, 242
Clinton, Hillary, 251
clothing, 209, 211–13, 217–18, 224
Commodore International Ltd., 30
communication, 220–21
commuting long distance, 146–48
computer industry, 20
Conant, Doug, 259, 260–63, 268
Conant, Sarah, 260, 263
Condé Nast, 85
conflicts of interest, 168–71, 172
*Congrats! You Have an All-Male Panel!*,
    267–68
Continental Bank, 89, 196
corporate boards, 225–42
    leadership lessons on, 241–42
*Cosmopolitan*, 84–85
Cox Communications Inc., 227
Cravath, Swaine & Moore, 168
customers, male, 202–5

Dancer Fitzgerald Sample, 140
Daniel (author's son), 143–44, 252–53
*Dare to Serve: How to Drive Superior
    Results by Serving Others* (Bachel-
    der), 123
Daytime, 33–35
Dillon, Mary, 150–51, 198–200, 207
Dillon, Terry, 150–51
Disney, 127, 162
Dolan, Janet, 42
Dolan, Jimmy, 178–79
Dollar General Corp., 89, 93
Domino's Pizza Inc., 123
door openings, 24–42
    allies in, 29–32

fathers and, 35–37
husbands and, 37–40
leadership lessons on, 41–42
in unfamiliar territory, 32–35
Dotlich, David, 215, 216
double bind for women, 102, 194
doubts, 41, 119–23
Dow Chemical Co., 248
Dow Jones & Co., 2, 28, 81, 158, 160
Doyle, Anne, 58
Drugstore.com, 6, 117, 119, 132, 170
Dublon, Dina, 65–67, 78
Dubuc, Nancy, 35
Dun & Bradstreet Corp., 37, 40, 195
DuPont Co., 115, 119–23, 154,
    166–67, 170, 236
Dyrdahl, Melissa, 50–52, 59, 77,
    173–75, 177, 214

earnings, 19, 22, 79–98
    leadership lessons on, 97–98
eBay Inc., 6, 126, 128, 161
economy, 15, 18
Edward Jones, 4, 177
ELI Group, 188
Ella Health Inc., 50, 173, 214
Ely, Robin J., 102, 193, 194
empathy, 97, 157, 201–2
engineering, 21, 27–28
entry-level jobs, 26
Equal Pay Act of 1963, 16
Ernst & Young, 136
*Esquire*, 85
European Round Table of Industrial-
    ists (ERT), 244
executive officers, women as, 3–5, 7,
    13–15, 19–20, 24, 93–94, 245,
    253
executive presence, 208–24
    gravitas, 210, 219–20
    leadership lessons on, 222–24

*Executive Presence: The Missing Link Between Merit and Success* (Hewlett), 210, 219
Exxon Corp., 202

*Facebook Era, The* (Shih), 184
Facebook Inc., 21, 134, 161, 183, 184, 218, 245, 248, 253–54, 269
Families and Work Institute, 252
Farrar, Straus and Giroux, 30
fatherhood, 149–51, 251–53
    parental leave and, 135, 252–54
    stay-at-home dads, 149–51, 253
    *see also* parenthood
fathers, career opportunities and, 35–37
Federal Reserve Bank of New York, 94
female allies and advocates, 182–87
feminine and masculine traits, 102, 194–95, 219
*Feminine Mystique, The* (Friedan), 16
*Financial Times*, 209
Fiorina, Carly, 10–11, 27, 60–61, 78
First City National Bank of Houston, 24–25
FirstRain Inc., 21, 64, 141, 205–6, 218, 223
first workplace, 42
Ford Motor Co., 201–2, 233
*(Forget a Mentor) Find a Sponsor: The New Way to Fast-Track Your Career* (Hewlett), 175
*Fortune*, 197
Fortune 20, 10
Fortune 500, 19–20, 69, 203, 213, 228, 239, 250, 259
Fortune 1000, 14
Fouad, Nadya, 21
Friedan, Betty, 16
Frontier Communications Corp., 10, 42, 156, 179, 186, 203, 227
FTD, 126–28

Galinsky, Ellen, 252
Gannett Co., 18–19, 81, 87, 105–7, 191, 192, 228, 256
GapJumpers, 249
Gateway Inc., 235–36
G. D. Searle & Co., 169
gender bias, *see* sex discrimination and gender bias
gender diversity, 14–15
gender roles, *see* sex roles and gender stereotypes
General Electric Co., 101
General Foods, 140
General Motors Co. (GM), 4, 8, 27, 54–58, 84, 155, 181–82, 186, 210, 253, 254, 269
Georgia State University, 149
getting ahead later, 116–32
    doubts and, 119–23
    leadership lessons on, 131–32
    setbacks and, 123–28
    "talk me off the ledge" moments and, 129–31
getting ahead sooner, 99–115
    leadership lessons on, 114–15
getting picked, 43–59
    leadership lessons on, 58–59
Gladwell, Malcolm, 213
*Glamour*, 82
glass ceiling, 13, 22, 243–57
glass cliff, 102–3
Global Summit of Women, 268
Goodyear Tire & Rubber Co., 232
Google, 10, 184, 248
Gordon, Ilene, 132, 206–7
Government Accountability Office, 136
Graham, Katharine, 14
*Grassy Road, The*, 206
gravitas, 210, 219–20
Greyhound Bus Lines, 31
Grillo, Valerie, 211

Grossman, Mindy, 41, 129–31, 153, 215–16, 228
Grossman, Neil, 130, 153
Gulfo, Adele, 206

Harrington, Brad, 252
Harsh, Griffith R., IV, 161–63
*Harvard Business Review*, 161, 194
Harvard Business School, 160–61
Harvest Power Inc., 28
Hasbro Inc., 128
Healey, Bruce, 133, 134
Healey, Melanie, 78, 110–14, 133–34, 142–43, 153
Hearsay Social Inc., 10, 41, 183, 184, 189, 193–94
Hearst Magazines, 84–85, 191, 223
height, 213–14, 223
Heller Financial, 90
Herrmann, Mary, 217, 220
Herscher, Penny, 21–22, 64–65, 141–42, 205–6, 214, 218–19, 223
Hewlett, Sylvia Ann, 175–76, 210
Hewlett-Packard Co., 10–11, 27, 59, 78, 84, 119, 126, 161, 162, 228
Hewlett Packard Enterprise Co., 59, 119, 126, 161, 228
high tech industry, 20–22, 52
History, 32, 35
*Holiday*, 85–87
Holliday, Charles "Chad" O., 120–22
Holt, Curt, 146–47, 149–50
Holt, Lauren, 146–47
Holt, Victoria "Vicki," 107–10, 146–47, 149–50, 154–55, 236–38, 241
HSN Inc., 41, 129–30, 153, 215, 228
Hudson, Linda, 20, 41, 68–69, 247–49, 269
husbands, 37–40
    conflicts of interest and, 168–71, 172
    leadership lessons on, 171–72

scheduling and, 166–68
two careers and, 158–72

IAC/InterActiveCorp., 129
Ibarra, Herminia, 194
*I'd Rather Be in Charge: A Legendary Business Leader's Roadmap for Achieving Pride, Power, and Joy at Work* (Beers), 74
Implicit Association Test, 247
imposter syndrome, 116–17, 119, 131–32
Inclusion Advantage, The, 249
Ingredion Inc., 132, 207
Institute for Women's Policy Research, 81
Institutional Shareholder Services, 225
Intel Corp., 52–54, 79, 80, 210–11, 221–22, 246, 247, 248
International Business Machines Corp. (IBM), 4, 84, 185–86, 221, 253
International Flavors & Fragrances Inc., 236

Jell-O, 99, 101
Johnson, William H., 263
Johnson & Johnson (J&J), 145, 177, 187, 190, 256, 269
JPMorgan Chase & Co., 67, 78
Juarez, Rosario, 136
Jung, Andrea, 43–46, 59, 101, 189
Juno Therapeutics Inc., 227
J. Walter Thompson, 74

Kaufmann, Mike, 250
Kelly Services Inc., 254–55
Kevlar, 119
KeyCorp, 10, 24, 26, 41, 103, 211, 238–39
KFC, 123–25

Kleiner Perkins Caufield & Byers, 63, 245

KLM, 209

Kolb, Deborah M., 88, 193, 194

Kool-Aid, 140–41

Kraft Foods Inc., 99–100, 105, 139, 145, 167, 231

Krol, Jack, 167

Kullman, Ellen, 115, 119–23, 154, 166–67, 170

Kullman, Mike, 121, 166, 170

labor force, women in, 16

Langer Research Associates, 62

Laybourne, Geraldine "Geri," 49–50

Lazarus, Shelly, 274

Leadership California, 231

Leadership in Action, 255

Leadership Lab for Women, 188

leadership lessons:
    on career couples, 171–72
    on executive presence, 222–24
    on getting ahead later, 131–32
    on getting ahead sooner, 114–15
    on getting picked, 58–59
    on male mentors, 189–90
    on manager moms, 156–57
    on managing men, 206–7
    on opening doors, 41–42
    on pay, 97–98
    on sexual harassment, 77–78

Lean In, 176, 245, 252, 255, 257

*Lean In: Women, Work, and the Will to Lead* (Sandberg), 21, 22, 134–35, 161, 185, 218

Lear Corp., 240

L'eggs, 203

Lehigh University, 227

Lepore, Dawn, 5–7, 117–19, 132, 170–71

Lepore, Ken, 170–71

Lewis, William, 81

Life Savers, 142

Lifetime, 32

Ligocki, Kathleen, 27–28, 56–58, 103, 132, 240–41, 242

line management jobs, 23

Lockheed Martin Corp., 233–34

long-distance commutes, 146–48

Lowe, Challis, 89–91, 93–96, 98, 196–97

Lowenstein Sandler LLP, 266

Lublin, Joann S.:
    daughter of, 144, 145
    husband of, 3, 88–89, 158–60, 169–70
    son of, 143–44, 252–53
    *Wall Street Journal* articles of, 3, 61–62, 136, 143–44, 163, 165, 166, 168, 174, 186, 228, 247, 248, 250, 252
    *Wall Street Journal* career of, 1–3, 13, 17–18, 22–23, 29, 67–68, 88–89, 143–45, 158–60, 170
    WSJ.com column of, 176, 187–88, 211, 217, 231, 236, 265

Lucent Technologies Inc., 9, 119, 223, 258

male champions of women, 258–69

male customers, 202–5

male mentees, 188–89

male mentors, 173–90
    leadership lessons on, 189–90

male peers, 54–56

management, 14, 15–16, 23, 96, 114, 156, 189
    accountability in, 256–57
    line, 23
    senior, women in, 15, 17, 19, 69, 93, 94, 96, 168, 176, 210, 220, 238, 239, 245, 248, 249, 250, 254, 255, 257

manager moms, 133–57
managing men, 191–207
   leadership lessons on, 206–7
"manels," 267–68
Manos, Kris, 238–39
Martore, Gracia, 18–19, 81, 105–7,
   228, 256, 269
masculine and feminine traits, 102,
   194–95, 219
maternity leave, 134, 135, 137–43,
   150
Mathew, Jacob, 37–40
Mathew, Sara, 37–40, 195
Mattel Inc., 236
Mayer, Marissa, 135
McCaw, Craig, 230
McCaw Cellular Communications Inc.,
   180–81, 230
McCluskey, Helen, 274
McCorkingdale, Doug, 106
McDonald's Corp., 151, 198
McKinsey & Co., 15, 23, 176, 187, 190,
   245, 252, 254, 255, 257, 263
McKinstry, Nancy, 147–48, 156,
   178–79, 208–10, 214, 244
media business, 19
men:
   as champions of women, 258–69
   as customers, 202–5
   managing, 191–207
   as mentees, 188–89
   as mentors, 173–90
   as peers, 54–56
menial tasks, 2, 25, 35
mentors and sponsors, 189, 190
   female, 182–87
   leadership lessons on, 189–90
   male, 173–90
Mercer, 16
Microsoft Corp., 67, 83, 181, 184, 246,
   248

Mike (author's husband), 3, 88–89,
   158–60, 169–70
millennial generation, 4, 136, 160,
   251–52
mission impossible roles, 99–115
mistaken identity, 193, 244
Mondelēz International Inc., 84, 99, 139
money, 19, 22, 79–98
   leadership lessons on, 97–98
Monsanto Co., 107–9, 146, 147
Mooney, Beth, 10, 11, 24–26, 41, 103,
   211–13, 238–39
Moore, Ann, 197–98
Morgan Stanley, 30, 210
Morrison, Denise, 9–10, 22, 179,
   202–5, 224, 231–32, 241, 259,
   261–62, 264–65
motherhood, 133–57
   pregnancy, 133–34, 136
Ms., 87
MSCI Inc., 228
Mulcahy, Anne, 46–49, 91–93,
   195–96, 210, 223, 230
Mylan NV, 206

Nabisco, 123, 142, 261
Nadella, Satya, 83
National Association for Female Exec-
   utives, 253, 270
National Cable Television Association
   (NCTA), 229, 230
NBC News, 22
Negotiating at Work: Turn Small Wins
   into Big Gains (Kolb and Porter),
   88
Nestlé SA, 231, 265
Netflix Inc., 135
Neuharth, Al, 87, 191–92
Newell Rubbermaid Inc., 236
New England Telephone Co., 147,
   178–79

*Newsday*, 28–29
Newspaper Fund, 2, 28
newspapers, 17, 28
*New York*, 87
*New York Times*, 33, 68, 168, 269
New York Times Co., 6
Nickelodeon, 49–50
Nike Inc., 129, 153, 215–16
Nixon, Richard, 179–80
Novak, David, 123, 124–25

O'Connor, Flannery, 30
office politics, 178
Ogilvy & Mather Worldwide, 74
OnBoard Bootcamp, 228–29
Oreo, 84, 99
Outback Steakhouse, 29

Paine Webber, 30–31
Palmisano, Samuel, 185
panels, all-male, 267–68
Pao, Ellen, 62–63, 83, 245, 246
parental leave, 134, 135, 137–43, 150,
    252–53, 254
  for fathers, 135, 252–54
parenthood, 189
  business trips and, 154–55
  fatherhood, 135, 149–51, 251–53
  child care and, 149, 152–54, 156,
    157, 167, 252
  leadership lessons on, 156–57
  motherhood, 133–57
  pregnancy, 133–34, 136
  stay-at-home dads, 149–51, 253
  travel and, 154–55, 157
pay, 19, 22, 79–98
  leadership lessons on, 97–98
  negotiating, 81–83, 86, 88, 93, 96,
    98
paying it forward, 186–87
Pearce, Harry, 181–82

Peat Marwick, 37
peers, male, 54–56
PepsiCo Inc., 67, 70, 151, 200
Pepsi-Cola North America, 70, 200
performance bias, 248
perquisites, 17, 88, 91–93, 98, 156
Perry, Richard, 127
Perry Capital, 127
Peterson, Sandra "Sandi," 145–46, 177,
    187, 190, 269
Pew Research Center, 136, 245
Pfizer Inc., 248
pink ghetto, 23
Playskool, 128
Polo Jeans, 215
PolyOne Corp., 237–38
Popeyes Louisiana Kitchen Inc., 123,
    125–26, 131, 142, 214
posture and body language, 214, 218,
    223, 242
*Powering Up! How America's Women
    Achievers Become Leaders* (Doyle),
    58
*Power of Many, The: Values for Success
    in Business and in Life* (Whitman),
    126, 161
PPG Industries Inc., 108, 236–37
pregnancy, 133–34, 136
presentations, communication in,
    220–21
PricewaterhouseCoopers LLP, 186
Procter & Gamble Co. (P&G), 38,
    39–40, 59, 78, 110–11, 112–14,
    127, 133–34, 142–43, 153, 203–5
promotions, 17, 59, 70, 107, 158, 174,
    176, 194, 211, 247, 252, 256,
    269
  considering, 45–48, 50–52, 189
Proto Labs Inc., 108, 147, 154, 238,
    241
Proudman, Bill, 251

Puget Energy Inc., 165
Pulitzer Prize, 3
PwC US, 240

Quaker Foods, 151
Quaker Oats Co., 150
Quantopian, 14
Qwest Communications International
    Inc., 59, 137, 188, 219, 220, 223

Raez, Lesbia, 153
Ralph Lauren Corp., 215
Raven, Abbe, 32–35, 41, 114
Reddit Inc., 83
Regan, Margaret, 247
relocation, 59, 90–91, 143, 158, 162,
    165–66, 172
    author's experiences with, 88–89,
    159–60
Republic Bank, 25–26, 212–13
Reynolds, Paula Rosput, 82, 96–97, 98,
    131, 165–66, 217–18
Reynolds, Stephen, 165–66
rising stars, 22–23, 71, 101, 110,
    181–82, 211, 215
Rice-A-Roni, 150
risk, 99–115, 129, 131
Ritz, 84, 99
RJR Nabisco Inc., 123, 142, 261
Robinson, Janet, 274
Rockwell Automation Inc., 246
Rometty, Virginia "Ginni," 4, 84,
    185–86, 221, 253
Rosenfeld, Irene, 84, 99–100, 139–41
R. R. Donnelley & Sons Inc., 226
Rumsfeld, Donald H., 169, 235, 263
Rumsfeld, Joyce, 263
Rumsfeld Foundation, 263
Russell 3000 Index, 225
Russo, Patricia "Pat," 9, 119, 223, 258
Ryder System Inc., 89, 93

Safeco Corp., 82, 98, 165–66, 217
salaries, 19, 22, 79–98
    leadership lessons on, 97–98
Salesforce.com Inc., 184, 246–47
Sandberg, Sheryl, 21, 22, 134–35, 161,
    176, 183–85, 218, 245, 248, 269
Sara Lee Corp., 69–70, 83, 84, 200–201
Särmä, Saara, 267–68
Schmidt, Keith, 25–26
Schwab, 117–19, 170–71
Scripps Research Institute, 146, 147
Searle, 169
Sears, Roebuck & Co., 72–73, 74
second-generation gender bias, 20,
    193, 194
Securities and Exchange Commission
    (SEC), 168
senior management, women in, 15, 17,
    19, 69, 93, 94, 96, 168, 176, 210,
    220, 238, 239, 245, 248, 249, 250,
    254, 255, 257
Sequoia Capital, 184
Sesame Street effect, 112
setbacks, 123–28
sex discrimination and gender bias,
    2–3, 4, 16–17, 22, 53, 197–98,
    207, 245, 246–47, 249, 269–70
    Pao case and, 62–63, 83, 245, 246
    perquisites and, 91–93
    second-generation, 20, 193, 194
    unconscious, 69, 244, 247–49, 269
sexism, 3, 9, 17, 245
sex roles and gender stereotypes, 4, 17,
    19, 20, 41, 59, 102, 116, 135, 191,
    193, 204–5, 247, 251
    and double bind for women, 102, 194
    feminine and masculine traits, 102,
    194–95, 219
    parenting and, 149–50, 252
sexual harassment, 60–78
    leadership lessons on, 77–78

shareholder returns, 14
Shih, Clara, 10, 41, 183–85, 189, 193–94
Silicon Valley, 52, 63, 245
Simplex Solutions Inc., 205–6
Sinclair, Christopher, 236
sisterhood, 182–87
Slaughter, Anne-Marie, 251, 252
small wins, power of, 196–98
Smith, Jack, 181–82
Smith, Liz, 29–32, 99–101, 103–5, 145, 152, 167–68, 189
Smith, Robin, 275
Smith, Sally, 36–37, 156, 157
Sonesta International Hotels Corp., 153, 163, 164
Sonnabend, Stephanie, 153–54, 163–65
Spartech Corp., 108, 236–37
Spence, Betty, 270
Spencer Stuart, 240
sponsors and mentors:
    female, 182–87
    leadership lessons on, 189–90
    male, 173–90
*Sports Illustrated*, 197, 198
spouses, 37–40
    conflicts of interest and, 168–71, 172
    leadership lessons on, 171–72
    scheduling and, 166–68
    two careers and, 158–72
staff jobs, 23
Standard & Poor's (S&P) 500 Index, 4, 5, 14, 228, 240
Stanford Brain Tumor Center, 161
Stanford University, 2, 15, 41, 184
Starbucks Corp., 10, 184–85
Stautberg, Susan, 229
stay-at-home dads, 149–51, 253
stereotypes, *see* sex roles and gender stereotypes

Steven Hall & Partners, 62
Stevens, Anne, 114, 201–2, 232–34
Stride Rite Corp., 127, 162
Sullivan, Dennis, 179, 180, 231, 259, 263–65, 268
Sun Microsystems Inc., 243
supervising men, 191–207
Synopsys Inc., 64–65, 141–42
Syracuse University, 227

Talent Deployment Forum, 255
"talk me off the ledge" moments, 129–31
Tampax, 112–13
Tatham-Laird & Kudner, 75, 76
Taylor, Teresa, 59, 137–39, 188–89, 219–20, 223
tech industry, 20–22, 52
Teflon, 119
TEGNA Inc., 19, 81, 105, 228, 256, 269
Tennant Co., 42
Textio, 249
Thirty Percent Coalition, 262
Thomas, Clarence, 2
*Time*, 197
Time Inc., 197
Time Warner Cable Inc., 230
Time Warner Inc., 256
Title VII, 16
*Tough Choices: A Memoir* (Fiorina), 60
Tower Automotive Inc., 28, 103, 132, 240, 242
Traub, Marvin, 44–45
travel, for work, 7, 18, 47, 157, 158, 163–64, 166, 177, 189, 190
    commuting long distance, 146–48
    parenting and, 154–55, 157
Tricon Global Restaurants Inc., 123
Trident, 84
Tumblr, 267
Twitter Inc., 246

two-career couples, 158–72
Tylenol, 145, 187

Ulta Salon Cosmetics & Fragrance Inc.,
    150, 151, 198
unconscious bias, 69, 244, 247–49, 269
*Unfinished Business: Women, Men, Work,
    Family* (Slaughter), 251
University of Chicago, 15
University of Wisconsin, 21, 243
*USA Today*, 18, 87, 191–92
U.S. Bureau of Labor Statistics, 14
U.S. Cellular Corp., 151, 198–200, 207
U.S. Census Bureau, 20, 149
U.S. Congress Joint Economic Com-
    mittee, 136
US West, 137–39, 219
Utah State University, 228

velvet glove, 97
Visa, 171
Vmware Inc., 248

wages, 19, 22, 79–98
    leadership lessons on, 97–98
Waitt, Ted, 235
Walgreen Co., 119
*Wall Street Journal*, 28, 149, 179, 186,
    203, 249, 252, 257, 261, 264
    author's articles in, 61–62, 136,
        143–44, 163, 165, 166, 168, 174,
        186, 228, 247, 248, 250, 252
    author's career at, 1–3, 13, 17–18,
        22–23, 29, 67–68, 88–89,
        143–45, 158–60, 170
Walt Disney Co., 127, 162
*Washington Daily News*, 35–36
Washington Post Co., 14

Washington University, 147
Watkins, Carole, 250
Wells, Frank, 162
Welty, Joe, 192
White, John W., 168
White, Mary Jo, 168
White Men as Full Diversity Partners
    LLC, 250–51
Whitman, Meg, 59, 84, 126–28,
    161–63, 213–14, 228
Wilderotter, Maggie, 10, 42, 156,
    179–81, 185, 186, 203, 227,
    229–30, 231, 259, 264–65
Wilson Sporting Goods, 83–84
Wink Communications, 181, 230
Wolters Kluwer NV, 147, 148, 156, 178,
    208–10, 244
Women's Network, 93
*Working Woman*, 39
working women, data on, 14, 20, 149
work-life balance, 8, 133, 144, 251
    *see also* parenthood
World War II, 16
WSJ.com, 266
    Lublin's column in, 3, 176, 187–88,
        211, 217, 231, 236, 265

Xerox Corp., 46–49, 91–93, 195–96,
    210, 223, 230

Yahoo Inc., 8, 20, 49, 78, 135, 152, 214,
    269
Young, Christina, 62
Yum Brands Inc., 123, 124–25

Zimmerman, Ed, 259, 265–67, 268
Zuckerberg, Mark, 253–54

# ABOUT THE AUTHOR

JOANN S. LUBLIN is management news editor for the *Wall Street Journal* and works with reporters in the United States and abroad. She frequently appears at conferences to discuss leadership, executive pay, and corporate governance. She created the *Journal's* first career advice column in 1993. She shared its Pulitzer Prize in 1993 for stories about corporate scandals. Joann earned a bachelor's degree in journalism with honors from Northwestern University and a master's degree in communications from Stanford University. She lives in Ridgewood, New Jersey.